POETS AND GOD

POETS AND GOD

Chaucer, Shakespeare, Herbert,
Milton, Wordsworth, Coleridge, Blake

DAVID L. EDWARDS

DARTON · LONGMAN + TODD

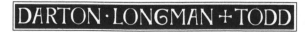

First published in 2005 by
Darton, Longman and Todd Ltd
1 Spencer Court
140–142 Wandsworth High Street
London SW18 4JJ

ISBN 0–232–52577–3

A catalogue record for this book is available from the British Library.

Designed by Sandie Boccacci
Phototypeset in 10/12pt Minion by Intype Libra Ltd
Printed and bound in Great Britain by
Page Bros, Norwich, Norfolk

To

CLARE

in thanksgiving

CONTENTS

PREFACE

THESE SEVEN POETS are at the centre of the cultural heritage of the English-reading world. That position may mean that some reluctant readers connect them dismally with examinations in school, but after early troubles they can come to be valued as useful and even enjoyable – indeed, even loved – escorts for life. And their work may stimulate some serious thoughts about life as a whole, for here is literature of the highest quality and of immortal power, and that may have a more lasting and profound influence than most of the material usually offered to us for our improvement or pleasure.

Both Chaucer and Shakespeare were very great storytellers and the abiding fascination of what they wrote ages ago results from their ability to make the characters in their stories as real to us as our own friends. Not always but often they can grab our attention, they can make us laugh or smile or look intently or feel moved, and in the end we have become a bit wiser about who we are and what our world amounts to. And although they do not directly tell us much about themselves, it is not true that Chaucer, being medieval, has become incomprehensible or that Shakespeare, being a dramatist who is not on stage, is unknowable. On the contrary, research has unearthed significant documents and reflection can enable us to see much of the story of their own lives half hidden in the stories which they told. In our gratitude for their work the least we ought to do is to get to know what can be known about them. So my treatment is biographical, defying those who warn us not to attempt to meet 'the author'. I have found that they are as interesting as the stories they told.

Inevitably a part of what they tell us about the characters in their stories, and about themselves, belongs to the areas of human life which are nowadays marked off from 'life-in-general' by notices announcing 'religion' or 'spirituality'. These two men belonged to a society which was officially Christian and was that in practice to a considerable extent, and England did not change completely although the Protestant Reformation occurred between the death of the one and the birth of the other. Christianity had soaked into what they wrote and what they were. They were both emphatically laymen, not hesitating to poke fun at the clergy and not hastening to get involved in theological arguments.

Indeed, they were practical men of the world keeping an eye on their incomes, the one a courtier, civil servant and diplomat, the other an actor, script-writer and businessman. But they could approach religion and spirituality through morality, through the almost universal habit of taking quite a tolerant attitude to 'human nature' in oneself and other people but nevertheless trying to distinguish between right and wrong. They did not moralise boringly, and they were not saintly in their own behaviour, but moral convictions can be detected in their stories. They are not firm in their answers to all questions but (for examples) they are very clear about authentic and faithful love before and after marriage, and what they praise as true chivalry or justice is not merely brutal. If we listen carefully to the tales told by those pilgrims on the road to Canterbury we can hear people revealing their own personalities, which Chaucer does not always admire. If we look closely at Shakespeare's tragedies, we can see that they are about the disasters which people bring on themselves after committing deadly sins condemned by the medieval Church. And if we think about his sonnets, we can see why he wanted them to remain private, because in later years he condemned the young man he had been. Or so this book will argue.

Both men were humanists, if we can use that term without the modern implication that to be a humanist is to be an atheist. They owed much to the Latin literature which was the intellectual and emotional diet in Europe's schools, and in particular loved its stories about people and almost-human divinities. That encouraged them to take a favourable view of human nature wherever possible. They wrote comedies with gusto, they tended to be sympathetic with almost everyone as they presented real or imaginary history, they applauded people who loved life as they did themselves, they could be robustly vulgar but could also cater for those who appreciated wit and subtlety. That is why they were popular with a large range of their contemporaries and why their work can still be read or watched with delight – in Shakespeare's case, in languages not his own. But they were not mere comedians, because they were not blind to the darker side of life; to self-inflicted catastrophes, to sheer bad luck, to the disillusionment which comes with experience. When they wrote about tragedies, at length or in miniature, they were unsentimental about the damage and loss, but ended by arousing some compassion for all the losers, by making us feel a little wiser, and by hinting that there remains hope.

Their ultimate hope lay in the reality of what, according to the convention which was observed in poetry and drama, they could call 'the gods' or 'Providence'. When they came to their own deaths, they called it 'God' as Christians. They accepted the common-sense opinion that 'Fortune' plays a large part in events, but when evil consequences follow evil actions they also saw the justice of the Judge who is above, in eternity. The man who wrote *Troilus and Criseyde* was not a sentimental fool, and the man who wrote *King Lear* was not a facile optimist, but they both believed that good can come out of bad and for both that means that there exists a mysterious power stronger than human evil.

Their Christian form of humanism was developed out of what they inherited as a Catholic or an Anglican in the late Middle Ages or the early modern period and if 'the Renaissance' is not defined narrowly it may be said that they both belonged to it, for the Renaissance took place inside Christendom, in England to the sound of church bells. Obviously it would be totally ridiculous to claim that what they wrote is all that we need as equipment for our own lives and tasks, but it does seem reasonable to suggest that in a century which is different in innumerable ways they have provided a spiritual resource. Their vision came out of a time when 'religion' and 'spirituality' were in the mainstream of life in Europe, as in Africa, Islam or India even now. Religion was not the defence and maintenance of beliefs, values and institutions which are widely rejected or ignored, and spirituality was more than a private feeling. And the religion and spirituality which they took more or less for granted despite their reticence were more or less Christian. So this literature can be a stimulus for those Christians or post-Christians who in our own time acknowledge the need to build new bridges between religion and life, and between spirituality and reality.

In societies which are modernising or modern, or postmodern, secularisation becomes one of the realities, either as a challenge beginning to disrupt traditions which are still supreme or as a climate of opinion which provides the background to the obstinate struggle of organised religion to survive on the margin of contemporary life and thought. Becoming secular may involve a decline in religious practices such as public worship, or the revision or abandonment of what used to be moral laws, or (most profoundly) a growing sense that God is distant, absent or unreal. It can therefore be important to discover that in their different ways two other Christian poets had to face some of these problems in the 1600s when modern societies were being born along with modern science. They too can be called Christian humanists, but they were disturbed by the first rumblings of an earthquake which was to change far more than did a reformation within Christendom.

To read George Herbert's prose and poetry as published in two small books after his death is to meet a man who resolved to be a totally dedicated but somewhat dictatorial pastor of a small rural parish, but who first had to go on a spiritual journey infinitely more anxious than the storytellers' pilgrimage imagined by Chaucer. In *The Temple* one solitary pilgrim is trying to feel near to the God revealed in Christ and is experiencing the ups and downs of a love affair. It is easy to see that nowadays Herbert's ideal for his leadership of a parish needs rethinking, but the real challenge is to ask what kind of holiness is rightly demanded from those who currently believe that they have a vocation to serve and influence fellow Christians, with or without ordination or pay. It is also easy to see that the poetry is more artificial than any heart-searching by a modern writer (R. S. Thomas for example), but it is more difficult, and potentially far more helpful, to think out what it can mean for us today. How often do these often brilliantly crafted poems, passionately sincere in their substance, either voice or answer the questions which can be raised after the 'death of God' in the modern process of secularisation (in English poetry, after Arnold, Hardy and Housman)?

John Milton hated the Roman Catholic Church and excluded it from toleration, and he did what he could to destroy the Church of England into which Herbert eventually fitted. In his prose he argued that the state should no longer control or favour any church and that every individual should be left free to interpret Scripture. He moved the emphasis completely from the ordained and appointed clergy to the laity gathered as a voluntary congregation. Such radicalism seemed very unrealistic at the time but may be taken more seriously in an age when many are asking how the Church, in an Orthodox, Catholic, Evangelical or Pentecostal shape now separated from the state, can have a good future. How can it be a people, not an institution? How can it be a community more credible and more lovable after a history which in many ways is not even respectable? How can the Spirit give it life?

Milton was also a pioneer in the work of reshaping Christianity in order that Christ's essential and permanent message might be conveyed in fresh images and words which could have something of the impact of the original parables and sharp sayings. Explorations of theology led him far from what George Herbert (for example) would accept as orthodoxy and his conclusions could not be published in his lifetime. What he could say in public had to be said in code: he could not talk about politics or theology but only about war in heaven or the Fall in the Garden of Eden. His imagination as a blind man had to be the medium of his message as a prophet. But during his life *Paradise Lost* and its two sequels were in print and beginning to have an impact which grew vastly after his death, and the attentive reading of them has continued into our own time. So has the controversy about them, for his style of poetry was special to his purpose and so was his handling of material from the Bible. But people who are aware of the multiple crises now confronting the Christian religion can at least agree that Milton's call for heroism needs to be heard. Whether or not he was right to think of Jesus as no more than the supremely heroic son of God, and to see God as the 'Task-Master' who demands obedience, he was himself heroic when in his blindness he imagined magnificently what had gone wrong for Adam and Eve, and for England in its civil war – and when no less splendidly he envisaged what could still be put right.

As a young man Wordsworth was an enthusiastic radical like Milton and he hailed the French Revolution as the dawn of a new age, as many more recently have hailed Communism, capitalism or consumerism. When Revolution became Terror and Napoleon, and a romance in France became flesh in a woman and a child whom he deserted, in shame and distress he turned back to nature, which had already been his real education. Like Herbert wrestling with God, or Milton wrestling with the Bible, he wrestled with nature before he could recapture the sense that a consoling and healing Spirit is everywhere. In the end he recovered also faith in God as Creator and as the source of new life through Christ after failure and death. He reported this journey to his contemporaries with such spiritual power that eventually his poetry became a new gospel. And it was not only a gospel about the creation and (with more hesitation) its Creator. It was also a message about the need to meet human suffering face to face, in particular the sufferings of the lonely and silent – the destitute, the bereaved, people usually thought mad, many women. And it was about daily duty.

The glory faded and he reacted with mere conservatism to the arrival of modern industry and urban democracy, but disappointment with his last period, when he was the 'lost leader' to Browning, need not mean that we have nothing to learn from what he wrote when inspired. In our time our situation is not totally unlike the younger Wordsworth's. Many who still live close to nature are again in poverty and distress. Many who have lived or half-lived in cities are now turning back to nature and natural living – and turn with questions at least as hard as those which troubled him as the eighteenth century became the nineteenth. Now that it has been experienced fully, exactly what in modern civilisation must be rejected? Now that scientific knowledge has expanded so largely, does what we know about nature support or contradict the belief that it is a creation by a Creator? It all had one source in the Big Bang, and it has included the marvel that this planet is inhabited, but does nature still seem to us as it seemed in Genesis and in Wordsworth's vision, 'very good'? Now that we have unprecedented power, does our place in nature encourage us to take care of the creation – or to take what we want? Now that we can, do we want to secure dignity for the whole of humanity? And now that we have unprecedented technical power and unprecedented appetites as consumers, can we halt our destruction of nature? These questions are familiar but answers are not.

Samuel Taylor Coleridge had a close and creative friendship with

Wordsworth until it was destroyed, like much else in his life, by his addiction to opium originally taken as normal medicine. He is therefore remembered mainly as a poet and a thinker not about nature but about the human power of imagination, with or without the drug's influence, and that leads us into some contemporary questions. Is poetry, or spirituality or religion, in the last analysis a drug which we take in order to escape from the pain of reality? If we seek an answer in the strange world of the Bible which is full of poetry, are we convinced by what the Bible dares to say – that our Creator imagined how beautiful our world could be, and we in it? And in our time is it possible to learn anything from Coleridge's idea of a 'clerisy' wider than the clergy to serve the people by spreading a civilisation rooted in the Bible? One problem is that too often the Bible is either dismissed as antiquated or mistreated as infallible – as Coleridge protested in his own day.

This book ends with some account of the seventh of these great poets, William Blake. A Londoner like Chaucer and Milton, he saw that a sweepingly new age was indeed coming and unlike Wordsworth and Coleridge he remained a persistent radical. He also saw that the new age would need a new image of the creative God, as love not power and wrath. So he longed for a revolution in society and in theology. But partly in order to avoid prison he had to clothe his vision in mysticism and mythology and in art, not plain words. Even without that incentive to be obscure, being reasonable was not his habit since he had never been given a formal schooling: Kathleen Raine called him a 'prophet against science'. Thus it remains the task of a new generation to discern what a vision of a far better world must mean for the urgently essential and necessarily drastic renewal of religion, spirituality and politics, and in that task the message of Blake can be no more than – but also no less than – an inspiration.

In this book I have not attempted to answer the great questions at which I have glanced in this Preface. In case anyone is interested in my thoughts, I may mention that I have written rather too many other books over what is now almost half a century. Here I simply try to share the experience of being struck by what seven poets wrote and by what some scholars have written about them. And in this book I have not thought it appropriate to add footnotes, to give references for all quotations or to reproduce the old spelling or punctuation (except in Chaucer's case). But in the hope that my non-academic presentation may persuade more readers to go not only to the texts but also to some of the scholarly literature which has added richly to knowledge and understanding, I have listed recent studies in the academic world to which I am very gratefully indebted. In the 1980s I included some short studies of these poets as essential figures in the three volumes of a history of *Christian England*, but since then there has been much to learn and to think, as I attempt to report.

Although I have offered some suggestions of my own, my main ambition has been to convey in a convenient package pearls of wisdom taken from the shelves of academic libraries. Perhaps, however, I ought to add that I have not found it necessary to depend exclusively on any one movement in literary criticism since the Second World War. With the formalists or New Critics I respectfully agree that a poem is good or bad as a poem, not as a manifesto; with the psychoanalysts that a poet often reveals interesting traces of being human; with the Marxist-materialists or New Historicists that a poet's background in class or culture is important; with the reader-response theorists or the deconstructionists that a work of art need not have a single, simple message; and with the feminists that these men were prejudiced. This failure to take sides may be because I do not understand the arguments, but I have the impression that in its internal divisions which are too exclusive literary criticism has recently been too like religion.

David L. Edwards

ONE

CHAUCER

GEOFFREY CHAUCER CAN BE SEEN from a number of angles. Since he was an Englishman born in or around 1345, when this island was firmly a part of Europe and Europe was influenced profoundly by the Catholic form of Christianity, he can be seen as an agreeably humane and humorous Catholic Christian. In G. K. Chesterton's *Chaucer* (1932) he was so seen with a brilliant clarity, at a time between Europe's almost suicidal wars. And within that civilisation he was also seen as very English. But very properly scholars led by Charles Muscatine in his *Chaucer and the French Tradition* (1957) became interested in, and knowledgeable about, the techniques of a sophisticated writer inspired by French and Italian poets and determined to match them in English. Then there was something of a return to Chesterton, insisting that this was an orthodox believer who drew on the medieval tradition in religion and morality, and that was the documented theme of D. W. Robertson's large *Preface to Chaucer* (1962). Chaucer was still seen as a storyteller but now the stories could be studied not as miniature novels but as disguised sermons, being allegories whose solemn purpose was to illustrate religious and moral teachings. It could be added that the characters in these stories were not individuals whom Chaucer might have met when out riding: they were fairly conventional embodiments of virtues or vices, classes or jobs, masculinity or the feminine. And the further point could be made that the representatives of the Church who are mocked or attacked in these tales, again in accordance with convention, do not represent the fuller reality, which was a general acceptance of Catholicism and its institutions.

Since then it has of course been agreed that Chaucer lived and thought in the shadow of the medieval Church but any suggestion that his poems were like medieval plays which naïvely popularised the truths of Bible and Church has been resisted. Constructively, it has been shown that he belonged to a time of religious and social unsettlement when the Middle Ages were beginning to disintegrate, and the new emphasis has been on the irony, satire and ambiguity in his work, or on 'radical' views which can be detected where his intentions can be discerned, or on 'radical' questions which can be seen to be raised, or at least on 'radical' interpretations which can be advanced by modern or postmodern critics. Robert Jordan's *Chaucer's Poetics and the Modern Reader* (1987) was one of the books which inaugurated this stimulating trend. But in his *Social Chaucer* (1989) a New Historicist, Paul Strohm, offered a useful reminder that this poet belonged to a period vastly different from Europe in the twentieth century. One difference was that, as Jordan wrote, Chaucer's 'vision upward toward God, though not free of anxiety, expresses confidence in an absolute that endures beyond the contingencies of this world'.

The facts are that he attended public worship like almost everyone else; he knew much about what the Catholic Church taught in Latin; he admired the virtues which the Church told him to admire; and the Church's influence on him grew as he grew older, overwhelming him when he was about to die. If he had any basic doubts he kept them to himself – as he kept any controversial opinions about politics to himself, for he was a civil servant. Yet he was to some extent independent. He was postmodern in this sense: he refused to fit everything which he knew, observed or imagined into a little box of ideology. In his greatest work, *The Canterbury Tales*, no tale-teller's viewpoint stands unchallenged and, as Helen Cooper has written, this collection of people and stories is so varied that it 'insists that in human experience, and in poetry and language, nothing can be regarded as normative'.

He was also, in a sense, a humanist. Human nature was what fascinated him and usually he liked it, or was merciful to it, or was amused by it. When dealing with theology, as he did occasionally, he was every inch a layman. He translated other people's philosophy but did not expound his own. He did not attack the generally accepted beliefs that the stars, and 'humours' in the body, are decisive influences on human behaviour. He took full advantage of the convention which then allowed a Christian poet to write about Roman or Greek gods or goddesses without always pointing out that they do not exist or always making clear their connection with the Christians' God. These divinities are used because they are prestigious (knowing about them shows that one is educated) and because they are semi-human; they have love affairs, quarrels, preferences and limitations. And he wrote about humans who are only half good; thus he imagined a pilgrimage which is tending in a religious direction but which meanwhile is telling stories about people and making personal remarks. He does not describe any visit to a wayside shrine and his account stops before the pilgrims reach Canterbury Cathedral. None of them is said to have been changed by their shared experience. They were all thoroughly medieval – yet we can see our own flawed humanity in these medieval versions of it. There was truth in what William Blake was to write in 1809: 'the characters of Chaucer's Pilgrims are the characters that compose all ages and all nations . . . for we see the same characters repeated again and again . . . and consequently they are the physiognomies or lineaments of universal human life beyond which Nature never steps.'

It is illuminating to consider the ways in which he was unlike the poet whose work was the climax to the English tradition up to that date: William Langland, very definitely a Christian but not a humanist. Pictures of Chaucer painted not long after his death suggest that he was genial and plump, but 'Long Will' Langland was so nicknamed because he was lean and tall; he could not afford to eat well and when in a poem he asked himself whether he ought not to earn his living by manual labour, his answer in a rare touch of humour was that he was too tall to bend close to the earth.

Although born only about fifteen years before Chaucer, and although like Chaucer he spent most of his life in London, his imagination belonged to an England older and more rural. His poetry was in a language and tradition going back behind the Norman conquest. It depended for any order not on rhymes but on alliteration and the need to find appropriate words beginning with the same letter could make it clumsy. And so could the sheer length of a poem, intended to be read to an audience or by a privileged individual with hours of leisure, probably in the evening. His masterpiece, *Piers Plowman*, seems to have been begun in or around 1362. In the later 1360s the initial draft was expanded; in the 1370s this version was trebled in length; in the 1380s it was largely rewritten. At no stage was it tidied up but it had power because it was undeniably sincere, with an urgent message but also with a full recognition that life, even the Christian life, is complicated. A mystic's total devotion to Christ was combined with a reformer's almost total indignation about the Church and the society around him – and with the sharp-eyed realism of a man of the people.

He was essentially a preacher who had to use poetry as a pulpit because his marriage to Kitte disqualified him for the priesthood. Reaching a considerable audience through the written word (some fifty medieval manuscripts of *Piers* survive), he stood in a long line of preachers who told stories full of everyday details but always teaching a religious or moral lesson. More than most preachers and more than most graduates he was an intellectual bursting with ideas, but in his passion to communicate he turned every idea into a story, a picture or a person, teaching by parables or allegories like the Christ whom he imagined vividly.

The poem begins in the Malvern hills, with the poet dreaming of a 'faire felde ful of folke'. Some of the folk are quietly getting on with the job of avoiding hunger by ploughing and sowing, but others are less truly respectable. Some sing bawdy songs, others make useless speeches, others tell worldly tales when they are supposed to be devout pilgrims. In the distance can be seen a society wedding in Westminster, between Lady Mede (Money) and Fals. Although the bride is accused by Conscience and Reason before the king, money continues to be the effective monarch. But on a high hill is the Tower of Truth and eventually a pilgrimage is led up there by Piers Plowman. This allegorical figure is not merely an honest labourer. He is Peter and he turns out to be Christ, wearing human nature like a suit of armour as he does battle with the Devil and 'harrows' hell like a conqueror in an invasion. Then Piers/Christ finds his way into the soul of every faithful pilgrim:

> For I, that am lorde of lyf, love is my drynke
> And for that drynke today I deyde vpon erthe.

At the start Holychurch has instructed the pilgrims about what they will need – prayer as the bridge before they make any progress, love as the only way, dependence on strength from God to reach union with Christ. The Christian life is at three levels: Do Wel (in practical work), Do Bet (in the spiritual life), Do Best (combining activity with contemplation). But the poem ends with Holychurch under attack by Antichrist from within its own ranks. Conscience has to go on another pilgrimage, this time to look for a good pope, needed before all the good can be gathered in the Barn of Unity.

Recent studies have uncovered the arduous development of the mind of this poet-preacher. At first he concentrated on the vision of disorder in society followed by the beginning of the pilgrimage to Truth. But what is Truth? Personifications of Thought, Wit, Study, Clergie and Scripture could explain the truth about the Christian life in some detail and in their somewhat different ways. Then he added five more visions in which all those secondary authorities were replaced by Christ the one Redeemer, yet the Church founded by Christ to be Christlike has been corrupted because it has rejected its Lord in favour of Pride and in pursuit of more and more wealth. The Franciscan friars, originally consecrated to poverty among the poor, were condemned in particular for granting priestly absolutions in exchange for cash. So the poet's development is increasingly radical, yet in essence the conclusion is already present early on, when Conscience is horrified by the king's suggestion that he should replace Fals as Lady Mede's husband: 'Crist it me forbade!' Langland was not a Protestant of the sixteenth century: although not an admirer of the fourteenth-century popes, he never attacked the Mass or the monasteries. But always he struggled hard to see how the whole money-fuelled apparatus of Church and State in his time – the Church of Lady Mede – might be subjected to Christ, the ultimate Judge who for now moves among the people as a ploughman.

The mind of this preaching moralist overlapped with Chaucer's very different personality because both lived in the same age. During Langland's adolescence the Black Death was a plague which killed about a third of England's population of about five million. He survived, to see London at the mercy of the Peasants' Revolt in 1381: so far from accepting attempts by the government to control where people might live and what they might wear or eat, and so far from paying the new poll tax affecting everyone, labourers demanded more freedom and more wages because their labour had become more valuable, and the Archbishop of Canterbury was among the bosses murdered. Capitalism was being born slowly and painfully; the feudal system which had chained a peasant to a lord and a land was being replaced by an economy based on cash and on bargains between buyer and seller. The sense of a sacred society, of a hierarchy ordained by God, of a community bound together by solemnly sworn loyalties, was being diminished. In the 1370s rival popes appeared, in Rome and Avignon, while England's king, Edward III, declined into senility and England's leading theologian, John Wyclif, launched the Lollard protest against the Church's corruption. These were all changes to which Langland felt close although he lived far from any centre of power. Chaucer, who did move in high circles but as an official, was for that very reason determined to keep his distance from any unpleasantness. Nevertheless, in his poetry he commemorated a duchess struck down by the Black Death, he compared the revolt of 1381 with chaos in a farmyard, he admired a saintly priest who could be called a 'Lollere', he did not admire people mainly interested in money – and we shall find more if we look closely.

Chaucer's life was far more privileged than Langland's. His surname comes from the French for shoemaker, but his grandfather entered the more profitable trade of the wine merchants and his father prospered in it, acquiring a connection with the royal court. Geoffrey was brought up in a house very near to London's excitingly busy river, educated by picking up sights and words in its crowded streets (although its population was then only about fifty thousand), and taught 'grammar' (which meant Latin) in one of its schools, the nearest being the one attached to St Paul's Cathedral. His later life was to show aptitudes for mathematics and languages.

At about the age of twelve he was given new clothes for Christmas – shoes, a short cloak and stockings in red and black, to wear as a page in the household of a princess. Some of his duties would be in the kitchen but he was now in a position to learn much about privileged life and to participate in it. And he made the most of his opportunities: he worked tirelessly in his career and made ambition hereditary, for his son Thomas was to become rich and a leading figure in the royal household and the House of Commons, and his granddaughter was to be a duchess.

A document of 1360 shows him in the army invading France: he was taken prisoner but the king contributed to his ransom. Seven years later he was given a senior position in the royal household, as an 'esquier'. In modern terms, he was now available for duties as courtier, diplomat and civil servant. For twelve years beginning in 1374 he was the controller who supervised the collection of taxes on the export of wool and leather from the port of London – a responsible position, for the money would be transferred to London merchants in repayment of loans to the king required to finance the government and especially its long war with France. Originally he was required to keep the accounts in his own hand although later he was allowed a deputy. As late as 1398 he was granted a safe conduct to travel through England while engaged in *ardua et urgencia* business of the king. In his poetry he could pretend to be stupid but that was not what he was paid to be in his profession.

He undertook at least a dozen official missions outside England. Knowing France helped him to know French literature at a time when chivalry and courtly love were being celebrated by Machant and Froisart, and he translated the first part of a key text, the century-old *Roman de la Rose.* Diplomatic work took him to Genoa, Florence and Milan at a time when poets of the stature of Dante, Petrarch and Boccaccio were either alive or well remembered. Returning to England with some of their books, he set himself to compete with those other Europeans. The French poets had celebrated chivalry and courtly love but he could be more discriminating about the individuals involved. Dante had set himself up as a judge of the dead as of the living, but he would remember his own humanity and be more tender. Petrarch had lamented the coldness of his mistress but he would look at a woman more shrewdly. Boccaccio had been a great teller of stories old or new and he would use them – but he would go deeper into characters, including even some touches of philosophy, and he never named Boccaccio as a source. So he sat reading and writing in his house above one of the gates which led out of the city of London, and he has left us a picture of himself absorbed in this escape. This gatehouse was quite near William Langland's cottage and in 1381 the rebellious peasants entered the city through Aldgate.

No doubt he found reading and writing more congenial than the collection of taxes but this was a time when a tax-inspector could be sent on delicate missions into the glamour of France or Italy, and even his main job did give him an audience as a poet. The royal court to which he was attached was a cultural centre with a tradition of enjoying poetry sung or read either by minstrels or by its own members, and rich people connected with the court would want their own households to resemble it up to a point. Also, the fact that an official with whom one did business in London was also a poet would be of some interest to merchants, who could be more educated than most of the nobility. Chaucer was thus in a situation where his enthusiasm about poetry would do him no harm and he knew that this was the best he could hope for. Authors were not paid royalties on the handwritten copies which might be made of their work. His friend John Gower could spend much more time as a poet because he was a considerable landowner.

He began by writing lyrics for songs about love; Gower claimed that England was full of his friend's 'ditees and songes glade' and although that compliment was probably exaggerated a collection of fifteen short poems in French by 'Ch' has reached us and may well be his work. A longer poem (like that collection, preserved in a single manuscript) is a devout petition for the prayers of the Blessed Virgin Mary, addressed in verses each of which begins with a different letter of the alphabet. That is a translation from the French, with short lines of French elegance.

When he felt ready to attempt something more substantial, what he produced in or around 1368 was full of echoes from recent French literature, but it rhymed in English and was much more than a translation. The Anglo-Norman dialect of French had been spoken by the upper class for some three hundred years but by the 1360s the language of the people was sufficiently respectable to be used for conversation at the royal court or in a noble household. Now Chaucer used English to mourn the recent death of a great lady.

The Book of the Duchess takes the form of a dream as does *Piers Plowman*, but it belongs to the court not to the fields. The narrator falls asleep after reading a Latin poem (by Ovid) about grief after love. In his dream he joins a hunt in lovely country but leaves the main party in order to care for a wounded puppy. The dog then leads him to the Man in Black who, when asked why he is so sad, speaks of his love for a lady called White. This broken-hearted knight seems to see her still, dancing, singing, laughing, as when they had been united in joy. 'She took me into her governance' and he still has no wish to escape. The slow-witted dreamer does not see that he is speaking with John of Gaunt, Duke of Lancaster, the most powerful man of England, a son of the royal Black Prince and the bereaved husband of Blanche ('White'). The dreamer eventually asks 'where is she now?' The reply comes in line 1,309 of the poem: 'She is ded'. The conversation then ends rapidly, for the dreamer offers no more than a sentence of sympathy: to say more might be impertinent and would certainly be beyond the range of his theological equipment. The poet finds himself back in bed – in real life, as a man still in his early twenties who can dream about his own future. The Man in Black goes back to his castle – in real life, as a duke who will soon marry again, very grandly, but fall in love with a different woman by whom he is to have four children and through whom he is to have a closer relationship with Chaucer (as we shall see).

A time of literary silence passed and then we are given two poems which show that amid his official duties Chaucer has armed himself with greater skill as a poet but is uncertain how to use that skill in order to achieve fame.

The House of Fame begins in some confusion about theology: he prays to the god of sleep but then to the one Creator and 'Jesus God'. Anyhow, he is granted sleep and his dream takes him to a temple of glass exhibiting a picture of a naked Venus. However, a brass plate on the temple's wall is seen as a reminder that love can end in tears, and the tale of the desertion of Dido by Aeneas is now retold with his sympathy all for her. And around the temple is a vast desert.

He is rescued by a giant eagle who lifts him into space travel. He is terrified but this eagle is not going to take him to hell, purgatory or heaven as Dante had been conducted in a more religious tour. Instead the learned bird explains how the sounds of earth can be heard on high. He offers an inspection of the stars but since he is a medieval poet the dreamer replies that he prefers to learn about nature from books (although Chaucer wrote a practical guide to the use of the astrolabe in astronomy, for the benefit of his son Lewis). He is taken instead to the House of Fame built magnificently on an iceberg which is melting in the sky. There he sees the goddess Fame giving or withholding her blessings according to her whims. Next door is the House of Rumour, spinning all the time and made of wickerwork through which the winds blow low sounds in and out.

So what is to be Chaucer's own fame? In the House of Fame he has seen great poets standing on pedestals around the goddess, each holding up a picture of the subject which has made him great. Excitingly, the dreamer is told that great 'love-tydyngs' are about to be announced. It is probably the engagement of Anne of Bohemia to marry England's young king, Richard II, after long and difficult negotiations in which Chaucer has been involved as a part-time diplomat (in Milan). But just as 'a man of great auctorite' arrives to make a statement, the poem ends and scholars have been left to speculate why. Was there some difficulty in the negotiations? Did the poet feel unable to compose an announcement with appropriate tact and grandeur? Or has the end been lost in all three of the surviving manuscripts?

The next poem, *The Parliament of Fowls*, seems to have been written in a far more confident mood connected with the celebrations soon before or after the royal marriage. It is in 'rhyme royal' (the lines have ten syllables and the rhyming is ababbcc). It begins with a reference to a dream known to the learned in the Middle Ages because a treatise by Macrobius cited it from Cicero's *Republic*: Scipio Africanus dreams of a heaven reserved for the great and the good who have laboured for the 'commune profyt'. But the narrator has a very different dream, about love – for Scipio pushes him into the Garden of Love which is a familiar feature of high-class love poetry. It is entered through gates which carry warnings that both delights and miseries are to be found within. The nasty bit is the temple of Venus, where the goddess 'withouten any atyr' is disporting herself with Richesse. But when he escapes from that hothouse of lust he finds himself in a garden presided over by a calmer and more sensible goddess, Nature, the 'vicaire' or deputy of 'almighty Lord'. She is arranging marriages between birds. The most impressive of these are eagles and three males are heard wooing a female, which probably represents the rivalry between the English king and two foreign princes for the hand of the beauty who is Queen Anne. The eagle who represents King Richard offers the most eloquent vow of lifelong devotion – a promise the king is to keep – but in the poem he gets no firm commitment from the bashful lady, as is the convention in poems about courtly love. Other birds of lesser breeds offer comments, polite or otherwise, but at length all join a song to 'welcome somer', in joy about their own marriages and in hopefulness about the eagles'. The implication may be that all classes should unite to celebrate the royal wedding which has taken place on 14 January 1383 although there is some evidence that it had not been popular among those who knew that Anne's royal brother, King Wenceslaus of Bohemia, had been 'lent' a large sum by the English government: so far from bringing a rich dowry with her, the bride had been sold.

A little puzzle is linked with this poem. Why did Chaucer make the 'smale foules' sing about summer and 'love' in honour of 'Saynt Valentyn'? If they are singing on 14 February 1383, it is exactly a month after the royal wedding, but why mention Valentine? Two martyrs honoured by the Church of Rome each year on that day were named Valentine but not connected with young love. A third Valentine is known to have been honoured in a festival celebrated in Genoa and that obscure festival came in May, a month when the sap rises in lovers as well as trees. So was the poem written to celebrate the marriage treaty in May 1382? An obscure French poem linking St Valentine and love may be earlier than Chaucer, but it is Chaucer who goes on about the link. In another poem by him a bird sings on St Valentine's day about love between Mars and Venus and in yet another a bird raises this chant:

> Blessed be Saynt Valentyn
> For on his day I cheese you to be myn.

Thus it seems possible that this poet of love was responsible for the addition of a festival of love to the English calendar.

What is clear, although equally odd, is that Chaucer had a special reason at this time to put himself forward as a poet of love. In 1366 he had married another courtier, Philippa de Roet. This is not clear in any surviving evidence, but it is generally accepted by scholars that she was the daughter of a knight close to the royal family, and also sister to Katherine Swynford, yet another courtier who was John of Gaunt's mistress and eventually his third wife. But in 1380 Chaucer was accused of *raptus* by a baker's daughter, Cecilia Champaigne. Those who love what he wrote have been dismayed ever since the relevant legal documents were discovered in 1873, and have been able to make some points in his defence. *Raptus* did not necessarily refer to what is now called rape although it usually did and it is difficult to think why Chaucer should have abducted her. Although she may have been blackmailing him when he had seduced her, or even when an affair of willing love had gone sour, because the accused did not wish the case to come to court he seems to have paid her off and to have been short of money for a period. Five distinguished friends were witnesses when the legal proceedings were ended officially and the scandal was not great enough to end Chaucer's career. But in this murky light we can see why he had a motive to acquire fame as a poet who could handsomely celebrate a royal wedding.

The Peasants' Revolt broke out only a year after the embarrassment of that Champaigne affair and it gave him a special motive to be hopeful, but perhaps also worried, about the future of King Richard. At the age of fourteen in 1381 Richard already had enough self-confidence to use the immense prestige of his kingship when confronting the very angry rebels outside London. They might have killed him but instead he pacified the mob and they remained respectful even when their leader was killed. Being an informed and shrewd walker along the corridors of power, Chaucer must have realised that the revolt revealed the instability of the whole feudal system, and he may have asked himself what role the young king could be expected to play. Would Richard's sense of drama combined with a mystical belief in his own sacredness equip him to govern acceptably (it did not)? Or would his self-confidence become tyrannical and alienate the aristocracy on whom even a monarch must depend (it did)?

Whether or not these events in 1380–81 were strong factors in the development, in the 1380s something made Chaucer think and write at a new depth. He confronted the great question which Arcite was to ask in *The Canterbury Tales*: 'What is this world? What asketh men to have?' One source of an answer was studied in depth when he translated *The Consolation of Philosophy* by Boethius, written in prison not long before its author was battered to death in 524. Although Boethius then confined himself to arguments used by philosophers in the ancient world, he was himself a devout Christian and had been a theologian of stature, even writing a book on the Holy Trinity. Now doomed to death as an alleged traitor to a regime which he had served eminently, he made himself listen to Lady Philosophy as she urged him to fix his mind on eternity. Her claim was that everything in history is foreseen by God, yet nothing is decreed inflexibly, and she attempted to explain this paradox by arguing that God lives in the 'eternal now': to him past, present and future are all alike because the past and the future are known to him as clearly as the present. Yet she also taught that humans have been given free will, the Godlike freedom of action. Thus the present plight of Boethius is not unknown to God or unexpected by him, but he has not commanded it: the unjust are free to do evil and Boethius is free to decide to be calm and brave in response. Here comes what is presented as the explanation: before they reach their decisions God knows how both his accusers and the prisoner are bound to behave. It is a little as if an observer standing at the summit of a mountain, and possessing uniquely sharp eyesight and intuition, can watch the apparently confused traffic in the valley below and predict who is going to move where.

The *Consolation* was written in a prison cell and its author knew that as an alleged traitor he would be released from prison only by death. Yet the teaching which he presents as coming from 'Philosophy' while he is 'cast into moornynge and into wepynge' enters his heart as well as his mind. In reality he is teaching himself how to endure. His translator into medieval English seems to have much the same motive for his work: he is a civil servant who wants to be a famous poet, yet he tackles the translation of this Latin text into about fifty thousand English words at a time when it would seem extraordinary for anyone to write philosophy in English. And he does not merely translate: he adds his own explanations of the text at many points when what Boethius wrote may not be quickly understood. He may well have been alerted to the merits of the *Consolation* by a reference to it in the second half of the *Roman de la Rose* (the half which he did not translate); Jean de Meuen, who had written that very worldly example of French courtly literature, had himself gone on to translate the solemnities of Boethius. But while Chaucer used that French version, he compared it in detail with the Latin original – itself no small feat for a man of business who had left school early.

Inevitably a modern reader is likely to question some or all of the logic used by Boethius. Before Philosophy begins her instruction she drives the Muses out of the prison cell: they belong to 'the fables of the poetis'. But the picture of the universe which she conveys is not the one painted by modern science. Here everything is obviously designed. Beyond all reasonable doubt it was God who decided to create all that exists and in its origin it was indeed all a perfect treasure, 'parfytely ymakid'. Things do not evolve from their beginning; things decline because corrupted. The only question is why God has allowed some things to be so imperfect that they harm humans. The answer is that these things discipline humans, who have become so corrupt that they tead to choose evil rather than good.

So humans deserve to be miserable, yet God can use religious meditation to rescue someone from misery. Boethius has fallen from high office to be 'turmented in this see of fortune' but in Chaucer's words he finds 'tranquillite of soule', the 'knowynge' which 'paseth in noblesse alle othere thynges'. What can be known is 'blisfulnesse'. In comparison, everything offered by the world becomes unsatisfactory sooner or later. Wealth leaves one anxious about what one has, yet wanting more; prestige, power and fame are all temporary; strength and beauty are mortal; even family life is so limited in its joys that Philosophy can quote 'my disciple Euripidis' as saying that 'he that hath no children' is a happy man. The familiar comparison is made between these perishable goods and the 'floures of the somer sesoun'. Chaucer also translated a treatise on the miseries of life written by a future pope, Innocent III (while he was waiting for the living pope to die), although this has been lost.

But the enjoyments to be had in the world are good up to a point. The desire for them is natural since every creature wants to be fulfilled, even if these things are not the fullness of 'felicite', not the 'soveryn good' of knowing God at the still 'centre of thynges'. 'Verray blisfulnesse is set in sovereyn God' and those who miss that are to be pitied because of the 'unselynesse of shrewednesse', the unhappiness of villainy. So the commandment of Philosophy is to love 'ryghtfully good folk, and have pity on schrewes'.

Evil people are punished, by pains or by their regrets, but Philosophy refuses to be dogmatic about the nature of hell. Her boldly positive teaching is that in this life 'alle fortune is good' because any event either punishes the evil 'by the resoun of justice' or rewards the good, or brings the good closer to God and their true selves by education through suffering. 'I deme that contrarious Fortune profiteth more to men than Fortune debonayre.' To believe this is to have a fixed point from which to view the ups and downs of life, and to be stable oneself although a disaster may be as overwhelming as the explosion of a volcano. The number of surviving manuscripts shows that this translation was welcomed quite widely and his poetry suggests that Chaucer was enabled by Boethius to find his own stability and his true voice.

He needed stability when he had to witness the political dramas which accompanied the literary and artistic achievements in Richard's reign. In 1387–88 aristocrats who resented the influence on the king of favourites other than themselves staged a political coup and were merciless to Richard's friends and closest servants. Those executed included some of Chaucer's professional colleagues and a poet who was a disciple, Thomas Usk. Chaucer, however, had not given offence and in 1386, seeing that a storm was coming, he had been shrewd enough to ask to be relieved of his duties in the collection of taxes. He had retired to Greenwich in Kent, where he undertook local and routine duties, for example as a magistrate. The government nominated him to represent Kent in the parliament of 1386 but it may be guessed that he stayed out of trouble. Some of his income continued but he could not stay completely out of debt and in this difficult period of semi-retirement his wife died. When the king regained power in 1389 one of his early acts was to appoint Chaucer as the 'clerk' in charge of the business side of work on the many buildings owned by the Crown, but this job lasted for no more than two years. He cannot have been entirely sorry when it came to an end, because he was attacked and robbed when travelling with cash on him. He kept himself available to serve the Crown but he could at last concentrate on work as a poet, unpaid but peaceful and absorbing.

During the 1380s he had set himself to produce a 'tragedie' – a word which he used in a new sense. In ancient Greek it had meant a song about a goat, presumably because a sacrifice of an animal to the gods had seemed to dramatise the human need to secure the gods' favour. Its basic purpose was still to reply to a turn in the wheel manipulated by Fortune to bring good or bad luck and a short poem called 'Fortune' was a plea to those responsible for making grants on behalf of the Crown to support men who have served well but are now down on their luck. But to Chaucer the wheel of Fortune was set in motion not by chance but by a strength or weakness in a human character and that was what he wanted to explore. Although he never wrote this, he may well have been thinking about the flaw in King Richard as a cause of the country's current ills; if Shakespeare was to see that Richard's vision of himself as a divinely anointed dictator caused his fate, it is likely that the closely involved Chaucer saw it too. It is also probable that he was examining flaws in himself, having come close to disaster through adultery. And from what he wrote next we may reasonably deduce that he was now thinking with a serious realism about chivalry as the ideology of the upper class and about marriage as cement or prison for the whole of society. He no longer fitted quietly into that society's system and he was now critical of hypocrites who took advantage of their positions in it but who in reality were interested mainly in their own comforts or profits. And he noticed individuals, with a new concentration on their personalities: in his new long poem seven out of eight lines were to be in direct speech by individuals and in his greatest work different pilgrims to Canterbury were to tell different tales, often self-revealing.

Because it shows again and again an unprecedented subtlety in the presentation of the characters of individuals, *Troilus and Criseyde* has been called the first English novel. But it is not in prose: Chaucer performs the feat of keeping up the pace of the plot although he writes more than 7,500 lines of poetry in the difficult pattern of the rhyme royal. It is a story which he owes to Boccaccio, about a lady of Troy who is wooed and won by a heroic prince but then transfers her love to one of the Greeks who are besieging the city. Chaucer presents Criseyde as a human being with fluctuating emotions, silly rather than wicked, vulnerable rather than unattractive, and it has been claimed that every man who meets her in print loves her and longs to protect her. At first she is a young widow who enjoys romantic fiction but is very nervous when told that a real prince loves her. Troilus also is very human: as a young soldier he visits the temple of Venus in order to poke fun at people who are there as victims of love, but the first sight of Criseyde instantly makes him love-sick. When she sees him riding in triumph home from a battle she too falls in love, but much cunning is required from her uncle Pandarus the match-maker to persuade her to come to supper one rainy evening and stay the night, and to get Troilus to be brave enough to visit and to hide himself. In the end Pandarus has to push him into her bed.

After three years as lovers they are parted because she decides that she must obey an order from the Trojan parliament to move to the Greek camp, to which her father has already deserted; he says he wants her to join him. She is exchanged for a Trojan general who has been captured. She promises to return from the enemy's camp within ten days – but does not. Troilus is distraught; he keeps on waiting and eventually he writes, to which she replies. Hers is a devastating letter. She blames him for making her cry when she is already sick, for thinking only about his own 'pleasaunce' when she is miserable, for being unfaithful to her, for failing to see that their continuing separation is 'the goddess ordinaunce'. And she hopes that he will not take her letter amiss.

The truth seen by the narrator is that because her 'corage' is 'slydyng' she needs a new man to protect her, the Greek soldier Diomede: her tragedy is that she always needs a man. And the sequel is also seen with understanding. The tragedy of Troilus is that he needs a woman – one, Criseyde. He throws himself into the war, first in order to kill Diomede and then in order to get killed himself. And then the narrator sees even more. The soul of the 'sleyn' Troilus arises from the battlefield and he hears the planets making 'hevenysh melodye'. The narrator cannot report that this pagan will enjoy the beatific vision of God which is the climax in Dante's exploration of eternity, but at least he can watch Troilus looking down on 'this litel spot of erth' – and laughing when he notices the mourners who weep for him.

On seeing that, the narrator revises his theology. As events have unfolded, his opinion up to this point has agreed with what has been believed by Troilus and Criseyde themselves: everything is decreed by Fortune. The only hope has been that God will grant a 'litel hertes reste' in each temporary position of Fortune's wheel. But now he knows something which he hopes will be known by all 'yonge, fresshe folkes, he or she', in whom love 'groweth'. He hopes that they will understand that the ultimate reality is rest in eternity. It is not 'this world that passeth sone as floures fayre'. Nor is it the pagan gods who are 'swich rascaille', such a contemptible mob. Nor is it Fortune. It is the purpose of the true God who made human lovers 'after his ymage' and who showed his own love 'upon a crois'. In comparison everything human, including our loves, is fragile, but at the end there can be a 'hertes reste' which is more than 'litel'. We can hear echoes of Boethius.

Like most plots, this one can seem silly: for example, why didn't the lovers marry, so that Criseyde's place would be with her new husband, beyond doubt? But Chaucer turned it into a story which is basically serious. He dedicated it to a more solemn poet, 'moral Gower', and to a theologian, 'philosophical Strode', and felt it necessary to ask that this 'litel book' should not be compared with the classics of Homer, Virgil and Ovid. And the possibility of such a comparison is not entirely ridiculous, for while maintaining a high level of poetry over a long stretch Chaucer has created characters with a skill without precedent in English literature and not common in the earlier literature of other cultures. At the end a reader can feel quite intimate with a man and a woman equally doomed, and will not be inclined to condemn in a hurry. So the reader has been guided to be more perceptive than Pandarus the go-between. A man of the world, he seems much cleverer and smoother than the others. He is always able to suggest a practical next step, never at a loss for a witty remark, never handicapped by a great passion or principle, always friendly and manipulative, perhaps bisexual. But at the end he simply hates Criseyde and says so, and he fails to understand why Troilus cannot forget her: he offers his own sister as a substitute. He understands nothing.

Chaucer may have been asked, or he may have invited himself, to write a sequel, the *Legend of Good Women*, which would be a long collection of short stories about women who were good in response to their bad treatment by men. Armed with plots derived from his wide reading, he set off confidently with yet another dream: before he falls asleep on the lawn of his house in London he remembers that a daisy is the symbol of Queen Alceste, the consort of the god of love. So when he is rebuked by Cupid for writing about love's victims he can hear Alceste rebuking her husband for speaking like a tyrant. Does he also hear the gentle Queen Anne restraining King Richard? At any rate he looks forward to presenting his new poem to Anne in the royal palace at Sheen. But Anne died in 1394, the whole palace was demolished by Richard whose mind was now unbalanced, and the poet had to write a new version of his prologue. However, he grew bored and, according to all the twelve surviving manuscripts, after about 2,700 lines ended abruptly.

It seems that he got fed up with moaning women and their misbehaving lords. Indeed, he wrote about these pathetic heroines with so little enthusiasm that more than one modern critic has suggested that the whole exercise was intended as a merciless satire on the medieval equivalent of feminism. Now he wanted to write about women and men who stood up for themselves and enjoyed life. As another critic has observed, he wanted to build with words something like a Gothic cathedral, with a richness more than compensating for the lack of symmetry and with a tower or spire rising above the exuberance.

In 1387, or a bit before it, his imagination was fired, and his energy aroused, by the idea of *The Canterbury Tales*. It would be an opportunity to exercise his literary skills in an experimental variety of styles and on a new scale, and also to preserve material already available. (There is evidence that he had already written the tales which were to be given to the knight and the second nun, and other old material may include the tales which look out of keeping because they are prose.) At last he could leave the royal court. If he could imagine a group meeting by accident in a tavern in London one April evening, he need not discuss kings or tackle the delicate task of describing the lords and ladies to whom he was subordinate in social status. Nor need he include peasants about whom he knew little, for they could not afford a holiday. But he could welcome the fresh air being brought into English society by men and women of, or near, his own bourgeois class; thus the Wife of Bath could be an independent merchant like his own father. He would be free to be honest about them, treating them partly as representatives of 'estates' (social groups) and partly as lively and quirky individuals. He could make them tell tales which would usually illuminate their own characters but the light thrown could be at an oblique angle so that the connection between tale and teller need not be boringly obvious. He could bring English people together as they had never been brought before; he could make them compete and argue with each other in a fellowship which no one would leave; he could make them all use the same kind of English, London-based. Most would not be spiritually minded but since they all belong to a society unified and dominated by the Church all could agree that the journey should be a pilgrimage. And by art he could conceal the improbabilities: it would not be asked how some thirty people riding along a narrow road could all hear a tale told by one person in the line, nor would readers wonder how the teller who was not a poet could speak at length in rhymed verse (or could speak intelligently when drunk, as in two cases). Chaucer would succeed brilliantly, being rewarded by fame not as a poet of love but as a poet of life. This fame began quickly (83 manuscripts of the *Tales* survive from the fifteenth century) and did not end when his language and his whole society ceased to be contemporary.

In his lifetime he felt confident enough about some of the tales to show them to friends (he refers to the Wife of Bath in a light, little poem in which he pretends to advise his friend Buxton against proceeding with his planned marriage), but he did not live to complete a project which was originally planned to include some 120 tales. He did not even revise fully what he managed to write; his prologue still announces the over-ambitious and abandoned plan, and some tales have been moved from one teller to another without changing the text. (A tough sailor is made to speak as a woman and a nun to speak as a 'son of Eve'.) And some people mentioned in the prologue tell no tale at all. The lack of a final polish is the more striking because Chaucer normally corrects a manuscript carefully, as in another, much shorter, poem he reminds his copyist, Adam.

The best explanation of this failure to leave behind a fully completed and corrected version of his masterpiece is that he became extremely depressed and mortally ill. This would be due in part to the tragic events of 1399–1400.

His ideals were standard in the society he knew and were expressed in three short poems of uncertain date – the nearest he came to preaching. One is 'Gentilesse'. It says very clearly that 'what man desireth gentil for to be' must himself love 'vertue' since no one can inherit that. No bishop, king or emperor is exempt from this rule. A true gentleman will speak the sober truth; he must be charitable and generous; he must be pure of heart; he must be hard working. In another poem he lamented the growth of lust for money or power, and liked to think that things had been better in a 'former age'. In another he complained that everyone who can oppresses his neighbour and 'no man is merciable'. He added a coded plea 'to King Richard': 'desyre to be honourable', fear God, love justice, 'cherish thy folk', 'wed thy folk agein to stedfastnesse'.

He watched this king – for whom, as already noted, he undertook difficult, dangerous and urgent missions – becoming a paranoid tyrant who defied the conventions in government, arranged the murder of the Duke of Gloucester and confiscated the estates of John of Gaunt's heir to the duchy of Lancaster. He cannot have been unmoved when Richard was dethroned by that heir, who became Henry IV, and then imprisoned and starved to death. He cannot have been as light-hearted as he pretended when he had to write a poem as a begging letter to the new king since his pension had not yet been renewed. In the last month of the year in which Richard's dead body was exhibited, he seems to have felt near his own death when he moved to a small house in the grounds of Westminster Abbey.

The last surviving document which mentions him comes from June 1400. When he died he was buried alongside other royal servants in one of the abbey's chapels, near the magnificent tomb which Richard had ordered in advance for himself and Anne. In 1566 he was reburied under his own tomb, more modest but respectful, in a transept of the Abbey which because of this beginning became Poets' Corner, with many graves or monuments honouring the great names of English literature. William Caxton, whose printing press was a few yards away in Westminster, published the first of the innumerable printed editions of *The Canterbury Tales* in 1478 and called their author the 'first founder and embellisher of ornate eloquence in our englissh'. Twelve years after his death Thomas Hoccleve had already acclaimed him as the 'first fyndere of our faire langage'. In late ages Philip Sidney lamented that Elizabethan poets 'walk so stumblingly after him' and William Wordsworth made a close study of Chaucer as an essential part of his plan to become one who would not stumble.

Famous words had begun *The Parliament of Fowls* at the height of his more youthful exuberance:

> The lyf so short, the craft so long to lerne,
> The assay so hard, so sharp the conqueryinge.

Those words have often been applied to his triumph as a writer but originally they referred to another preoccupation: 'al this mene I by love'. And as he looked back over a life which was not short by medieval standards, Chaucer became convinced that no good eternity lay ahead for him if he did not repent of having paid so much attention to what the parson in the *Tales* calls 'fables and such wrechednesse', about human love. So he added to the parson's exposition of ethics his own 'retraccIouns' in the hope that 'I may be oon of them at the day of doom that shulle be saved'. He did not regret 'the translation of Boece de Consolacione and othere bookes of legends of seintes, and omelies, and moralitee and devocion', but he begged for prayers that he might be forgiven for having learned how to write everything else, for he had been guilty of writing 'worldly vanitees'. They included 'the book of Troilus' and the book of the 25 ladies (he could not remember exactly how many he had covered); and also 'the tales of Caunterbury thilke sowen unto synne'.

So at the end, in that mood, Chaucer shared the verdict that the *Tales* encourage sin, or at least have no moral purpose. In the Victorian Age Matthew Arnold was of the same opinion, lamenting Chaucer's lack of 'high seriousness', and in our own time the postmodern suspicion about any grand narrative intended to improve us has turned that lament into praise. And certainly Chaucer is often non-judgemental. The 'Chaucer' who is one of the pilgrims is deliberately made unimpressive. The group's leader teases him about being fat and always looking on the ground nervously, and he is slow to speak. The two tales which he contributes are not intended to be authoritative pronouncements about the meaning of life: one is in tiresomely humorous verse, the other in tediously moralistic prose. And had the pilgrims returned to Southwark for their promised dinner and prizegiving, the prize for the best tale might have gone to the one which most mocks moralism, told by the 'nun's priest'. Although it may be conceivable that the original project envisaged an account of the pilgrims' devotions in Canterbury when they had been moved by the parson's sermon, in the *Tales* which we have the only expression of penitence is the author's own, in that brief epilogue.

The tales have not been arranged in a system which would convey a clear message. Ten fragments of the incomplete work are all that we have and they seem to make connections between the tales only in order to make contrasts. The lofty tales of the knight and the physician are followed by randy comedies about low life; the Wife of Bath's gusto about marriage is matched by stories by men who are very much unmarried; the thoughtful clerk is followed by the insensitive merchant, the hardboiled shipman by the tearful prioress, the lugubrious monk by the funniest man in the party, the pious second nun by a magician's assistant. Since the suggestion was first made in 1915 many readers have thought it both legitimate and illuminating to link tales with tellers, and that will be the strategy which is about to be tested (in a new form) in this book. It is, however, likely that hearers or readers will not always make such connections easily because the order in which the pilgrims are introduced in the general prologue does not correspond with any arrangement of their tales – and any connection which may be real is no more than a link between the dominant characteristic of the storyteller and the dominant characteristic of the story. And the link may be a piece of irony which may not be recognised as such immediately.

So the spiritual dimension of the *Tales* is not a simplifying morality which is quick to condemn and denounce. But that does not mean that Chaucer never implies an opinion about people's behaviour: on the contrary, it means that by this stage in his life he firmly occupies a moral position which is generous because mature. As John Hill put it in *Chaucerian Belief* (1991), he is sure that 'fiction has truths to tell, although not necessarily the truths of propositional assertion or logical demonstration'. All the time he is making moral judgements although he does not thrust them at us and as the climax he produces a good priest who simply repeats the medieval Church's teaching. At the end of *Troilus and Cressida* he gave hearers or readers a glimpse of eternity. At the end of this pilgrimage he gives us a glimpse of holiness as then understood.

Some of the tales are coarse; in 1700 John Dryden, who famously praised 'God's plenty' in Chaucer's work, refused to include these when he translated the book into poetry considered proper: this medieval poet, he explained, was a 'rough diamond' and needed polishing. But medieval people took the body and all its functions for granted, as the earth where any ladder must start. It is relevant that they seldom wore any clothes in bed.

A sordid story is told by a 'reeve' who is efficient at managing a lord's estate, at terrifying anyone who tries to cheat him – and at cheating the lord. It is a story about a miller who has been cheating his customers in a Cambridge college. Bent on punishment, two students ride over to his small house in a nearby village. Night falls and they are pressed to enjoy a good dinner and to sleep in the one bedroom, only to find that they are kept awake by the miller's drunken snores. Complicated manoeuvres between the adjacent beds result in sex for the students with both the daughter and the wife, who do not complain. By accident the miller is told about it all and by another accident is knocked out by his wife. The students then ride away without having paid for a large loaf. We can almost hear the merriment of an audience not unlike the people in the tale but we are instructed by historians that stories of this type, in French *fabliaux*, were also acceptable to people who enjoyed laughing at the mishaps of their social inferiors.

The narrator has previously apologised for telling such tales, and has offered two excuses: no one is compelled to listen or read, and he is merely reporting what was said. But in the *Tales* the context provides a better explanation, for we are told that before he became a dishonest estate manager the reeve had been a carpenter. This offensive story about a miller is a response to an offensive story about a carpenter told by a miller.

In the miller's tale, an old carpenter has a 'wylde and yonge' wife who is unsurprisingly glad to yield to the advances of a student who lodges in their little house. The exhausted sleep of wife and lodger is interrupted by a singer with a guitar at the window. He begs a kiss and the wife presents her bottom. Swallowing his indignation, he returns to ask for a proper kiss. The lodger, already out of bed 'for to pisse', offers his own bottom in order to 'leet fle a fart' – only to be branded by a red-hot piece of iron. His cry of pain awakens the old man who has been persuaded that the Flood which had drowned everyone except Noah's family is about to be repeated – so he had better sleep upstairs, suspended in a hammock from the roof. In his panic the old man cuts the rope holding him up and crashes through the floor, where everyone is united in chaos.

That is the farce and it is too funny to be merely obscene. And it is too humane. When he panics the old man thinks first about the danger to 'my wyf' Alison and earlier he has tried to share his simple faith with Nicholas, the student who, he thinks, is too interested in astronomy. Actually both Nicholas and Alison are young animals who perhaps do not deserve to have stones thrown at them. Before he is tricked into kissing the wrong part of Alison, Absolom (who works as a verger in the parish church) has a pathetic image of himself as a gallant gentleman. And so it seems significant that the divine Judge does not send that Second Flood to exterminate such humanity.

Chaucer withdrew from writing a story which might have been merely obscene. The story is begun by the cook who has been brought along by the five guildsmen who think themselves entitled to a special menu although their own trades are humble; their wives are even bigger snobs. The cook has an uncovered ulcer on his skin and when drunk he begins a dirty story: an apprentice who has been sacked for dishonesty becomes a lodger in the house of an addicted gambler, and his host's partner supplies the household's income from her earnings as a prostitute. But at this point the story stops.

However, tales which were completed poke gentler fun at people who think themselves morally superior. One such person is the prioress who is very anxious to be ladylike. Her name is Eglentyne (a flower's name); her old-fashioned Anglo-Norman language is elegant although not the French of Paris; her habits while eating are very delicate; she weeps if she sees a mouse in a trap; she feeds small dogs with roast meat and expensive bread; 'all was conscience and tender herte' – but does all this make her a seriously holy nun? She tells a tale about a 'litel' boy who sings a 'litel' song in honour of the Virgin Mary. This irritates some Jews who cut his throat and throw his body into a sewer, but he resumes his song and the miracle encourages a massacre of the Jews. The tale is an obvious example of the medieval anti-Semitism which was of course a great evil fed by such nonsense rather than by any experience; nobody admitting to being a Jew had been allowed to live in England since 1290. But here Chaucer seems to be intent only on teasing the prioress about her sentimentality – which is totally lacking when she mentions the fate of the Jews.

A more prominently flawed moraliser is a monk, but Chaucer exposes him only as we look back from his tale to his portrait in the prologue. His tale is a list of sudden disasters which by a change of fortune have overtaken worldly men – a list cut short only by protests about its 'hevynesse'. Some of the victims fall because of their pride: Lucifer the first bad angel does, as do tyrants such as Nebuchadnezzar or Nero, but Canobia's life is wrecked only by her husband's death and strong men are ruined by women, as are Adam and Samson, Hercules and Alexander. Caesar's only fatal mistake is not being on his guard against a 'mishap' inflicted by Fortune (a woman). So fortune has many ways of wrecking happiness. But the portrait is of a complacent 'monk out of his cloystre', a 'manly man' who is devoted to hunting with greyhounds and well dressed, with the body of 'a lord ful fat'. He expects no change in his good fortune and his knowledge of other people's misfortunes adds to his contentment.

Another pompous fraud is a senior barrister. Chaucer seems to have allocated his tale to him after writing that this 'Man of Law' would speak in prose, but now a tale told in verse devastates a hypocrite by implication. It is a version of the old story of the adventures of Custance (our Constance). Although she is the daughter of a Christian emperor she is married off to a sultan in the East, is ill treated, and is sent back home by sea. The storms during her voyage are so fierce, and her rudderless boat is so fragile, that she is shipwrecked on the coast of pagan Northumberland. After other adventures she finds herself back in Rome and throughout she has been rescued by miracles. But this tale of a saint's constant reliance on interventions by God is told by a lawyer who relies on his learning in the law and on his skill in an argument, and who rewards himself by buying up land with the money he makes. He receives many fees but what interests him most is the 'fee simple', the legal term for the possession of land without restrictions. In his profession he seemed 'bisier than he was' but in his private life he was really busy – and always on the make.

Another unrealistic tale is told by a dishonest physician who praises the beauty and innocence of the only daughter of a knight, and who exhorts his hearers to make sure that all young ladies are brought up as strictly as Virginia was. A wicked judge wants sex with her and conspires to have her made a ward of court after arranging an accusation that she has been stolen from her true family by the knight. The grief-stricken father then kills her with her consent, in order that she may die a virgin. Her severed head is sent to the judge, who commits suicide in prison. But the very prosperous physician who relates this nonsense has been described as a wicked old fraud in the prologue: when the patient can afford to pay he adds gold dust to his prescriptions. The meaningful comment is made in the prologue that 'gold in physik is a cordial'.

To these tales which, when thought about, can be understood as mockery of humbug, is added a story which treats all moralising comically. Chaucer attributed it to the chaplain who accompanies the prioress although he did not get around to describing this 'nun's priest' in the prologue. Perhaps a man in that job gets tired of sentimentality?

The story begins with a portrait of a widow who keeps a few hens and a cock: in her silent simplicity there is nothing wrong. Also conventional in medieval poems is the ability of birds and animals to speak. Here the cock, Chauntecleer, is very handsome and very pompous as he lectures his wife about the power of dreams to foretell the future, citing many literary authorities and telling stories to prove the point. Chaucer is surely laughing at himself: it has been his habit to introduce into his poems both allusions to great literature and stories about dreams. But Chauntecleer's down-to-earth wife tells him that his dream of being carried away by a dog-like beast was probably caused by an upset stomach and she recommends a laxative. Then a fox appears and persuades the vain Chauntecleer to sing a song, with neck stretched and eyes closed in self-admiration. The cock is promptly seized and abducted. The farmyard is thrown into an uproar but the fox is persuaded to hurl insults at his pursuing enemies. As he opens his mouth, Chauntecleer escapes.

At least four truisms of morality are offered as the lessons to be learned from this comedy: keep your eyes open, keep your mouth shut, do not take a risk, do not trust a flatterer. Some modern commentators have discerned much more subtle teachings in the story but the listener or reader is probably still laughing and Chaucer may imply that laughter is the best medicine.

Such tales are not to be taken too seriously, yet they do reveal Chaucer's attitudes to various kinds of human hypocrisy and folly. Rather more serious are the tales which hint at his maturely moral attitudes to the social system, to marriage and to the Church.

At the head of the pilgrimage he places a knight who is 'verray, parfit, gentil' – true, complete and noble. His tunic is stained by rust from the chain-metal armour he has been wearing until recently. This elderly knight has fought in fourteen 'mortal batailles' over a period of almost fifty years, as we learn through a list of campaigns stretching from Russia to Algeria. These were almost all crusades against non-Christians although he had once been a mercenary in a civil war between the 'hethen' in Turkey. His refusal to get involved in expeditions against Christians in France is implied and there is explicit praise for his behaviour when not on military service: then he is 'as meeke as is a mayde'. He loves an appropriate combination of virtues, 'chivalrie, trouthe and honour, freedom and curtesie' – courage in fights, fidelity to vows, generosity of spirit and refinement of manners. He seems perfect in the modern sense of that word, and William Blake saw him as 'a true hero, a good, great and wise man'.

Yet questions can be asked, as Terry Jones did when he treated Chaucer's knight as a 'medieval mercenary' in 1980. Had he really taken part in all those campaigns? When he had fought, had he been paid to kill? And when Chaucer chooses a tale to be told by this soldier who is presented as being more truly Christian than the prioress or the monk, it is a long story about two knights, Arcite and Palamon, which is decidedly unromantic although they are both smitten by courtly love.

They are prisoners from Thebes, which has been conquered by Theseus, Duke of Athens. The duke has married the queen of the Amazons whom he had conquered earlier and through a window the prisoners spot the queen's sister Emelye. They both fall in love with this vision of beauty and although they are cousins they have a bitter quarrel about who saw her first and loves her most. They continue this quarrel when one escapes and the other is released from prison. When they meet they fight like a lion and tiger, with blood up to their ankles in their iron shoes. The duke arrives, stops this fight and arranges a tournament in which hundreds of other knights can join under the code of 'chivalre'. Before the battle Emelye prays to be spared marriage or, if that cannot be, to be married to the man who loves her most. Arcite prays that he may be the victor and Palamon prays to be the husband. All these prayers are granted: Emelye is married to Palamon because Arcite, having won the jousting, is wounded mortally when his horse stumbles as he rides off the field. Chaucer has never been one of Arcite's supporters: one of his earlier poems which has been lost told of this knight's earlier mistreatment of a lady, Analida. And here we are told about the chapels dedicated to Mars and Venus where the cousins say their prayers: both tents exhibit pictures which symbolise the ugly realities of war and sex.

The narrator claims that all these events have been controlled by the gods who live in the planets but the duke, who seems to have read Boethius, makes a more elevated claim: everything is held together in a 'faire cheyne of love' by 'the First Moevere' of the creation, who 'stable is and eterne'. If this world is experienced as 'wrecched', even as a 'foule prisoun', a man must 'maken vertu of necessitie' and at least keep his honour, his 'good name'.

If we reflect about this tale as a whole, we can see that it means much to Chaucer, who (scholars agree) wrote it before he began *The Canterbury Tales*. But what does it mean? He would not wish to attack the pilgrim-knight who is now associated with it, or to disagree with the narrator who speaks about control by the gods, especially if the pagan gods are understood as deputies of the duke's 'First Moevere'. But he does not fail to notice the stupidity of knights who are eager to fight and the importance of sheer accident in the outcome of their violence. He is also sceptical about chivalry in the tales which he allocates to 'Chaucer'. One is in doggerel verse about Sir Thopas, a knight with a beard coming down to his waist and a career in farce and failure. He seeks an 'elf-queene' and is challenged by a giant but does not manage either to woo or to fight. This is a parody, a burlesque. The other tale is in excessively sober prose, about Melibee who is persuaded by his wife Prudence not to do battle with his enemies: it would lead to nothing good. It has been discovered that this is a translation of the French version of a story written in Latin in 1246 and Chaucer may have added it to the more easily digestible tale about Sir Thopas because he did not want to waste work already done as a translator of morally improving material. At any rate, it is a plea for behaviour not in the code of chivalry: when insulted, it says, turn the other cheek. This deserves to be taken seriously because nowhere else in *The Canterbury Tales* does Chaucer attach his own name to such a serious statement about ethics – and here is a plea for forgiveness and peace, put into the mouth of a woman who is as charming as she is prudent.

Also relevant is the story given to the knight's son, the 'squire': it is a tale so far-fetched and so tedious that it is stopped by a 'franklin' who is lower than a knight in the social system. This franklin is a country gentleman, fond of food and drink but also full of good works and much liked by his neighbours as he lives in peace with all. He interrupts the knight's son very politely: he praises the story as a young man's good effort, full of modesty and promise, and laments that his own son is worse behaved. Nevertheless he does stop the inexpert talkativeness of his social superior, whose head is crowned by golden hair, whose body, eager for love, attracts the ladies by a rich costume, and whose imagination lives in a world very different from his father's. And another relevant fact is that the pilgrims do not insist on the knight being their leader: they accept Harry Bailly (a real man's name) who runs the Tabard Inn in Southwark. As the group leaves Southwark, in the front is a red-bearded miller playing the bagpipes: this pilgrimage is going to be something of a democratic carnival.

The official theory about an ideal marriage is stated in the tale told by the franklin about right behaviour among the 'gentil' people above his own class: the man must be 'servant in love and lord in marriage'. Putting things more crudely, Chauntecleer reminded Pertelote that 'woman is mannes joy and al his blis', did not take her advice about how to recover from his nightmare, and knowing the most agreeable way of restoring his contentment 'fethered' her 'twenty tyme'. But before they are married, women must like Virginia be willing to die rather than lose their virginity; when told whom they are to marry they must, like Emelye, express an opinion only in prayer; and when they are married they must obey the husband who has taken over the sovereignty of the father.

One of the tales about marriage is told by the 'clerk' or scholar from Oxford. His story is about Griselde, who is picked up out of poverty by a rich lord, Walter. She is then subject to a prolonged series of ordeals in order to test her submission to God and her husband, the two not being sharply distinguished. She has to consent to the removal of her two children who, she is told, are to be killed; she is herself cast off and sent back to poverty; she is summoned back in order that the lord's house may be made ready for a new bride. She never disobeys and therefore, after years of this treatment, she is reinstated as his wife and reunited with the two children. So what is the scholar's motive in telling such a story? Quietly he subverts any linkage between the husband and Christ: it is the wife who is Christlike. He says nothing to contradict the official theory, but the absurdity of Walter's demands suggests that this unmarried clerk's sympathy is wholly with Griselde, for whom the only alternative to slavish obedience in marriage is grinding poverty. He knows that without a strong man to protect her a woman may be as helpless as Criseyde is in the Greek camp or Custance on the stormy sea. What he rescues from his version of an old story is an old moral: let a wife's patience be a model for a Christian's acceptance of God's mysterious ways.

Sometimes, however, a wife can be a successful rebel. At the end of this tale it is pointed out that few wives would be as saintly as Griselde under anything like such treatment. Wives should be patiently strong like camels, but if men behave too badly women should speak up, if need be fight like tigers, and make their oppressors 'wepe, and wrynge, and waille'. This advice is explicitly called 'Lenvoy de Chaucer' – his own opinion – in the manuscripts.

In another tale a merchant's own marriage is unhappy because he believes that it must depend on an obedience which his wife refuses to give, but what he also says to his fellow pilgrims unintentionally invites applause for a wife who rebels against a husband who is blind to her emotional needs. He tells a tale about the marriage between January who is old and rich and May who is young and restive. He has married her because he wants sex although he is not a ready performer in bed, and then he wants comfort because he goes blind. He does not notice when May throws herself at a willing squire in the household, young Damyan. He literally cannot see that Damyan is up a fruit tree in the garden – the Garden of Love as in the tales of courtly love – to which this pathetic husband has taken May for her marital duty. He helps her up the tree and so up to Damyan. Then Pluto the king of the fairies restores his sight and Pluto's wife enables May to think up a good excuse. So now January can see – but he still does not see much.

A manciple, in charge of housekeeping in a little college, tells a much shorter tale about why crows are black. Originally they were white and Phebus the sun-god kept one as a pet. But the crow told him that his wife had committed adultery and so Phebus committed murder, killing her and then repenting. The god curses the crow: henceforth it will be black and incapable of speech. A lesson to be learned is that it is wise for humans to hold their tongues when tempted to gossip about other people's marriages, which are liable to be imperfect, and presumably the manciple feels that a little lapse by a goddess ought to matter no more than his own cheating of the lawyers who employ him. But he shows no feeling for any of those involved: about gods, women or birds, as about his employers, he is a cold cynic. When the drunken cook falls off his horse into the mud most of the pilgrims are concerned, but he contemptuously offers the bruised drunk sneers and more wine.

Another cynical tale about marriage comes from the shipman, a man who is tough enough to throw the passengers he robs overboard. A wife finds her rich husband obsessed by money-making and she prefers a monk who borrows money from him in order to pay for sex with her. When the husband asks for the loan to be returned, the monk says that he has given it to the wife, who says that she has spent it on clothes. But even less romantic is the fact that in the social system known to Chaucer a much younger wife could be married for the sake of the financial dowry accompanying her. Although they may have fallen in love after marrying, it is probable that Duchess Blanche was initially valued because having no brother she would inherit the vast estates of the duchy of Lancaster (jointly with her sister, who died).

Into this often sordid reality of medieval marriage rides the Wife of Bath who shamelessly parodies the use of biblical texts to defend a husband's supremacy: the texts which men have found supportive are left in tatters. With an equal daring she uses anti-feminist stereotypes in literature and folklore outside the Bible to assert the reality of a woman in control. As Helen Cooper has said, 'Chaucer's extraordinary achievement is to turn an embodiment of the worst dreams of every henpecked husband or celibate cleric into a vibrant personality.' She exploits or bullies men – and wins every time. Instead of echoing laws made by men, she says that she relies on her own experience. She made herself financially independent by exploiting three 'riche and olde' husbands in a row (her first marriage was at the age of twelve) and by investing the proceeds in her own business. She has avoided having children but is skilled at the 'olde daunce' of married sex. She flirted with others – no more than that – when her fourth husband proved unfaithful, and then noticed the legs of a young man from Oxford carrying the coffin at his funeral. This Jenkyn became her fifth husband but proved difficult to tame. When she objected to his reading out to her stories about rebellious wives, she tore pages out of the book. In the resulting fight she was deafened in one ear but then she lived at peace with him – on her terms. And as a merry widow she now says 'Welcome the sixte!'

Theories that she was in her depths unhappy because she wanted both power and love seem too solemn, but her tale does deal with those two objectives of men and women. It seems that originally she was to contribute the bawdy tale now told by the shipman, but now she has been allocated one with a far less cynical message: Chaucer likes to surprise. Another surprise is the change he makes in a story, which had been used by Gower to tell how in the good old days of King Arthur a knight accused of rape cleared his name, chivalry's 'honour'. Chaucer tells the tale from a woman's point of view, although the woman is not the one who has been traumatised. For him it is a tale about a 'lusty bachelor' guilty of raping a virgin. He is spared capital punishment if he can discover what women want most. The answer is given to him by an old hag to whom he has to promise marriage (such is his desperation) and it is 'sovereynetee'. The case against him is now dropped but he is condemned to keep his promise, which he does with immense reluctance. The poor and elderly woman who is now his wife rebukes his snobbery: it is Christ's will that 'we clayme of him oure gentillesse'. Then she asks him whether he would prefer a woman to be beautiful and disloyal or ugly and faithful. He begs her to decide, at which point she is revealed as being a young beauty, at least in his eyes, and the prospects are good. May they be good for an old woman such as the Wife of Bath!

An obvious moral emerging is that a marriage works for both partners when it is based on solid love, not on any law about it. This moral is driven home in the franklin's tale, set in Brittany. A knight marries a lady within the law of the land and also within the code of chivalry, as is demonstrated when Averagus soon leaves Dorigen in order to be chivalrous in Britain for two years. Alarmed that his ship may be wrecked before they can be reunited, she uses a light-hearted promise of her sexual favours to persuade Aurelius to arrange a magic spell which is successful. On his return the husband insists that his wife must keep her promise as if it had been meant seriously but Aurelius releases her from the vow, the magician releases him from his promise to pay, and the married couple are expected to live happily ever after. It is an incredible story but we may believe that the franklin told it because of his own wedded bliss.

Was Chaucer a feminist? Should that be our conclusion when about 140 generalisations about women are in the *Tales*? Yes, for he always treated women as interesting people with their own feelings and rights, and he was happy or amused when these were asserted by women in his stories. But no: he was a man who accepted the man's leadership in marriage as in the rest of life, and who believed that Eve needs Adam as much as Adam needs Eve. The two are best when bound together by 'trouthe', which means true love, not a legal relationship between master and slave.

Was he a Catholic Christian? The only possible answer is yes. One of the ways in which he shows his commitment to the Church is that like William Langland he gets seriously angry when its representatives are scandalously disgraceful.

In the company is a trio of representatives of the Church whose aim is to extort money out of gullible people. A Franciscan friar vowed to poverty avoids the poor, concentrating instead on extracting money from people who have it, and he operates by smooth talk. In particular he makes women his victims before he celebrates and seeks fresh prey 'in taverns well in every toun'. He tells a tale about an ecclesiastical official, a 'summoner', who is employed to summon people accused of sins (mainly sexual) to the archdeacon's court. During one of his journeys on this job he makes friends with the devil – but finds himself sent to hell because he has tried to get a bribe out of a poor widow who is monstrously accused of adultery. She curses him. We see that what the friar says about the summoner's fate will come true for himself.

The point of that story is driven home when a summoner in the company tells a tale directed against the friar. A friar demands money from a poor man on the brink of death, pleading that there are twelve hungry men in the friary. The dying man sees that this begging is so much hot air and responds by giving a large fart. Now the only problem is how to divide that answer by twelve. It is a problem which would only occur to a summoner close to the law – and close to hell.

A 'pardoner' is also a member of the pilgrimage. Normally he is employed as a fund-raiser for a hospital, selling promises of divine pardon and also exhibiting bogus relics of the saints in order to encourage generosity. His tale is of three louts who kill each other in their rivalry to get at buried gold – and we see that the teller is himself already dead spiritually. Thus all three men, whose trade is religious rhetoric, condemn themselves by their tales.

It has been suggested that all three are homosexuals and that Chaucer may regard this condition as a reason for their sense of alienation from society. In the Middle Ages this characteristic of some men would have been associated both with effeminacy and with disease, and some touches in the *Tales* reproduce this conventional image: the friar speaks with a lisp, the summoner has a face of which 'children were aferd', and he has a 'freend' in the unpleasant shape of the pardoner. He and this friend sing together a 'ful loude' song, 'Come hider, love, to me'. The pardoner's very appearance identifies him in the sight of medieval onlookers: his hair is blond and shoulder-length and he cannot grow a beard. The narrator knows 'he was a gelding or a mare', which means a eunuch or a homosexual. Thus his condition seems to be clear in Chaucer's own eyes also. But there may be some doubt about the other two, for the friar has a special relationship with 'worthy women of the toun' (and when he serenades them his eyes twinkle 'as doon the steeres in the frosty neigt'), while the summoner is entrusted with the secrets of 'the yonge girls of the diocise'. Their ability to charm women is their most deadly weapon and it may be that Chaucer accepted the belief that normal women will find abnormal men repulsive.

So does Chaucer accept homosexuals? No: he denounces a group which includes at least one. But also yes. At the end of the tale he makes the pardoner attempt to persuade the pilgrims to pay for the privilege of kissing a fragment of a bone which is claimed to be holy. The host and leader of the pilgrims, Harry Bailly, then explodes with an obscene protest and the other pilgrims laugh, but the knight intervenes to stop this breach in their fellowship on the road:

> 'Sire Pardoner, be glad and myrie of cheere;
> And ye, sire Hoost, that been to me so deere,
> I prey you that ye kisse the Pardoner.
> And, Pardoner, I prey thee, draw thee neere,
> And, as we didden, lat us laughe and pleye.'
> Anon they kisse, and ryden forth hir weye.

It is probably the bravest thing that Chaucer ever did.

So does he attack the use of religion for extortion? Yes, obviously. But although he can see the fires of hell at the end of the roads which three criminals take into the homes and minds of the defenceless, he does not attack the bishops, the archdeacons or the authorities in charities such as hospitals, the men who control the system in which dishonest subordinates are no more than parasites. This is because he accepts the system as the context in which everyone lives, and he cannot imagine an alternative.

The system is also challenged when the question of alchemy arises. A canon of a cathedral, accompanied by a yeoman as his servant, joins the pilgrimage but rides away when a conversation shows that he is interested in alchemy, the transformation of one kind of matter into another, preferably gold. The yeoman then proceeds to explain in detail how alchemists work and the very detail shows that Chaucer, too, is fascinated. But the conclusion is that the Church is right to condemn alchemy because the differences in matter are decreed by the Creator. Chaucer hints at this conclusion by making the yeoman confused as he gives his long account of a 'science' which attempts to confuse what God has made distinct.

In contrast with such scandals, two churchmen receive nothing but praise in the *Tales*. The 'clerk' is a graduate student in Oxford whose only ambition is to have a small library of books over his bed but Chaucer's praise for him is the lesser of these two tributes, presumably because he is too bookish. The hero of the *Tales* is the 'parson' (rector) who is practical as well as holy, devoted to his urban parish, tireless in visiting, generous to the poor, no despiser of 'synful men' but a faithful preacher of 'Christes gospel' who 'wroghte' before he 'taughte'. He is accompanied by another saint, his brother who is not a serf (a peasant tied to a lord). He is a free man who can plough a field if paid but he is also a good man because he is willing to do it for a poor neighbour without charging.

The saintly parson's 'tale' concludes the book. No one is allowed to reply to it although it defies the plan to tell entertaining stories: it ends that 'game'. It is lengthy, vigorous and uncompromising as it catalogues sins which the medieval Church condemns in accordance with a long tradition. The instruction about how to examine one's conscience before repenting sincerely is done with a pastor's skill. It is a heroic effort to make people see that they are on a pilgrimage to 'Jerusalem celestial'. The only touch of unreality is that it reads more like a manual to be used by priests – as indeed it was in the Latin sources on which this 'tale' is based – than it is like an account of what might be said to the average layman making one of the annual confessions which were compulsory.

It does show that 'doing penance' after a confession could be an experience very different from Martin Luther's agony as he felt dragged down into ever deeper levels of failure and guilt. 'Men shal hope', says this pastor, 'that every tyme that man falleth, be it never so ofte, that he may arise through Penitence.' The Christian will find that the solution is to love God, for 'the law of God is the love of God' and no one who truly loves God is any more under sin's complete control. However, he (this advice is man to man) will find that he is still tempted. Those who know the *Tales* will not be surprised to be told that 'al the while that a man hath in hym the peyne of concupiscence, it is impossible but he be tempted somtime and moeved in his flesh to synne'. Even St Jerome in the desert found that 'lecherie boyled in al his body'. But there are other sins: 'superfluitee' or 'scantnesse' of 'clothynge', 'pride of the table', envy ('the worst synne that is'), dishonest speech ('flaterers been the develes chapelleyns'), sloth, 'wanhope that is despeir', avarice which includes keeping things 'beyond rightful nede' . . . This list is indeed daunting and no one would be left untouched. But the key idea is simple. 'Whan man loveth any creature moore than Jhesu Crist oure Creatour, thane is deadly synne' – sin which, if there is no repentance, leads to spiritual death and to hell. But 'veniall' or somewhat lesser sin 'is it, if man love Jhesu Crist lasse than hym oghte'. That, too, needs repentance, for such sins do not measure up to 'the love that men sholde han to God moore and moore'.

Since this was the Church's standard teaching, it is not difficult to see why the very human Chaucer's 'retraccions' were added to the parson's warnings at the end of the *Tales*. Nor is it difficult to be moved by the fact that this highly sophisticated man of affairs and poet took the Church's teaching so seriously that he spent a lot of time translating it and destroyed a lot of his pride by applying it to himself as he was about to die. But was he too penitent? When writing about the characters in his stories he has been discriminating and in the end charitable, but now he condemns too much, as five centuries of praise have already demonstrated. And he may have had himself a small feeling that he was going too far in self-condemnation. When he confesses to writing 'many a song and many a lecherous lay', he does so in a fragment of poetry: it is in iambic pentameter.

Even in his work which he could condemn as 'lecherous' he was an exponent of a faith more humane than was much of the religion of his time. On 8 May 1373 a woman (nowadays called 'Julian') in Norwich had, while seriously ill, meditated on a crucifix and believed that she was seeing into the loving heart of God – a vision which made love the heart of Christianity. Chaucer never wrote anything like her *Revelations of Divine Love* and never lived like a nun. Two weeks after her vision, he submitted a claim for expenses incurred while on an official visit to Italy. But he did believe in making love not war the best thing in chivalry; he did teach honesty, generosity and hard work by his own example; he did attack the exploitation of the poor and the gullible by representatives of Christ's Church; he did praise authentic holiness; he was sympathetic with the weak – especially with women in that society – and tolerantly saw all humans as weak in some way. He was the first Englishman we know about who articulated in any detail a truly Christian response to everyday humanity, and the first giant in the literature of the English-reading world.

TWO

SHAKESPEARE

William Shakespeare was born in 1564 into an England where the medieval Church had been overthrown, as was illustrated by his purchase in 1605 of the right to receive tithes (a local tax on agricultural produce) which in the Middle Ages had been paid to the clergy. But that did not mean that Christianity had been overthrown. On the contrary, some sort of a church seemed an indispensable feature of life in village or town, and whatever may have been their feelings which might delay their submission most Elizabethans quietly conformed to the Church of England as established and privileged by the state. It is clear that he was one of them. Anyone who did not take communion in the parish church at Easter could be reported to the government as a potential traitor – which happened to his father but never to him. At the end his monument was grandly positioned in his parish church, near the site of the medieval altar. Being buried there was by tradition the right of a holder of tithes but he must often have sat in that church, for his plays resound with echoes of the Book of Common Prayer of 1559, in particular quoting its version of the psalms. Whether he went to church so often in London, where he lived in lodgings and was comparatively unobserved, we do not know. We know that in retirement in Stratford he was the kind of parishioner who could be asked to entertain a visiting preacher, the wine being paid for by the town council. His plays also include many references to customs of the Catholic Church and he is certainly not at sea when writing about Catholic countries or about England in its Catholic centuries – but to say that he was knowledgeable and often respectful about that part of England's heritage, and that the Warwickshire in which he grew up was slow to become Protestant in sincere belief, is not to say that he thought of himself as a committed Roman Catholic in conscience bound to obey the pope.

Nor did he belong to the 'school of night', a group of intellectuals which can be named thus because of an obscure reference, possibly to it, in his play *Love's Labour Lost.* The group met in the London of the 1590s. It was alleged to be atheistic but it is not certain that it included any a true disbeliever in the existence of God. Sir Walter Raleigh, sometimes said to have been the convenor, was to occupy his time in prison by writing a history of the world which relied heavily on the Bible and strongly affirmed that the world had been created by the Almighty and was governed by Providence. At the end of his most famous play Christopher Marlowe, said to have been the Elizabethans' chief spokesman for atheism, left Faustus, the over-reacher who had aspired to be equal with God, in the hands of devils dragging him off to hell. It is of course possible that in the book or the play belief in God was used for a literary or dramatic purpose and was not the author's own sincere belief, but Raleigh went to his execution with the prayer that his pilgrimage would soon end in eternal life and Marlowe's plays seem serious in affirming God's existence while eloquently questioning or denying his love.

To say that 'we cannot know what he believed or disbelieved', as Harold Bloom does in his *Shakespeare* (1999), is in one sense true and can be said as a tribute. His plays are ambiguous: they open up many questions and they penetrate an astonishing number of different minds and hearts. That is what Keats had in his mind when he praised a 'negative capability' – 'being in uncertainties, mysteries, doubts, without any irritable reaching after fact and reason'. This absence of dogmatism means that the plays may not clearly preach royalism, family values, class distinctions and militarism, and need not protest loudly against discrimination on grounds of class, gender or race, despite interpretations along one or other of these lines offered in the 1940s or 1960s. It also means that the plays need not proclaim a bleak nihilism about human existence despite an interpretation of 'Shakespeare our contemporary' which meant much in the cold 1950s. And it means that they are unlikely to echo a religious authority. However, Shakespeare is also unlikely to conform to postmodern doctrines about the desirability of decentring or deconstruction, for a play has to have a substantial unity coming from the mind of an author (or group of writers) if it is to make a sufficiently rapid and strong impact on an audience, and this impact will reveal what the author 'believes' or 'disbelieves' in the wider sense of supporting or rejecting a vision of life as shown most easily in a conviction about what is right or wrong in behaviour. Some evidence about this has been supplied by recent developments in Shakespearean studies: it has been stressed how radically he changed the plots from their sources in order to make the point or points he wanted to make, and how often he or the actors made little changes after the early performances reflected in the early printed versions in order to get on with the story and strengthen its impact. Moreover, there was then no equivalent to the modern director of a film, making the actors conform to his own vision. If actors wanted advice about how their roles should be presented, presumably they asked Shakespeare.

His tragedies show a great sympathy with questions or denials in the darkness of human suffering, but they do not record admiration for the response of full atheism. In *King Lear* the atheists are the villains – Goneril and Regan who never mention the gods except once in an oath, and Edmund who says 'Thou, Nature, art my goddess.' Edmund argues against religious belief with a bitter eloquence seldom matched in the literature of atheism, but he is clearly not the play's hero. Lear himself comes very close to atheism in his misery: he acknowledges that he has been unjust, he sees human injustice all around him, he has a vision of the injustice of nature to powerless individuals who are left to be 'dead as earth'. But that miserable old man whose own behaviour has caused at least some of his miseries is not presented as a calm teacher of philosophical atheism, any more than Macbeth is when his ruthless ambition has led to nothing except defeat and death. At the end of each tragedy – even including *King Lear* in its final version – we are given a glimpse of something which lies beyond tragedy and what he wrote after the tragedies points to what this something is.

Frequently the plays communicate a belief that divine 'Providence' works mysteriously, and even inscrutably, before finally prevailing – a belief that allows room for human actions, for what seem to be accidents, and for times of unrelieved darkness. That may seem to be a very cautious, even evasive, understanding of God's method of working, but many passages in the Bible, or in venerated works of theology (even Augustine's or Calvin's), could be quoted in its support. Moreover, despite the mystery which surrounds it Providence is repeatedly seen by Shakespeare to be successful in some of the most important areas of human life: it brings lovers together so that a new generation may be born, it reunites parents and children in a new birth for a family, it establishes good government after a long time of deadly troubles. Atheism is a very different philosophy, which in Shakespeare's lifetime was denounced far more often than it was openly expressed, and since he never clearly advocated it we may conclude that he was not so unusual as to accept it.

On the contrary, his plays are full of references to the majesty, power, justice and mercy of God, the gods or heaven, and his expositions of a world-view which is essentially the same as Chaucer's include the lay sermon by Ulysses in his version of the story of Troilus and Cressida: God created and presides over a universe which is on the whole orderly and therefore human society ought to respect 'degree, priority and place'. In *The Merchant of Venice* Lorenzo tells Jessica that the stars sing like angels and that such harmony ought to be in human souls. And this vision is not destroyed when the behaviour of the manipulative Ulysses shows that he does not know his place in the hierarchy of the Greek army or when the response of the obstinate Jessica declares that she is not turned on by music.

Because everything is bound together and linked to God, the stars can influence, or be influenced by, human behaviour, and God's direct influence can be supplemented by other supernatural agents – angels, demons, ghosts, fairies and spirit-possessed witches. Preachers could throw the Bible at astrology, 'superstition' or magic, but Shakespeare seems to be happy to use popular beliefs when they suit his purposes: in his plays the stars shine or grow dark on cue and his Prospero, the benign equivalent of Marlowe's Faustus, practises white magic and ends in Italy not hell. How much of all this he took literally we cannot know but obviously it matters less than the basic belief in 'Providence'.

Man stands at the centre of this vast creation and Man's salvation is the creation's supreme purpose; and of course 'Man' does not mean only half of humankind. At the centre of history stands Christ, to whom serious references in the plays are always devout: he is the Saviour, on his cross. But Christ is also the Teacher of the morality which Shakespeare accepts. Through almost forty plays he explicitly or implicitly praises love and pity, humility and patience, forgiveness and reconciliation. Christ may not be named but through at least one Christlike figure (who may be a woman) the message is clear. The major deviation from the moralising 'homilies' officially appointed to be read in the churches he knew is his refusal to condemn the suicides of frustrated lovers or defeated Romans, but that was a convention of the theatre and could become more than a convention when Antony and Cleopatra live in the Roman empire. Even Macbeth who feels 'tied to the stake' like a bear being baited by dogs in a little arena near the theatre, does not applaud his wife's suicide and even Lear, a pagan at the bottom of despair, is not tempted to kill himself.

So whether or not we like that Elizabethan form of Christianity, we can see from the evidence that in 1899 George Santayana exaggerated when he reported 'The Absence of Religion in Shakespeare', as did Tolstoy who made the same mistake. They correctly saw that Elizabethan Anglicans were not so passionate in their religion as Spanish Catholics or Russian Orthodox, but if does not follow that they were godless. The evidence also suggests that in 1999 a biographer, Anthony Holden, was over-confident when he claimed that by his early forties Shakespeare was 'abandoning the last vestiges of religious belief'.

Why, then, was he not more explicit about religion?

Once he was old enough to be discriminating in such matters, the

Elizabethan Church of England cannot have appealed to him aesthetically or intellectually apart from its importance as a vehicle conveying the Bible in English. Its churches had been, or were being, stripped bare in order to exhibit their Protestant rejection of visual images, and in almost all of them any music was a crude versification of the Hebrew psalms (hymns were not sung by English Protestants before the eighteenth century). Its theology as set out in its Thirty-Nine Articles of Religion (1562) was a version of Calvinism; salvation was confined to those whom God had 'predestined to life'. Other Calvinists could be more plainly and brutally narrow-minded, talking explicitly about the predestination of the many to hell, but it is easy to see that some of these official doctrines of the Church of England were glaringly incompatible with Shakespeare's vision of humanity. 'The flesh lusteth always contrary to the spirit; and therefore in every person born into this world, it deserveth God's wrath and damnation . . . Works done before the grace of Christ, and the Inspiration of his Spirit, are not pleasant to God . . . They also are to be had accursed that presume to say, That every man shall be saved by the Law or Sect which he professeth, so that he be diligent to frame his life according to that Law, and the Light of Nature.'

Another reason why he was not a keen churchman was that he was not a saint or a man interested in becoming one. Although he earned considerable wealth, he was not generous to the poor or a benefactor to the local community. Although he was liked and admired by people connected with London theatres, towards his neighbours in Stratford he seems to have been hard-headed and although he was as eloquent as anyone has ever been about lovers and parents he does not seem to have seen much of his family. Although in his plays he let no one speak about any religion without respect, he let no one preach for long; one can see why Dr Johnson complained that 'he seems to write without any moral purpose'. He knew enough about saints to be able to write about women who are devout as well as innocent, and about good men such as Horatio and Kent in the tragedies, and in a sense they preach with their lives, but there is a contrast between Chaucer's high praise of the poor parson in the *Tales* and Costard's more casual remarks about Nathaniel the curate in *Love's Labour's Lost*: 'a foolish, mild man; an honest man, look you, and soon dashed. He is a marvellous good neighbour, faith, and a very good bowler'.

Occasionally Shakespeare can show that he is not completely ignorant of theology; for example, his poem 'The Phoenix and the Turtle' uses terms taken from learned discussions about the relationships between the three persons of the Holy Trinity. But that poem is an allegory about a perfect marriage between humans and we have no reason to suppose that he had an ambition to be a theologian. He was of course the cleverest man in England in his period (as Chaucer had been in his) but his mind was so unacademic that at one stage T. S. Eliot could compare his poetry with music which cannot be put into words – and could suspect that any philosophy which he may have learned was a 'rag-bag': 'you can hardly say that Shakespeare did or did not believe in the mixed and muddled scepticism of the Renaissance'. For Eliot this was not a damning criticism, for he did not believe that a poet's business is to organise ideas into theories: it is to 'express the greatest possible emotional equivalent of thought'. He thought that 'Shakespeare became a great poet by writing for the theatre' because a drama intensifies emotions and calls for words like strong music. Nevertheless, the evidence does not agree with what was then Eliot's verdict. Shakespeare did not express his religion clearly, as Eliot did, but his mind was not totally hidden or merely muddled. Nor, for that matter, was the mind of the age to which he belonged, despite the degree of scepticism to be met in *Hamlet*.

And writing for the theatre gave him a particular reason for not writing explicitly about religion.

Playwrights were then warned off religious territory; when he had rashly picked on the name of a Protestant martyr, Sir John Oldcastle, for an unedifying character, he changed it to Sir John Falstaff and drew attention to the change. No play could be staged until it had been licensed by an official, the Master of the Revels, who would veto anything likely to offend the bishops. An Act of Parliament in 1606 prohibited the use of words such as 'God' or 'Christ' if their use was 'jesting or profane', a dangerously unclear definition of a crime which could incur a large fine. References to pagan gods were still allowed and could be used as a code in which to refer to the Christians' God, as was the case in all Shakespeare's plays after *Macbeth*, but the writer who supplied scripts to an actors' company under the direct patronage of the king was bound to exercise great caution. And such caution did not result merely from anxiety or discretion after a law imposing censorship. All clergymen we know about were very sure that the pulpit and the stage were, and ought to remain, very different places, and people did not go to plays expecting to be exposed to religious edification. In the Middle Ages 'mystery' plays had been performed in churches or on the streets in order to retell biblical stories to the people, and 'morality' plays had dramatised the moral lessons, but those had been the Middle Ages and the theatregoing public now demanded more sophistication just as the educated had already demanded something smarter in Chaucer's day.

They would be more comfortable if the action of the play could be located in a pre-Christian country or at least outside the world of the

Bible or of the Church. This could be done because intelligent Elizabethans such as Shakespeare did not believe that there should be nothing but war between Christianity and pagan mythology or philosophy. As we saw when thinking about Chaucer, in the Middle Ages an unquestionably Catholic poet would write about pagan gods as if they existed and about pagan morals as if they agreed with the Bible. In the age of the Renaissance, also inherited by Shakespeare, this respect for the Greeks and the Romans was even stronger; it formed the basis of his education. The pagans' gods could be treated as agents of the Christians' God and good behaviour advocated by pagan philosophers as natural could be seen as also Christian. At the same time questions which were really about the Church's presentation of God could be voiced with impunity by phrasing them as criticisms of pagan religion or superstition.

In his *Appropriating Shakespeare* (1993) Brian Vickers was therefore right to include among his attacks on misinterpretations a protest against Christian readings which refer directly to the Bible or the Church and which may proceed on the principle that 'any resemblance to anything in biblical or legendary material will do'. Shakespeare's consuming interest, like Chaucer's, is in human behaviour – in how Falstaff lives and feels before he dies after saying 'God, God, God' and being told that it is not yet time to trouble himself with such thoughts. Like Chaucer he is a humanist within Christendom and we can see what Harold Bloom meant when he wrote that 'he invented the human as we continue to know it'. Not only were the people in his plays so often life-like. No one before him – not even Chaucer – had imagined characters so complicated and so changeable as the story unfolds. He allows people to be themselves, and to speak up for themselves, so that when they discuss religion or morality it is out of their own lives, within their own settings and in their own styles. They need not be spokespeople for the Bible, or for the Church, or for any philosophy, or for him. They need not even be consistent in what they say.

Yet if he had no wish to embrace the Thirty-Nine Articles or to be reckoned among the saints or the preachers, it is equally true that he had no wish to be counted as having 'no religion'. Like Chaucer and very many other people in any period, he paid more attention to religion and morality as he grew older; after 1601 he did not write a straightforward comedy. Although we shall never know the precise extent to which the will which he dictated on his deathbed represented his personal opinions in 1616, that last testament should not be excluded from the evidence: 'I commend my soul into the hands of God my Creator, hoping and surely believing through the only merits of Jesus Christ my saviour to be made partaker of life everlasting.' What we do know is that he signed a will which begins with that formula, omitting the 'blissful Moder and alle the seintes of hevene' included in Chaucer's retraction of his sinful writings. The rumour that 'he died a Papist' was first recorded seventy years later and the suggestion that he died an atheist was not made until our own time. He wanted it to be thought that he died as a Protestant Christian.

At least the fact that he can be recognised as an 'early modern' person with 'early modern' beliefs or doubts will enable us to treat him as a figure who belongs neither to a remote age of faith nor to a secular today. He was not a dogmatist but he had no wish to escape completely from the religion which dominated his society. He was not an unbeliever but he was, as Ben Jonson remembered, 'honest, and of an open and free nature'.

Obviously it was a marvel that he became what he did become, it can be ranked quite high among the wonders of nature, and people who believe in God can call it a miracle in some sense. But up to a point it can be explained.

It was a marvel that he survived infancy. His parents had already lost two children and shortly after his birth an epidemic brought death to many other homes in Stratford-upon-Avon. It was also a marvel that what he did with his life still seems so significant to so much of the world, for Stratford was then a market town of some 1,500 inhabitants and he lived to see about half of them in poverty.

His parents did not sign their own names although Mary Arden had a grander background than John Shakespeare, a farmer's son who made and sold gloves and other leather goods. John was for a time a respected figure in that small and tightly regulated community, rising to serve for a year as bailiff or mayor, but when William was aged twelve he ceased to attend the town council and had to be excused from paying some local taxes. Probably the main reason was that trade was now bad, but he got deeper into trouble when he tried to get out of it: he traded in wool without the permit which was required and he lent money at a 25 per cent rate of annual interest when usury was still frowned on and the maximum permitted was 10 per cent.

What was his religion? All his children were baptised in the Anglican parish church and in 1563, while he was the chamberlain or treasurer on the town council, he paid for the 'defacement of images' in a beautiful medieval chapel built for the celebration of Mass. The rood screen from which the figure of the crucified Christ had profoundly impressed worshippers was pulled down although pictures on the walls were covered by a thin layer of whitewash and may be seen today. It is probable that like many of his contemporaries John Shakespeare was not sure that the Act of Uniformity establishing the Church of England as the only legitimate church in 1559 was right or would prove permanent. There had been many changes in the government's religious policy since Henry VIII's break with Rome in the 1530s and the average member of that generation could quietly prefer to stick to the Old Faith: it had been taught in childhood, it would be a comfort in death. This, however, did not necessarily mean accepting all the old teachings: John tried to be a greedy money lender in defiance of the Old Church.

In 1592, when there was a scare about the possibility of an invasion, he was included in a list demanded by the government of non-churchgoers. His former colleagues on the town council explained that he feared arrest for debt but the excuse was a cover-up, for he did not hesitate to institute his own legal proceedings against neighbours with whom he felt aggrieved. In 1757 a document was produced which was said to have been found hidden in the house which had been his home: it was a 'spiritual testament' affirming that he would die a Catholic even if no priest was available to administer the last rites. It was made in a standard form distributed by underground missionaries. But although it may well show where John's heart lay it does not make him a lifelong Catholic so strict that after the pope's decision in 1570 Elizabeth was no longer his queen.

It was a marvel that such a man's eldest son fitted into the Elizabethan world so well that he made a small fortune and was able to arrange for John to be officially registered as a gentleman in 1601 although an earlier application had been rejected. But we need not think that the genius of William Shakespeare wholly defies rational explanation. He had to relate to four brothers and two sisters and, having been socialised by family life (but how often do his plays stress rivalry between brothers!), he came under two influences which shaped his imagination and intellect.

One force was the Bible. In an Elizabethan home which tried to be respectable a boy would be taught 'courtesie' and manners would include daily prayers and grace at meals. He would be taken to church as a Sunday routine and would hear the Bible read in English with solemnity and even with excitement about a translation now permitted to reach the people. The Great Bible of 1539 was only a quarter of a century old when he was born and the Geneva Bible, which was to be his favourite version, only four years old; it was to reach 139 editions, with elaborate notes and arresting illustrations, before its last in 1644. The 'Bishops' Bible' was the officially blessed alternative to that work done in Geneva, and was first published four years after his birth. He was to be able to handle the King James Version of 1611, at first unpopular but destined to be the only part of English literature more influential than his own plays. And having an English Bible open in the middle of a town was like having a time bomb in a market.

In the Old Testament he would find stories told as well as stories have ever been told. He would see how a great variety of private emotions could be revealed in the psalms and how public history could be reduced to order by an insistent theme: God rewards his chosen people with victories to be remembered 'from this day forth to the end of the world' but only if they obey his commandments, and he punishes them when their ruler is wicked or incompetent or when subjects divide or rebel without a very good reason. Young William would also begin to learn from the Bible the strength of evil and the depth of suffering: in his plays there were to be 25 explicit references each to the murder of Abel by his brother Cain and to the torments of Job inflicted by Satan. And in the New Testament he was to meet not only the four gospels (to which his references were to be almost innumerable) but also the letters of Christians with their probing of hearts and consciences. In his plays he was to quote from 42 books of the Bible. Equally striking is his expectation that theatregoers would understand his references.

The other great influence on his early years was his education in the King's New School, a short walk from his home; the schoolroom is still to be seen. In *As You Like It* the generally gloomy Jaques pictures 'the whining schoolboy . . . creeping like snail unwillingly to school', but when our mentally hungry William walked to school he walked into the civilisation of Rome. He did not walk away from the Church of England: every morning in school began with Scripture and prayers and it was a legal obligation to make sure that the boys knew by heart the theological and moral questions and answers set out in the Prayer Book. But the curriculum was based on a clear philosophy of education about which we can know a great deal although no records of this particular school survive from this period. Much more was involved than needing to know Latin in order to enter a university or profession. The teacher of teachers was a great Christian scholar, Desiderius Erasmus, who earlier in the century had provided both inspiration and material. In *De Copia* he had expounded the aim of education, to be eloquent; his *Colloquia* had supplied examples of good conversation; his *Adagia* had collected wise sayings for use in such talk; and his *Institutum Christiani Hominis* had stated very clearly his conviction that eloquence and learning should adorn a good life as a Christian in the world (not in a monastery). We also know which Latin authors, or excerpts from them, were used when facility in the language had been gained through many exercises and tests. Caesar or Livy would teach the art of history and Ovid the art of enjoyable poetry while opening up a storehouse of mythology. Virgil would be a model for grand poetry and Horace both an example of the lighter touch and a systematic teacher of *Ars Poetica.* Cicero would should show how to speak with unhesitant dignity, Plautus and Terence would introduce the delights of comedy. Seneca would begin thoughts about grim tragedy. For about ten years this would be a boy's work for about ten hours each working day and Ben Jonson's claim that his friend and rival had 'small Latin' was false. The curriculum was narrow but it was drilled into small classes by repetition and strict discipline and it did produce what the state wanted: a supply of men with well developed minds and an ability to use tongues and pens without fumbling for words. Indeed, it produced an eloquence richer than English in any earlier or later period.

William's teacher while he was a senior pupil in this grammar school (1575–79) was Thomas Jenkins, a good scholar from Oxford. He was repaid for his labour by his pupil's marvellous plays, but when schoolmasters were characterised in these they were treated with some affection combined with broad hints that they taught Latin rather than anything useful for life. Such are the woes of the teaching profession.

William would have left at the normal age between his fifteenth and sixteenth birthdays; his father's financial embarrassment would not have prevented this, since no fees were charged. Some boys moved on from Stratford to Oxford or Cambridge but a university was not a possibility for this one. It was therefore a further marvel that in 1592 he was to be attacked in a pamphlet said to be based on scribblings left by Robert Greene, a Cambridge graduate and a London playwright who had died in squalid poverty. Shakespeare was denounced as a newly arrived outsider; as 'an upstart crow beautified with our own feathers', implying that he had stolen material from educated and experienced writers; as a man 'wrapped in a player's hide' but with 'a tiger's heart', implying that as an actor he was deceitfully but ruthlessly ambitious; as an 'absolute Johannes Factotum' or Jack-of-all-trades, implying that he would do anything for money; as a novice who was 'in his own conceit the only Shake-scene in the country'. Some thirteen years after leaving school Shakespeare was so successful that he could arouse such a hostile tirade – and was so respected that after protests by admirers an apology was issued.

Seeking an explanation, it has been suggested that he left Stratford to gain experience in Italy or wherever, but all we know from allusions in his plays is that he had a extraordinary ability to pick up ideas, images and phrases from conversation or rapid reading rather than travel. A somewhat less unlikely suggestion is that he became a junior schoolmaster but that would have needed a bishop's licence and none has been found naming him. Some recent biographers have thought it likely that he was the William Shakestafte mentioned in a will by a rich and defiantly Catholic ('recusant') landowner in Lancashire, in August 1581. Had he been recommended as a reliable Catholic from Stratford? John Cottom was its schoolmaster from 1579 until his return to his native Lancashire in 1581 after his brother's execution as a Jesuit 'traitor', and 'John Cotham' also received a legacy. But 'Shakestafte' was a faithful servant who deserved to be given a year's wages, promised an annuity of £2 for the rest of his life, and placed in a similar job in that district – whereas Shakespeare, aged eighteen, would be in Warwickshire in August 1582.

We know that our man was there then because he was in contact with a woman who was eight years older, Anne Hathaway. Their contact led to their marriage at the beginning of December and the birth of a child about six months later, at a time when about a fifth of all brides were pregnant. Their daughter was called Susanna, after a biblical character vindicated after being accused of sex outside marriage. In the plays can be found condemnations of intercourse between those who intend to be married to each other, most notably in *Measure for Measure* and in Prospero's stern warning to young Ferdinand in *The Tempest*, but we can only guess about the young Shakespeare's feelings when problems followed ecstasy – and no more than guesses are possible about the history of the long marriage. Twins, Hamnet and Judith, were born in 1585 but there were no more children in an age when it would be worrying for parents to have only one son, who might die young as Hamnet did. It may be relevant that in this period the delivery of twins could so damage the mother that a full marital relationship would become dangerous and might be abandoned. In a poem which is very close to music, 'The Phoenix and the Turtle' (1601), he was to celebrate the married union of the legendary bird with an entirely delighted turtle-dove, but we do not know that his own marriage was like that – or never was. It seems probable that one of his sonnets (145) refers to Anne Hathaway: 'hate away she threw, and saved my life'.

So probably he and his Anne had to live, and make themselves useful, in the house which served also as his father's shop and workshop. Some mind-broadening entertainment would be provided by troupes of actors visiting nearby Coventry or Stratford itself, but as preparations for what lay ahead such experiences were so inadequate that there have been speculations that William Shakespeare never wrote the plays attributed to him despite what all his contemporaries thought.

In *The Winter's Tale* an old shepherd was to say that 'I would that there were no age between sixteen and three-and-twenty, or that youth would sleep out the rest; for there is nothing in the between but getting wenches with child, wronging the ancientry, stealing, fighting'. But it is impossible that Shakespeare spent these years so lamentably. It seems more reasonable to guess that when not making or selling leather goods in his father's shop he took more delight in the countryside which was to spring up again in his plays (including *The Winter's Tale*); he drank and talked with humble neighbours who when remembered would make theatregoers chuckle; he read when he could get hold of books; and hour by hour he learned by experiments how to write his own poetry in English, an art which required not many books but plenty of blank paper, the cost of which was probably quite a problem.

When he had access to theatres in London – most usefully to the Blackfriars theatre where boy actors performed comedies by John Lyly – he was to be marvellously quick to absorb the skills needed by professional actors and their servants, the men who supplied the scripts. The extent of his rapid achievement once he had the chance suggests a point not often made: he deserves some praise for staying with his wife and children for about five years when after an excellent education he must have been longing for the wider world in which they would have been out of place. In that world life in Stratford, while remembered with some affection, would seem another, much smaller, existence and the religion absorbed in Stratford, while in the background, would seem considerably less interesting than the new panorama of this-worldly excitements.

It seems that he went to London when about 23 years old, in or around 1587. No evidence is available about how he made the transition. It has been suggested that he was recruited by a troupe of actors visiting Stratford when one of their number had been killed in a brawl. But this was the leading theatrical company, the Queen's Men; there is no evidence that he ever belonged to it; and had he been given such a job in Stratford it would have been for him a fantastic piece of good luck. If no such miracle gave him a flying start, he must have begun his career at or near the bottom, even if the story that he was hired to hold the reins of patrons' horses is no more than a good story.

In 1577 a preacher dismayed by the opening of 'The Theatre' in a suburb of London had warned that sin causes plagues and plays cause sin, therefore 'the cause of plagues is plays'. Many arguments could be produced in support of the view that theatres were Satan's chapels. Certainly they seemed a major threat to health, with crowds packed into a small space. They could also seem a danger to security, for excited audiences could get out of control. Those were to be the two main reasons given for the long-term closure of all the London theatres in 1642. But there were other objections. Actors could seem to be parasites who wasted the time of citizens who ought to be at work or at home instead of theatre-going for a performance which consumed two hours of an afternoon. They could be suspected of spreading heresy and treason; in 1587 the queen's council wrote to the Archbishop of Canterbury and the Lord Mayor urging them to keep an eye on players who had taken 'upon themselves certain matters of divinity and state'. They could be accused of corrupting audiences as men and women together laughed at comedies about sex. They might encourage crime; actors were so ready to express emotion that they could murder each other (Ben Jonson did) in addition to what they did on stage. And actors were shameless sinners because in plays and rehearsals men assumed to be immoral mixed closely with boys who were trained to dress, act and speak like women. So by law a company of actors needed a nobleman as patron and supervisor.

Actors were not even well rewarded for their sins. A bit-part actor would be paid like a labourer and a star like a carpenter. Not even the writers who supplied the fifteen or twenty new plays which a troupe would need each year were well paid and one of the mysteries is how they gained access to the expensive books needed to suggest plots, for there were no public libraries. Their scripts belonged to the companies of actors which paid £6 (an artisan's average annual income) for the completed play although a few writers commanded a regular salary. And fame was not a reward, for many scripts resulted from collaboration between hacks who supplied scenes or acts as directed by the 'plotter', who was thus more or less the author. The only draft believed to be in Shakespeare's handwriting reaches us in three pages of a script about Sir Thomas More written in haste with many abbreviations and some revisions. Elsewhere in the manuscript four other hands have been detected. And after all this work, that play could not be performed, it seems; probably the censor rejected it because, although Shakespeare's bit showed More lecturing an unruly mob, it was about a Catholic martyr. It was first printed in 1844.

An early play on which he collaborated was not edifying: it was *Titus Andronicus*, a drama of many sensational horrors likely to excite the groundlings who paid a penny to stand and chew nuts right in front of the blood-soaked stage. The rhetoric is bombastic because too much influenced by memories of Seneca from schooldays; one of the longest speeches is made by Marcus when he meets Lavinia, who is bleeding to death because her hands and tongue have been cut off after rape. In Sonnet 111 the young man employed to write this stuff was to lament that he had to please the public, so his 'manners' had to be 'public' or vulgar. Like a dyer who has to dip a cloth into colour, so his hand must be stained.

An Elizabethan theatre could also function as an institute of adult education. If it tackled subjects less sensational than the material of *Titus*, eloquence would be needed by writers and actors because it was necessary to hold the attention of the audience without a roof to shelter it during an English afternoon and without scenery to dazzle its eyes. But it is striking that audiences then had an appetite for talk at an intellectual level which would never be allowed on modern television. So there was a market ready for it if the subject was English history, with rich robes to provide glamour.

People could be fascinated by revelations about the private lives of their social superiors as plays gave them glimpses of what 'really' went on in royal courts and semi-royal mansions, but they could also want to know about history because it helped to explain the time in which they lived. It was itself an age full of dramatic events. Shakespeare's arrival in the capital almost coincided with the defeat of the Spanish Armada by the more mobile English ships and, as was believed, by a storm contributed by Providence. The fifteenth century could be made relevant to the sixteenth because it had been a period of civil wars (the Wars of the Roses) from which the nation had been rescued by the Tudor dynasty now reigning and now the centre of resistance to the might of Spain. English history had not been on the curriculum in Stratford but a writer in a hurry could consult the enormous *Chronicles* of Ralph Holinshed in its new edition of 1587, together with the earlier and shorter history by Edward Hall which suggested the clear theme: the Tudors had come to England's rescue by ending the civil wars between Lancastrians and Yorkists.

Consulting other recent plays and probably in collaboration with other writers, Shakespeare presented the long reign of Henry VI (1422–61, 1470–71) as a series of dramatic episodes. The rhetoric was still overblown as it had been in *Titus* but he did manage to create some convincing characters, including Joan of Arc the tough peasant-warrior, to English eyes a bit of a witch and a bit of a whore, and Queen Margaret with her 'tiger's heart in a woman's body'. Then the series was made compulsive viewing by the arrival of a male villain, the deformed Richard III with much blood on his hands but with a witty tongue and an attractive way of confiding in the audience in order to reveal his secret thoughts. There had never been a series of history plays like this one.

There could also be a market for light-hearted plays about the private lives and thoughts of gentlemen, and this observant product of a grammar school, although not yet a gentleman himself, could supply what was wanted. It is often thought that the earliest comedy was *The Comedy of Errors*, a farce partly based on a play by Plautus as taught in Stratford: identical twins have servants of the same name and complications follow in rapid succession.

The Taming of the Shrew, also influenced by Plautus, would have caused amusement rather than offence. It takes for granted the conventional wisdom that a wife must obey as well as love her husband, but the tests reported are as exaggerated as in Chaucer's tale about Griselda and the monstrous Walter. Petruchio and Kate are both tough. He humiliates her systematically but she has defied a family richer than his in order to marry him. She loves him for his swaggering vitality and after their verbal wrestling – for she has a mind of her own – it all ends in bed. And some women may have applauded because a male actor given the role of Kate had been compelled to put himself inside a woman's place. One day John Fletcher was to write a sequel, about Petruchio's second marriage, and was to call it *The Tamer Tamed* – and Shakespeare might have called *All's Well That Ends Well* (about a reluctant bridegroom) *The Taming of the Man*. As in Chaucer's day, England was not then so crudely masculinist as is sometimes thought.

In contrast, *Two Gentlemen of Verona* (unaided by Plautus) was too immature to be successful: the two gentlemen and their beloveds are less memorable than the clown and his dog.

In August 1592, however, the theatres were closed because of an outbreak of plague and they did not reopen for a long period before the end of 1593. The frustrated playwright could tour the provinces with his fellow actors but his ambitious energies found their main outlet in the writing of poems. The two longest were published by Richard Field, a friend since they had sat together in school, and another connection with the Stratford years was their common origin in stories told by Ovid.

The first, *Venus and Adonis*, proved to be a bestseller despite the claim in Latin on the front cover that it was not vulgar. It was escapist, erotic and written in lushly sensual verse, and was dedicated to Henry Wriothesley, the immensely rich third Earl of Southampton who was not yet twenty years old, very handsome and very conceited. He was being urged – even ordered – by his widowed mother and by his guardian Lord Burghley (the queen's chief minister) to marry a suitable young lady, preferably Burghley's granddaughter, and beget an heir. (When he refused he was fined very heavily.) Desperately needing a patron, Shakespeare saw his chance. The poem was a reminder that marriage need not be unpleasant: even women getting on in years can be both passionate and available. Such is Venus the goddess of love, who lusts after the exquisitely beautiful but unexcited Adonis. As he flees from her hotly explicit advances he is savaged by a wild boar in the groin, evaporates into air and returns to earth as a flower, somewhat consoling Venus but not breeding a new god.

The dedication to the Adonis-like earl promised a 'graver labour' and this turned out to be a poem of almost 2,000 lines recounting *The Rape of Lucrece* by Tarquin, the last king of the Romans. The trouble about it is not any lack of eloquence: it is that the story is too laborious. The rapist's lust is described powerfully, as is his victim's sorrow, but the pace is leisurely. Although every reader will agree that Tarquin thoroughly deserves to be exiled, it may be noted that for all her distress Lucrece does not cry out to arouse her nearby servants: instead, there is talk. In *Venus and Adonis* the author had not been personally involved as he told a tale which was clearly mythological and essentially comic, but *The Rape* was meant to be about an action like a murder – not a literary exercise reporting a debate. The poet's own awareness of this absence of drama may have been what finally convinced him that his future lay in the theatres despite their exposure to epidemics. But the poem sold (although not as well as the more sexy *Venus*) and in 1598 a young clergyman recorded the admiration of a considerable circle by praising both poems as 'honey-tongued'.

Francis Meres also recorded that some 'sugary' sonnets had been shown to the poet's 'private friends' but it seems that he used that adjective because he had not been among those friends, for if these sonnets were among the 154 to be published eleven years later they were in a style very different from both *Venus* and *The Rape*. They were not quite sugar-free. They, too, made a formal pattern out of words which were clearly eloquent; they, too, were rhetorical and that involved exaggeration in praise, condemnation or self-pity. But they were not about a sex-mad goddess or a royal rapist. They were about realities in the private life of a very anxious poet.

These poems will always intrigue inquisitive readers because their emotional content may reveal the personality of a genius who normally did not expose himself. Recently scholars have tended to stress their artificiality; their most recent (2002) editor, Colin Burrow, found in them 'rhetoric and play', not autobiography. Yet readers who obstinately want to meet the man behind the poems can appeal to William Wordsworth, who wrote rather too many sonnets, most of them artificial, and who after years when he had thought otherwise decided that 'in these poems Shakespeare unlocked his heart'.

The facts seem to support Wordsworth's mature opinion. In the early 1590s the poet had a patron: in Sonnet 87 this benefactor is 'too dear for my possessing' but may grant 'riches' if the poet is 'deserving'. The only patron known to have stirred his emotions and energies to any great extent in any period of his life is Southampton, whose personal situation in this period corresponds with many lines in the sonnets. Needing a patron desperately, Shakespeare worked so intensively and so successfully on these poems that he wanted them to be preserved, but also so emotionally that so far as we know he did not want to see them made public. And the sonnets suggest that he wanted to attract the rich young earl by displaying himself in two roles at once: as servant-to-master he would flatter shamelessly while as man-to-man he would be equally unreserved in confessing his intimate anxieties, even his sense of despair as the earl won their competition for the favours of the Dark Lady. His reward for such a laborious and extensive abasement, rhetorical but also painfully real, could be very considerable. He might be appointed as Southampton's secretary and companion, with leisure and encouragement to develop himself as a poet: such an arrangement was not unknown in that age. Or if he remained in the theatrical world which was his first love, he could be given a sum of money which would lift him out of the insecure drudgery of a hack in a team of script-writers. He could also be allowed access to a good library. Above all, if he listened carefully to the talk in the sophisticated circle around the young earl he could have material as a writer which Stratford had not supplied. Such hopes could seem realistic, for Southampton was always determined to use his wealth as he chose: in different periods he defied Lord Burghley, Queen Elizabeth and King James, knowing that plenty of money would be left after paying for such eccentric and very risky behaviour. For a needy poet, this eccentric multimillionaire was the ideal patron and he seized his opportunity. It is indeed difficult to think of any other reason why in a period when he had much more ambition than money he spent so much time writing poetry which would not be sold to the public. He could not afford 'rhetoric and play' for his own amusement.

The first seventeen sonnets have an urgent message: for the future's sake marry – you were begotten and you have a duty to beget. With the extravagance expected from poets in that period the next nine (and others) celebrate the patron's beauty, claiming that nature had intended to make him a woman but had added the 'one thing' that prevents the physical expression of the poet's 'true' love. This has stimulated the modern discussion of Shakespeare's attitude to 'homosexuality'. The word had not yet been coined and talk about the subject was not loud. The rape of a boy could be punished by death and even lesser contacts between adults could arouse disapproval; an informer told the government that Shakespeare's patron fondled the Earl of Essex in public while they were supposed to be leading a military expedition, and tongues wagged when King James made no secret of his infatuation with a handsome young favourite. But many people, including Shakespeare, were relaxed about more discreet feelings which may, or may not, have included lust. In his plays men have very close friendships with men, and women with women, and as in the sonnets the language can sound homoerotic if that classification is wanted. But there is no evidence that he was other than heterosexual in his own basic orientation. In his plays the evil characters are almost always men, and the women are almost always lovable, and the whole point of the romantic comedies is that 'Jack shall have Jill'. Few poets have written with such passion about a woman he desires as he did in these sonnets and none has been so eloquent about the duty of a man to make a woman a mother. He did not 'come out' as 'gay' when he offered *The Rape of Lucrece* to the Earl of Southampton with the public assurance that 'the love I dedicate to your Lordship is without end'.

In his sonnets he sounds utterly captivated by a relationship which has lasted for three years (Sonnet 104) and he hopes that his patron's magnificent beauty will have an 'eternal summer', but he knows that it will not and the contemplation of the decay which time inflicts on everyone helps to make these sonnets more introspective than any previous writing in English. While sleepless he curses his life without privilege and worries that he will lose his patron's love, but he also hugs to himself the hope that his verses will outlast his patron's beauty. He broods on the approach of his own death (soon, from the plague?). In Sonnets 76–86 he is alarmed by the appearance of a rival poet with 'the proud full sail of his great verse' (probably Marlowe) and from 127 onwards he records different agonies. He is both lured and rejected, both enchanted and disgusted, by a woman with whom his patron also has a sexual relationship. She is dark in complexion, eyes and hair but her identity cannot be known despite many theories. In 1594, however, a clever student in Oxford published a satire based on the latest gossip from London, and *Willobie his Avisa* claimed that both 'H.W.' and 'W.S.' had caught an infection from an innkeeper's daughter. The last few sonnets also seem to point to venereal disease and the unhappy poet writes about a 'waste of shame' after 'lust'. But there are hints in the sonnets that the Dark Lady was socially superior and therefore preferred an earl to a poet.

This self-revelation was not printed before 1609. Then a publisher calling himself a 'well-wishing adventurer', Thomas Thorpe, brought out *Shake-speare's Sonnets* with many misprints and without any aid to understanding. The little book was dedicated not to Henry Wriothesley the earl who might have been called 'H.W.', but to 'Mr. W.H.', described as its 'onlie begetter'. This clearly implies that someone had supplied the manuscript but much investigation by literary detectives has not determined who this someone was. Sir William Harvey has been proposed; he had been the third husband of the earl's mother who had recently died, so he would have had access to her papers. But it seems very unlikely that most of the sonnets would have been sent for approval and safe keeping by a widowed countess. A more favoured candidate is William Herbert, the third earl of Pembroke; fourteen years later Shakespeare's collected plays were to be dedicated to him and his brother with thanks for unspecified favours shown to the author in his lifetime. Conceivably some of the sonnets may have been about this W.H. but while these earls probably subsidised the solemn and expensive printing of the plays it is not likely that in 1609 Pembroke had any motive to give or sell sonnets to Thorpe, and if such a strange transaction had occurred, addressing an earl as 'Mr' would not have been a tactful way of expressing gratitude. The same considerations apply to Southampton whose patronage had almost certainly begotten the sonnets in the first place. Around 1593 he had presumably been delighted by the flattery but now he was older and more respectable, in good standing at the court of King James although this did not last; he did not need either money or publicity for what he had been some fifteen years previously. So it seems that the identity of the supplier will never be known.

He was not Shakespeare (whose surname strangely includes a hyphen in the title) although this, too, has been suggested. The reference by Francis Meres shows that as late as 1598 the circulation of the sonnets was still restricted to 'private friends'. In 1599 a printer included two in an unlicensed pamphlet called *The Passionate Pilgrim*, claiming that the whole little collection was 'by W. Shakespeare'. And next year another printer secured the official registration of the forthcoming *Amours by J.D. with certain other sonnets by W.S.*, but *The Passionate Pilgrim* must have made Shakespeare indignant and the proposed collaboration with John Donne seems never to have got into print, for no copy has been found. If he had been behind the publication of all his own sonnets in 1609, surely the poet would have dedicated it himself, and to Southampton, and would have taken care to have his work printed accurately and presented attractively. It has been claimed that he was anxious to make money because, after providing a large dowry for a daughter married in 1607, he had seen his income drop as a result of the closure of the theatres from July 1608 to the end of 1609. But in recent years he had spent large sums on purchases of property, land and tithes and there is no record of the sale of any of these investments. And had he been in dire straits, it is unlikely that he would have turned to a publisher. It was argued in a recent (2001) biography that the sonnets were 'highly marketable' for a 'substantial sum', but their fate shows why Thorpe is unlikely to have produced any such sum for a first edition to be sold in only one shop. There was to be no second edition before 1640, when some of the love poems were to be readdressed to a woman, some were to be merged with others, and some were to be replaced by the more accessible work of other writers.

Thorpe may, however, have been willing to pay a small sum to someone who supplied the manuscript and that would be understandable: *Venus and Adonis* had at least sixteen reprints before 1640 and even *The Rape* had eight. He knew how to advertise, for he boasted that these sonnets by our 'ever-living poet' were 'never before imprinted' and aroused gossip by being mystifying about the identity of their 'only begetter' who nevertheless was promised 'immortality' as a reward for his good deed. And these poems were a revelation of the sex lives of celebrities, in no age a hindrance to sales.

Why, then, was the book not a commercial success? It seems probable that Shakespeare, so far from sponsoring its publication, did all he could to suppress it, with Southampton's help. It was illegal to sell a new book without the approval of the Stationers' Company and both the earl and the poet could report that the manuscript had been stolen. They would also be able to threaten or bribe the single bookseller named on the cover. And we need not look far to find a motive for such a reaction by the aggrieved author whose status had been shown by the title of the booklet published in the previous year: *Master William Shakespeare and his True Chronicle History of the Life and Death of King Lear . . . Played before the King's Majesty.* Already in 1592 Robert Southwell the Jesuit had protested that a gifted poet, named 'Mr W.S.' in the reprint of 1619, ought to write about Christ.

Now, in 1609, a definitely Christian poet whom we shall study in the next chapter, George Herbert, then a first-year student, complained about ungodly verse and assured his mother that in due course he would write in praise of God. A poet who in many ways articulated Victorian religion and morality, Robert Browning, commented to the effect that if Shakespeare did indeed unlock his heart here, many readers must be disappointed – not by the quality of the poetry, but by the quality of the young man. More recent commentary, accustomed to treat this poetry with great respect, has not considered seriously enough what reasons their author may have had for action to limit the damage to his reputation. He had written that in the sonnets 'every word doth almost tell my name' and what his words could now tell the public was that in his early years he had been so open to criticism that he could judge himself harshly. The rhetoric of his flattery or self-condemnation was far beneath his present status as a writer who could take a detached view of the strengths and weaknesses of famous kings. So was the passion in this married man's adultery with a woman who was promiscuous ('the bay where all men rise') and who in the end preferred as a lover someone younger and richer. And so was his reaction to his disappointments: 'I alone beweep my outcaste state . . . desiring this man's art and that man's scope.' Sonnet 66 had not been his only admission that life had defeated him, so that he hoped for 'restful death'. These poems were like a nude appearance on stage.

He had also been ungodly to an extent which would shock many besides George Herbert in 1609, when Puritanism was rising fast. He may 'shun the heaven that leads men to this hell' in Sonnet 29 but that is because he is a man infected by a woman he would like to be his mistress. Sonnet 145 has him at the 'poor centre of my sinful earth', but only because he has bought clothes at 'so large a cost' which he could not afford. He resolves to 'buy terms divine' but does not explain how he intends to make that further purchase. In some sonnets there is self-loathing; in none is there repentance. Certainly he will not confess his sins to a Catholic priest: in 124 he smugly contrasts the 'hugely politic' constancy of his love for his patron with the folly of priests who are traitors not martyrs. They are justly executed because although it is claimed that they 'die for goodness' in fact they have 'liv'd for crime'. His extreme humility – in 72 he is a 'slave' begging for the favour of his 'sovereign' – is addressed to his patron, not to his Maker. Sonnet 29 has him praying to 'deaf heaven' and in 108 he is still praying 'every day', but his prayer is that his love for the 'sweet boy' may be eternal. He has such love in mind when he makes his famous claim that 'Love's not Time's fool'.

In the course of time Shakespeare and Southampton seem to have drifted apart and as we shall see the poet did not get into trouble when the earl did. The arguments that most or all of the sonnets were written after 1594 seem weak. Comparisons have been made between rare words used in the poems and post-1594 plays but the same words may have been in this crowded mind before as well as after that year. There may be unclear references to events after 1594 – or may not be. What does seem decisive is the certain fact that after 1594 Shakespeare, although not exempt from troubles and not unable to write about them, prospered in his career. It seems very unlikely that he had the time or inclination to work on many sonnets that are full of abject flattery and self-pitying desperation. And if the evidence points to the writing of all or most of these sonnets before 1594, and to action against their publication in 1609, then we do indeed hold in our hands a key to a part of Shakespeare's heart. What we have is almost his diary in his years of hellish anxiety, and this suggests almost a certainty that fifteen years later he wanted the key to remain hidden, because he was ashamed of what he had been before he had changed.

One of the wonders in the story of this 'ever-living' poet is, however, the wide popularity of some of the sonnets from the nineteenth century onwards. Many readers have felt that the characters on view were real people experiencing normal emotions. Originally the sonnets were (it is likely) highly sophisticated expressions of emotions connected with two loves which a self-respecting and respectable married poet ought not to have experienced and expressed so intensely – loves for a patron and a mistress. But history has shown that the sonnets are sufficiently ambiguous for it to be possible for readers to be able to treat them – and to make gift books out of them – as very beautiful expressions of happy heterosexual love. In the sonnets such love is not happy. Some of Shakespeare's own memories lie behind Lear's claim that women are like animals – only, the women have 'the more riotous appetite'. The gods may rule women 'to the girdle' at the waist, but beneath it

> There's hell, there's darkness, there's the sulphurous pit,
> Burning, scalding, stench, consumption . . .

The second half of his life started in an outburst of relief that he had survived the plague and had been rewarded financially by Southampton (this is the most likely reason for the fact that he now had some spare cash) yet had been liberated from dependence on a single patron. He seized the opportunity presented by the death of Marlowe, killed in a brawl and probably by agents of the government, scandalous as Shakespeare had not been – a blasphemer, a homosexual, a spy in the service of the government before he was dismissed to die. But he had also been spectacular and had he matured might have been a lifelong rival. Death also removed Thomas Kyd, who was tortured severely during the investigation into Marlowe's circle: his *Spanish Tragedy* had been a theatrical sensation.

It was, however, unrewarding financially to be unrivalled in one's art unless one became a shareholder in an actors' company. Only then could one be sure of steady employment and entitled to a regular slice of the takings. Shakespeare was again fortunate: a new company was formed under the sponsorship and protection of the courtier who arranged the queen's entertainments, the Lord Chamberlain, and he became a shareholder, probably buying the share but possibly in exchange for a promise to write a stream of comedies. These can be analysed as festivals which mark the great transitions of life: from darkness to light, from winter to summer, from adolescence to adulthood, from confusion to simplicity, from enmity to forgiveness, from separation to unity, from ignorance to knowledge. Such have been some of the great themes of religion, embodied over many ages in great myths, but on an Elizabethan stage these myths had to be presented as stories not totally unlike soap operas on our TV. They had to appeal to instincts deep down in humanity – but they also had to be fun which people would pay to enjoy.

The central theme of some of the plays which now poured from his pen is the difficulty, the 'labour', which can turn into the glory of young love. The new richness of language is striking: he had developed fast in his few years of concentration on the public or private work of a poet. In *Love's Labour's Lost* four bachelors including the King of Navarre form a little college for study without the distractions of female company. Four highly eligible women including the Princess Royal of France arrive and of course the men want to marry them – but first they have to develop emotionally while the women hold themselves aloof. Berowne, for example, is sent off to work for a year in a hospital. The play cries out for a sequel about the marriages and *Love's Labour's Won* was probably that, but if so only the title has survived, in a bookseller's catalogue.

Better still are *A Midsummer Night's Dream* and *Romeo and Juliet*, both written in 1595–96. The ultraromantic plot of the *Dream* was thought up by Shakespeare and rescued from absurdity by what was now undeniably his genius in imagination and expression. In a moonlit wood the fairies make mistakes with their magic: Lysander is made to fall in love with Helena although Hermia has run away from home in order to marry him, Helena seems fated never to marry Demetrius on whom she dotes, Titania becomes infatuated with Bottom the clownish weaver. But better magic sorts things out: the women marry the right men, Titania and Oberon live happily ever after as queen and king of the fairies. And the best magic is Shakespeare's own as he pours out lyrical poetry about a spirit-filled but recognisable countryside and glorious humour about down-to-earth humanity. Homage to Chaucer is hinted at: the plot of *Pyramus and Thisbe* comes from his *Legend* and that tragedy-turned-into-farce is performed to celebrate the marriage of Theseus Duke of Athens, who is infinitely happier now than he had been in the knight's tale. In the end everybody is given what Theseus wishes all the married: 'joy and fresh days of love'. In the background is a medieval custom: on this night, although it begins the Church's commemoration of John the stern Baptist, young men escort young women into a wood.

Romeo and Juliet is his first tragedy. Romeo Montague and Juliet Capulet fall in love at first sight but are 'star-crossed' and more than the stars are against them. After killing Tybalt Romeo is banished and after rejecting Paris Juliet is ordered to marry that unwanted suitor, and thus the situation is created in which the lovers kill themselves. But in contrast with the source of the story (a poem of 1562 by Arthur Brooke), this is far from being an unmitigated tragedy about the follies of the young. Romeo's sharp-witted friend Mercutio and Juliet's no-nonsense nurse – for the girl is only fourteen – could be in a comedy. The lovers live, speak and die in the 'high' style which the Elizabethans so admired, and their love is supported by a priest who is depicted favourably, Friar Laurence. He warns the lovers to moderate their enthusiasm but blesses their marriage against the anger of their parents; he supplies a drug so that by a pretence of death Juliet may avoid the sin of bigamy; he summons Romeo to the rescue; he is dismayed when the summons is delayed by an accident; he uses their grief to reconcile the two families previously locked in hatred; he shows that 'church' and 'sex' need not be divorced. All this takes place in Verona, but Shakespeare's development since *The Two Gentlemen* is staggering. The two young lovers are of course open to criticism: they are infatuated with each other, they both commit suicide, Romeo kills Tybalt and Paris as well as himself. But the purpose of the play is not to attack them. Again we seem to hear an echo of Chaucer's humane voice.

The Life and Death of King John has another Chaucerian theme: love for England. It is an attack on a king but not a demand for democracy: *Magna Carta*, which anyway was not democratic, is not mentioned. Its point is that John ought not to be king: not only is he as foolish as he is cruel, he is a usurper while the rightful king is Arthur the son of his royal brother against whom he has rebelled. He is excommunicated by the pope as Queen Elizabeth was in 1570, but Cardinal Pandulph hands the crown back with the words 'take again your sovereign greatness and authority'. Such greatness ought to belong to Arthur, who dies in a bid to escape murder. This gives some of the English a good reason to collaborate with a French invasion but of course the ideal is the nation's independence.

King John was a reworking of an anonymous and mediocre play of 1591 but *Richard II* was all Shakespeare's own work and all in verse. It again dealt with a question about who is the rightful king, with the answer that Richard, although civilised and eloquent in a way which must commend him to any audience in a theatre, is not suitable as a king: he is self-dramatising without knowing how to be self-assertive in a way which other selves will respect and accept. He uncrowns himself, both literally and metaphorically. The usurper Bolingbroke is a hard man who lets his actions speak for him, yet after victory he becomes penitent about his success. In defeat, before he is murdered Richard speaks the message: kingship is sacred, whatever may be the humanity of one king or another. No baron and no pope can destroy it, for it is the instrument of God for the good government of God's people. Shakespeare would add that to conform fully with God's will, the government must be good. There must be leadership given in a style which will make less gifted people glad to be followers, and despite his guilt Bolingbroke is the agent of Providence.

In these plays the defects of two kings are not allowed to damage Shakespeare's love for the kingdom of which they are unworthy. In *King John*

> Come the three corners of the world in arms,
> And we shall shock them. Naught shall make us rue,
> If England to itself do rest but true.

And in *Richard II* England is

> This royal throne of kings, this scepter'd isle,
> This earth of majesty, this seat of Mars,
> This other Eden, demi-paradise . . .
> This land of such dear souls, this dear, dear land . . .

But it is not easy to see what is being celebrated in *The Merchant of Venice* (1596?). The play rises a few inches above Marlowe's *Jew of Malta* in its treatment of Jews and its presentation of Portia rises further above *The Taming of the Shrew*. She triumphs in a man's world (admittedly, disguised as a man and played by a boy) and she is the first of a line of heroines who are both nicer and more effective than the men. Yet Shakespeare does not fully rise to the question about mercy in contrast with strict justice. When she has failed to commend mercy to Shylock as 'an attribute of God himself', Portia falls back on a legal argument: Antonio has promised a 'pound of flesh' if he fails to repay Shylock's loan (is there a hint of the Jewish law of circumcision?), but since the pound now demanded would be near the heart that would draw blood and therefore be contrary to the law of Venice. And when Shylock has been found guilty, no mercy is shown to him. His cry was to reach the century of the Holocaust: 'If you prick us, do we not bleed? If you tickle us, do we not laugh? If you poison us, do we not die? And if you wrong us, do we not seek revenge?' But the Venetians who nominally adhere to the religion to which this Jew is now forcibly converted seem to notice only his mention of revenge: having baptised him, they ruin him financially.

If *The Merchant* falls short of greatness, an explanation may be psychological. Shakespeare seems to have been basically ambiguous in his attitude to money. He did not write mainly in order to make it: he was a great artist exercising his gifts. But having made it, he spent or invested it as shrewdly as Shylock or the self-styled Christians in Venice.

As a shareholder profiting financially from such plays which had every merit except the highest, he was now in a position to prove that for him a training as an all-round man of the theatre had been better than a university and had brought rewards in every sense. He would not die like Greene or Marlowe. Instead, three years after the reopening of the London theatres he bought the second-largest house in Stratford. By making up a story about his ancestry, and by paying a fee, he persuaded the heralds to acknowledge his father as a gentleman entitled to display a coat of arms with the motto *Non sanz droict*, 'Not without right'. Ben Jonson parodied this as 'Not without mustard' and a scrawl beneath a herald's drawing survives to show us that he was sniffily aware that it was being done for a mere 'player'. But the new gentleman's class-conscious son would be unable to pass on these signs of status, for in August 1596 his only son, Hamnet, died before his twelfth birthday. There is an echo of his grief when Prince Arthur dies in *King John* (probably written at this time) and a calmer reference can be found in the much later *Macbeth*, when Macduff has been told that his entire family has been murdered and Malcolm has advised him to bear it like a man. Macduff replies very simply:

> I shall do so,
> But I must also feel it as a man:
> I cannot but remember such things were,
> That were most precious to me.

But Salisbury's words over the prince's dead body in *King John* seem to be closer to what Shakespeare felt at the time:

> Kneeling before this ruin of sweet life,
> And breathing to his breathless excellence
> The incense of a vow, a holy vow,
> Never to taste the pleasures of the world,
> Never to be infected with delight,
> Nor conversant with ease and idleness . . .

In the sonnets he had recently told his patron that if a man dies without an heir he will have lived in vain. But if these were his emotions when Hamnet died, he would seem to have done his best to drown them by proceeding with his plan to establish himself as a gentleman and by working hard at his plays. However, he aged. Among these plays his romantic comedies show that he could not revive the simple and full zest of the *Dream* and *Romeo and Juliet* about young love. *The Merry Wives of Windsor*, written hastily in 1597, is merry about the efforts of Falstaff to lure married women into his middle-aged arms but the merriment seems to be manufactured. Then the very titles of his next two plays suggest that he is becoming detached and even melancholic in his own middle age. 'All the world's a stage' is probably the most famous quotation from his work in this period when he became a spectator not always able to stay fully awake.

Much Ado About Nothing (1598) presented two pairs of lovers, Claudio and Hero in their more conventional courtship, Benedick and Beatrice in their mock-battles of wit. The 'much ado' comes when the wicked Don John manages to persuade Claudio that Hero has been unfaithful and he denounces and almost kills her by calling her a 'rotten orange' just as they are about to get married. Don John is exposed but only by a comically blockheaded constable, Dogberry. The banter between Claudio's friend Benedick and the equally sharp Beatrice develops from rivalry in showing off into seriously strong love only when Benedick is willing to accept Beatrice's challenge to kill Claudio in revenge for his treatment of Hero. All ends well but the clever talk about nothing very much has always been the play's chief attraction. Perhaps, however, 'nothing' here refers to what about a woman is most desired by a heated man, as in Elizabethan slang.

As You Like It (1599) adapted the plot in a recent French novel. Rosalind is the daughter of a duke who has been deposed, Orlando is almost killed according to a plan devised by his brother Oliver, and the two fall in love when exiled to the deposed duke's court in the forest of Arden although Rosalind is now disguised as a man. Again all ends well, with Oliver and the wicked duke repentant and the two central lovers married – but again, it almost ended in tears. And minor characters including Touchstone and Jaques supply a commentary which is far from romantic, while the forest which is idyllic in the novel is not so in this sweet-and-sour play. Here a clown called William, asked 'Art thou wise?', answers 'I have a pretty wit'.

Twelfth Night, the last and best of his ten romantic comedies, is shown by its title to have been connected with the end of the Christmas festivities. Whether or not it was first performed at court during the visit of an Italian duke, Orsino, in January 1601, it made prominent use of that name and was partly based on a popular Italian play. But it was unlike that play both by being more of a high-spirited revel and by having an undercurrent of middle-aged disapproval. Its first lines refer to a 'dying fall' in music meant to be the 'food of love', a food which can sicken. When a member of the audience wrote up his diary after a performance in 1602 he did not mention any new Romeo: the only character he remembered was Malvolio, the austere steward of the play's most hungry lover, the widowed countess Olivia. A spoil-sport, he could be treated as a tragic hero in some nineteenth-century performances and as a protester against upper-class frivolity and sport in the twentieth century. Maria calls him by the new sixteenth-century term 'puritan' and Sir Toby Belch accuses him of being against 'cakes and ale'.

This outsider, full of self-righteousness and 'self-love', is therefore tricked into believing that his widowed employer is in love with him, and he with her, but in the end the laughter dies down. In keeping with the tradition in these comedies others proceed to weddings after much confusion, but he leaves the stage vowing to be 'avenged on the whole pack of you'. Then Feste the clown ends the play with a song of disillusionment, about rain 'every day'. It almost seems possible that Shakespeare has foreseen the Puritan revolution which forty years later will close the theatres completely and thus make sure that 'our play is done'.

Beatrice, Rosalind and Viola dance out of the plays as Shakespeare's dream-women, beauties with brains, but there are to be no more like them for many years. It seems that even his imagination was now exhausted in this department and that a cause can be found in the fact that while he saw his wife and daughters only for short periods, the women he met in London's taverns (and brothels?) cannot have been very like these imagined heroines. For him, the road ahead in the rain will not be romantic until he meets the heroines of the tragedies.

The histories also continued, again by popular demand, again full of glamour, but again with signs that he has grown more detached. Now older, he would not commit himself totally to any cause, knowing that every human project is flawed, but his empathy and sympathy have become such that no cause is completely condemned – and some great plays can be written in that mood.

The two parts of *Henry IV* and their sequel (1597–99) show that Shakespeare, having been the pioneer, was now the master. Needing to celebrate England amid many dangers, he concentrated on the invasion of Scotland and the defeat of rebellions in Wales and in England itself. Needing to support the English Crown, he depicted the king as careworn and as anxious to go on a crusade to prove his penitence for the way in which he had taken the crown from Richard II. Needing to please the public, he created a friendship between the Prince of Wales and a rogue with 'more flesh' and therefore 'more fraility', the purse-stealing, woman-embracing, life-enhancing Falstaff, who ought to have had an opportunity to marry the Wife of Bath. He praised heroism in battle, with Prince Hal beginning to perform in that role although outclassed by the rebel Hotspur, but he was equally at home in London taverns or Cotswold villages and was clearly sympathetic with the recruits to the army whom Falstaff calls 'food for powder'. He seemed to mock the Prince Hal who wore the crown prematurely as his father lay dying, but he did not criticise the new King Henry – the legitimate king as his father had not been – who emerges from his coronation to tell Falstaff not to come near him again. So on whose side was Shakespeare? Did he intend to praise Hotspur's dedication to 'honour' above Falstaff's commitment to fun and 'fellowship'? All that is certain is that he intended to write a very good play in two parts; and to follow it up with a play about Henry V, who right at the beginning of *Henry IV* says that he intends to learn about his future subjects by living among them as the sun lives among mists before it shines. And he thinks deeply about the relationship between father and son, here as in *Hamlet*.

At the end of *Henry IV* the king advises his son and heir to use a war abroad in order to distract the barons from rebellion at home – and that is what Henry V now does, encouraged by the Archbishop of Canterbury, who offers a learned justification of the invasion in exchange for a promise to protect the Church's wealth. Through 'dead men's blood' the reborn Henry now wades to victory at Agincourt and to the diplomatic version of rape, his marriage with the daughter of the French king. It may not be obvious that Shakespeare sees this: the chorus merely applauds a conquering hero and Henry's wooing of his bride is treated as a comedy about learning French. When alone, however, the king has the honesty to tell himself, God and the audience that monarchy is 'ceremony' accompanied by anxieties which make his life more wretched than a slave's. *Henry V* is moving both when the king in disguise talks with soldiers trying to warm themselves in the night before the battle and when a far less vulnerable 'Harry the King', this 'mirror of all Christian kings', urges them into battle with a speech which sounds more than ceremonious:

> We few, we happy few, we band of brothers . . .

And the patriotism of this play stirred many hearts in, for example, the 1940s. But the few were fewer after this expedition to France in the 1510s – as later.

A magisterial detachment from any partisan feeling also marks Shakespeare's first use of Roman history, made possible by Sir Thomas North's splendid translation of Plutarch's *Lives* (1579). Its centre is the assassination of Julius Caesar but it is full of self-revealing and thought-provoking oratory. Caesar is a highly successful leader who still needs an ambition to keep him going ('he would be crown'd'); Mark Antony is a brilliant speaker who uses words as he has used a sword, to win a battle; Brutus is an admirable idealist who is not practical enough to fight and kill; Cassius is a lean and pale conspirator, hungry for power and calculating about realities which need to be faced if power is to be won and held. And from behind all that talk come whispers of the great political issues. Granted that democracy is out of the question because it would involve rule by the stupid and fickle mob, is a republic led by men such as Brutus and Cassius worth saving when a dictatorship can work better – and can appeal to the mob?

For Shakespeare these issues are moral as well as political, yet he is not crudely pro-Richard or anti-Richard, pro-Hotspur or pro-Falstaff, pro-war or anti-war, pro-Caesar or anti-Caesar. And this man from Stratford who can never have been treated as an equal by men with political power has seen the questions so seriously and so perceptively that the prophecy by Cassius has come true:

> How many ages hence
> Shall this our lofty scene be acted o'er,
> In states unborn and accents yet unknown!

Those plays were among the first to be staged in the Globe, a theatre rebuilt on the south bank of the Thames in the early months of 1599; *Henry V* refers to it as the 'wooden O' because its centre was open to the sky. The buildings had been removed from a site on the north bank when the company's lease on that had expired. It rose above the brothels, the gambling dens and the bear-baiting arenas and defied the respectable who deplored theatres along with the other entertainments, and who controlled the City of London on the opposite bank of the river, under St Paul's Cathedral.

Shakespeare was driven to work on more plays – driven partly by the demands of his job as his company's resident writer but also by the demands of his creativity as a genius now with a large platform. Five among these plays are usually ranked among the greatest tragedies ever, but first let us glance at five others. They show that between masterpieces he could still produce work below his best, not because the poetry was always poor (it was often excellent), nor because the plot was unrealistic (the plots of better plays often were), nor because an audience would not wonder what would be the next turn in the plot (a performance can be truly dramatic), but because he did not throw enough of himself into the writing. He did not make it easy for the actors to persuade the audience that here was a reality so important that disbelief about incidents could be suspended. He might have made them plays which preach a clear morality, and by implication they do condemn evils – marriage without love, government without mercy or justice, war without a good purpose, wealth without a heart, strength without service. But he was occupying a stage, not a pulpit, and even as a storyteller he was not so creative as he had been. So these plays are nowadays usually called his 'problem' plays and the main problem about them is why, coming from Shakespeare, they were not better.

In two plays probably first performed in or around 1604 he revisited the situation in which he had found himself when he had made Anne pregnant. In *All's Well That Ends Well* Bertram fully accepts Helena as his wife only because she is pregnant with his child. In *Measure for Measure* Claudio narrowly escapes death as the punishment for impregnating his betrothed Juliet although their contract to marry is of the sort that is legally binding, while his judge Angelo, 'affianced' to pregnant Mariana by a promise which can be broken, breaks it on discovering that she is not going to bring to the marriage a dowry as big as he had expected. But Shakespeare's treatment of these three conceptions is not passionate. In his own case he had accepted his responsibility and the hasty marriage had been blessed by the Church, and it seems that he could not really understand people who made a fuss.

Both plays are full of eloquence. In *Measure* the Duke of Vienna, disguised as a friar, speaks to Claudio out of a long tradition which recommends contempt for life before death. No period of mortal life is more than 'an after-dinner's sleep', while death brings not awakening but a longer rest. So 'be absolute for death!' Claudio speaks more realistically about his fear: when we die 'we go we know not where' and while our bodies rot in a grave our spirits may find that all our previous suffering has been Paradise in comparison with everlasting life in hell. At the end he agrees with the serious argument that death is to be accepted if life is to be enjoyed, so 'let it come on': he will 'encounter darkness like a bride'. But the whole conversation is based on hypocrisy, for the self-styled priest who offers this consolation to a doomed convict is in reality the legislator who has been grossly unjust in making what has been done a crime deserving capital punishment. Such a law was out of the question in England at that time although in 1650 the Puritans were to secure what several bishops had previously demanded – death for adultery.

Unreality also damages what these plays might teach about mercy. In *All's Well* it is finely said that 'the web of our life is a mingled yarn, good and ill together: our virtues would be proved if our vices whipped them not, and our vices would despair if they were not cherished by our virtues'. In *Measure* there is for once poetry about Christ:

> Why, all the souls that were, were forfeit once;
> And He that might the vantage best have took
> Found out the remedy. How would you be
> If He, which is the top of judgment, should
> But judge you as you are? O! think on that,
> And mercy then will breathe within your lips
> Like man new made.

But unlike *Romeo and Juliet*, this play is not a plea for mercy on young lovers. The poetry comes from Isabella who is shown to be coldly judgemental. Instead of rebuking Angelo the judge for a wildly excessive sentence, she has just told him that Claudio is guilty of the 'vice which I must abhor' and deserves the 'blow of justice' which is death, so that her only plea can be for undeserved mercy. When Angelo has offered to commute the sentence to life imprisonment in exchange for sex with her, and when her doomed brother has begged her to consent, she refuses as is her right, but she does so with cruelty: she tells her brother that 'mercy to thee' would be wrong and 'I'll pray a thousand prayers for thy death'.

The title of *Measure for Measure*, which has been wrongly praised as his 'most Christian play', is taken from the Sermon on the Mount (Matthew 7.2), where the boundless mercy of God is promised to the merciful who do not insist on measured justice. Such a title could have been used for a magnificent sequel to Portia's plea in *The Merchant*, but here as there Shakespeare does not seem to be able to get beyond a story about human failures to be merciful – and here a government is not only merciless: it is also flagrantly unjust. Admittedly this play can look like one of the comedies with a happy ending: Claudio survives to marry his Juliet; Isabella is asked to be the duchess; and the bad and sad Angelo is reappointed as the duke's deputy in the administration of justice. But Claudio is alive only because the severed head of a pirate who looks like him has been used to satisfy Angelo's bloodthirsty justice; Isabella, who has repeatedly declared her vocation to be an exceptionally strict nun, does not reply to the duke's offer of marriage; and Angelo becomes a married father because he has impregnated Mariana when under the illusion that she is Isabella. And it was not right for Wilson Knight to claim that 'the duke's ethical attitude is exactly correspondent with Jesus'. Duke Vincentio decreed the unjust law which Angelo enforces, but out of laziness rather than wisdom he did not enforce it himself: instead, he allowed brothels to flourish during his reign of fourteen years. He delegated his difficult responsibilities because he wanted to move around the city in disguise, snooping on Angelo and others and claiming the right to hear the confessions of sinners. He is creepy and his reappointment of Angelo is a perversion of the criminal justice system. This Vienna (inhabited by Italians) seems a long way both from reality and from the Sermon on the Mount, and the reason may be that without a clear message it reworks the plot of a play of the 1570s by George Whetstone. It is one of Shakespeare's most thoughtful plays but here as in *The Merchant* he seems to be thinking aloud. One difficulty for him was that in his age neither 'justice' nor 'mercy' seemed to have a close connection with Christian humanism.

All's Well That Ends Well transforms Boccaccio's story about a young aristocrat who is compelled to marry a woman he does not love, mainly because she is inferior to him in social status, and who refuses to have sex with her. The change is that in Shakespeare's play Bertram is deeply unpleasant while his wife is a saint who first heals the King of France and then heals Bertram's sexual problem by getting pregnant and exchanging rings when he is very happily in bed with her under the illusion that she is the woman after whom he lusts, Diana. She then heals the audience's dislike of him by forgiving him so generously that he repents and a full marriage can begin. But his repentance is unconvincing and the bed-trick also met in *Measure* is even more unrealistic here. The contrast with the romantic comedies is again great: the wine is now sour.

In three other plays his imagination took him to Troy, Athens and Rome but he was not fully excited. *Troilus and Cressida* reworked Homer's epic and Chaucer's tragedy but with a weary cynicism: Thersites sums it all up as 'wars and lechery'. Cressida is 'false, false, false!' and without any authentic soul-searching and the men around her talk very cleverly but to little purpose while the siege of Troy drags on. Ajax is 'sodden-witted'; Achilles prefers to be in bed with Patroclus his 'masculine whore'; Hector is sure that the more conventionally lustful Helen of Troy is not 'worth what she doth cost'; he is the nearest to heroism but his killing is accomplished by Achilles, here the envious antihero; Pandarus tells the audience that he has syphilis and proposes to spread it. An anti-war attitude was widespread during the last years of Elizabeth's reign, a time of inflation, bad harvests and an apparently endless war against Spain. But since this is Shakespeare, the lapse into the unbalanced condemnation of everyone is dismaying – until we learn that in the 1990s the examination of its language by computer showed that he wrote *Edward III*, or much of it, in the 1590s. For in that immature play the launch of the Hundred Years' War is praised without any hesitation. One fact which makes us applaud Shakespeare is that unlike Homer he learned to hate war.

Like that failure *Timon of Athens* seems to have been left unperformed until long after Shakespeare's death. A play about money from which Karl Marx was to quote more than once, its central character is a man who so wastes his wealth in order to buy friendship that he bankrupts himself. He then insults the friends who become less keen on him. He goes to live in a cave but when digging on a beach finds gold which he gives to a new friend, Alcibiades, in order to finance an army which will massacre the ungrateful Athenians. But Alcibiades relents on hearing that he is dead and few people have cared greatly one way or another. The defences can be that Shakespeare was only the joint-author, and that the script was abandoned before completion.

Coriolanus is also about a man who becomes isolated. He fights heroically for Rome but cannot bring himself to be polite to its people when he needs their voices if he is to become consul: he cannot 'ask it kindly' as a citizen demands. Not even his wounds, about which he is usually proud, can be used as an advertisement in an electoral campaign. So he is not elected but banished, replying 'I banish you'. The anger of his wounded ego is now so great that he joins his country's enemies and leads their army against Rome, only to relent on the order of his mother – with the result that Rome's enemies kill him. It seems that although Shakespeare shared this general's lack of respect for the mob, and was no doubt alarmed by anti-poverty riots in the English Midlands (while he was writing this play in 1607?), he could not get far into the thick skull of Coriolanus who, having been brought up by a mother who equates virtue with virility, becomes what a much later generation would call a Fascist.

In the five years 1602–07 he put titanic energy into five tragedies, his supreme achievement. Here detachment from human passions contains no trace of boredom or contempt. Instead we find grandeur and insight with an almost Godlike mixture of judgement and pity. In *The Canterbury Tales* the monk had recited lugubrious stories about catastrophes of previously lucky men struck down by Fortune, but in *Troilus and Criseyde* Chaucer had been more thoughtful and in the fifteenth century John Lydgate had also been, telling of fallen because sinful 'princes' from Adam downwards. From 1559 successive editions of the *Mirror for Magistrates* had shown how men had earned disaster by abusing their positions of power. Now Shakespeare could write at a level new in England, about famous men who became tragic because there are great flaws in their characters – flaws which widen out to let in an ocean of suffering. And thus he revived a great tradition. He was not alone in this: Ben Jonson turned to tragedy in this period and John Webster came close to Shakespeare as a master in this gloomy genre. In part the demand for such plays was due to King James, who liked sadness as well as alcohol because his own early life had been so tough, but there was also a change in the people's mood: even before James arrived in 1603, Elizabethan optimism was over.

Long ago Aristotle had discussed Greek tragedies. They were performed during religious festivals enacting purification and they cleansed their audiences by releasing and discharging the emotions of pity and terror – of compassion for the sufferer, and of awe because his suffering shows the vulnerable condition of humanity under the reign of the gods. Pity and terror were stronger when the central figure had been prominent in society and not inhumanly wicked, but his great error, his *hamartia* bringing *nemesis*, had been *hubris*, some action which had broken the good order of *dike*, the proper arrangement of gods and humans in harmony, and *moira*, the lot which has been allocated. From that Greek conception of tragedy the idea of a 'fatal flaw' had evolved, as Elizabethan books about tragedy show. But what flaws are likely to be fatal? A. C. Bradley wrote *Shakespearean Tragedy* in a time of optimism ten years before the time of horrors which began in 1914, and to him a flaw could result in calamity when it was no more than a 'tendency to identify the whole being with one interest, object, passion or habit of mind'. So we are invited by Bradley to contemplate 'all the nobility and sweetness' in Hamlet, to feel for Othello 'nothing but love and admiration', to find Macbeth 'sublime' and to think that Lear has saved himself. But Bradley took Hegel's philosophy where all tensions end in 'synthesis' more seriously than he took the Christian tradition, and it would be more natural for Shakespeare to think that a fatal flaw is a sin. In Seneca's tragedies the Greek idea of the 'error' was strengthened into the idea of the crime against the law or the serious offence against the code of honour. But the Christian interpretation, which Shakespeare had absorbed, declared the worst errors to be more than crimes or offences: they are extremely serious sins against God.

The traditional list of such 'deadly' sins included seven (expounded by Chaucer in the parson's tale and mentioned in *Measure for Measure*). That list did not exclude any other sin from consideration, but it did teach that at a particular time one of the seven could be chief among the others. This idea would have been at the back of Shakespeare's mind, if not at the front, while he wrote his tragedies. Many other interpretations have been based on some evidence but it seems worthwhile to try out a suggestion that (envy and gluttony being insufficiently dramatic) he was thinking about sloth, anger, pride, covetousness or lust as he wrote *Hamlet*, *Othello*, *King Lear*, *Macbeth* or *Antony and Cleopatra*. For if that was the case, then what gave him a new depth of insight was a new awareness of the destructive strength of evil. The plays of this period which were in comparison failures were also about evil, but these five tragedies reached further by thinking of evil as sin, condemned by divine justice which is slow but not finally powerless, and by thinking of these sins as possible for Shakespeare himself.

In *Hamlet* the sexual element has a depth not found in any earlier play, and that depth is dark. True to his wider theory, Freud claimed that in his earliest years Hamlet wished to marry his mother in the Oedipus complex. We cannot know about this but we can see that his early closeness to his mother has so influenced him that when he imagines her sexual intercourse with his father's brother, very soon after his father's funeral, he becomes distressed, even before he is told that his father was murdered by the man she has married, in order to make himself king. We can also see that, whether or not his distress includes real insanity, he is now so maddened by the thought of the sexual act that he is abominably rude both to his mother and to Ophelia whom he had planned to be his queen. We can also see how, and why, his brutal rejection of her disturbs the balance of Ophelia's mind and leads to her suicide. These are all very important factors in the tragedy – but they are not quite at its centre, for they offer no explanation of why Hamlet does not kill the criminal swiftly.

If we look for that, let us begin with what we can know about the political background in England. Robert Devereux, Earl of Essex, was for a time the queen's favourite and seems to have hoped to become her husband. But he fell from favour and became a close friend of another in that position, Shakespeare's patron the Earl of Southampton who, having incurred a large fine for refusing to marry Lord Burghley's granddaughter, instead carried off a lady-in-waiting to the queen, who never forgave him.

The subsequent careers of both earls were a mixture of dithering with actions which were equally disastrous because so impetuous as to be manic if not mad. In a brief return to favour, Essex was entrusted with the command of an expedition to crush a rebellion in Ireland (it is mentioned in *Henry V*) but was forbidden to put Southampton in charge of the cavalry. When he did precisely that, the outraged queen vetoed the appointment. Instead of fighting a battle, he delayed and then made an unauthorised pact with the leading rebel and rode back to England, bursting into the queen's bedroom before she was dressed for the day. He was then placed under house arrest and Southampton was kept under surveillance; their punishment was lighter than would have been expected in that age, presumably because Elizabeth remembered past days sentimentally. They plotted against the government but ineffectively. In February 1601 they attempted to stage – and that is the right word – a coup. Shakespeare's company was bribed to put on a special performance of *Richard II* with its drama of a king's deposition and murder. This was intended to inaugurate a revolution during which the earls were to force their way into the queen's presence in order to demand the recognition of James of Scotland as her successor and of themselves as the ministers in charge of the transition. Would they have assassinated her, had she refused? The revival of *Richard II* had given a hint in that direction and we also know about the recent success of *Julius Caesar*. But the government had been alerted by the sudden, one-off performance of the meaningful play and now London refused to rise. The earls were arrested, tried for treason and sentenced to death.

Southampton's sentence was commuted into imprisonment in the Tower for the rest of Elizabeth's reign; probably he was not thought to be a danger to anyone except himself. But Essex was executed, as was his agent who had bribed the actors.

The queen was also to blame, for her earlier indecision about punishing Essex was not unique. She dithered before signing an order for the execution of Mary Queen of Scots who was at the centre of Catholic plots against her. She also refused to make clear that she wanted Mary's son James as her successor although he was Protestant and the obvious next of kin. She did not like to think that any queen could be beheaded (so, privately and in vain, she sent another order, for murder). Nor did she wish to contemplate an England without her. But fortunately for England, the smooth transition of power from Elizabeth to James was being arranged secretly by Lord Burghley's clever and coldly determined son, Robert Cecil.

We do not know exactly when *Hamlet* was first performed (an inaccurate version was printed in 1603, showing that it was already popular), but this was the political atmosphere in which it was written. In part it is a play about a play: the prince has strong opinions about how a play about a murder should be acted ('trippingly on the tongue') and is sure that, if acted properly and with a few lines added, it will have great consequences: it will be a mousetrap to catch the murderer. The actual results are, however, unforeseen like the results of the revival of *Richard II*: the wrong mice are caught. And up to a point it is a play about a rotten situation in politics: Shakespeare makes Polonius a caricature of Lord Burghley, Southampton's enemy, worldly-wise in his own estimation but classifiable as a pompous old fool; no respect is shown to the old queen, and the king who reigns is due for replacement. There are strong links between *Hamlet* and the recent *King John* and *Richard II*. But he was of course too clever to make his criticism of contemporaries obvious. There had been a dangerous moment when *Richard II* had been acted: the queen was reported as saying 'I am Richard II, know ye not that?' We may presume that the Lord Chamberlain's Men were rebuked for their indiscretion by the Lord Chamberlain but he remained their patron. They were forgiven since they were actors who could be bribed to do anything, and pointedly they were summoned to act at Elizabeth's court amid the relaxation on the evening before the beheading of Essex.

Shakespeare now wrote a play so full of material that it could not be acted within the customary two hours, but it does have a centre: Hamlet is flawed by the kind of sloth which in the Middle Ages had been called 'accidie' and which to us means dithering while depressed. As interpreters began to see more clearly when the eighteenth century became the more disturbed and introspective nineteenth, this thinker is so absorbed in his thoughts that he fails in his duty. And many of his thoughts come from uncertainty about truth in religion. At the start of the seventeenth century some of the exceptionally intelligent, or some of those disillusioned by violence linked with religion, were asking Michel de Montaigne's question: 'What do I know?' In 1605 Francis Bacon's *Advancement of Knowledge* was to be an English manifesto for the coming revolution in thought, for he was to argue that the discovery of facts by scientific investigation is the only reliable source of knowledge – apart from divine revelation, as he was careful to add. As it began to face this modern challenge, traditional Christianity found itself cut in two by the Protestant Reformation. Neither Catholicism nor Protestantism could be embraced without knowing that other Christians thought it false. And since Shakespeare was among the sophisticated it is not surprising to find what seem to be direct allusions to Montaigne's essays in *Hamlet.* Although they were not published in English until this play had been completed, he would almost certainly have been able to read them in French and he certainly had a link with their translator, John Florio, who was tutor in Latin to the Earl of Southampton. Presumably he could have had access to the manuscript. But *Hamlet* is only one of his plays which carry a warning that too much scepticism can damage your life.

Presumably when he had agreed that his son should be named Hamnet (after a godfather) he had been hoping that the boy would be both loyal to his father and effective in life, and that was indeed the character of the hero whose career in the imagination of Europe has been traced back to the appearance of Amleticus around 1200. In a French collection of tales in the 1570s, Amleth avenges his father's murder, kills the usurper Fegan and reigns in his place. In England a play of the 1580s, now lost but probably by Kyd, had given rise to the popularity of the phrase 'Hamlet, revenge!' But Shakespeare now makes it clear that what is demanded of Hamlet is more than revenge. Claudius is a traitor who has acquired the throne by murder. In the eyes of the Church his sin is specially heinous because the victim is the murderer's brother and his marriage with his victim's wife is therefore incest. He is a sinner in his own eyes also, as we are told when we watch him trying to pray. Hamlet must perform the execution himself because the last king has ordered it, because he is now the rightful king, and because no court would attempt a trial of a reigning king. Not for nothing does Shakespeare call his story the tragedy of 'Hamlet, Prince of Denmark': it is a story about a prince who does not do his duty.

So why does he delay? Act I explains that confusion about religion and the morality taught by religion is at least one reason why he is indecisive and in the Elizabethan term 'melancholic'. He has studied philosophy in a Protestant university, Wittenberg, made famous by Professor Luther. His friend and fellow student Horatio has imbibed so much philosophy that he refuses to believe in ghosts until he sees one. It is the ghost of Hamlet's father, on an outing from the flames of purgatory, a place strongly believed in only by Catholics, for a Protestant must find it difficult to believe that a man's 'foul crimes' can really be 'burnt away' by torture after death. When the confused Horatio is reminded of a tale that ghosts do not walk on Christmas Eve, he replies 'So I have heard and do in part believe it'. When Hamlet appears he announces immediately that the world seems 'weary, stale, flat and unprofitable' and that 'self-slaughter' would be the best way out, had it not been forbidden by 'the Everlasting'. Those few phrases, spoken before Hamlet has become aware of the full horror of his father's murder, point to the great disturbances in the European mind which were gathering force as the seventeenth century began. 'There is nothing either good or bad, but thinking makes it so' and can a man born into such a time 'set it right'? Hamlet doubts that he can, for he confesses 'my weakness and my melancholy'. That is the flaw in him and he tells Horatio that 'one defect' in a man, put there by nature or by fortune, can corrupt all his virtues and wreck him.

Act 2 shows that unease about religion, while not yet banishing God, can destroy a man's self-confidence. How good is the earth, how majestic the sky, how full of God's glory is the whole of his creation! And yet humanity now seems no more than 'this quintessence of dust' – dust in a 'prison' under a sky full of 'foul vapours'.

Act 3 shows the confusion about religion getting stronger and more disastrous. Is there 'something after death'? Yes, but it may be worse than a life which tempts a man to suicide. Is the ghost to be trusted? Yes, but he may be a devil. Hamlet has become a coward, irresolute, inactive, 'John-a-dreams' as he calls himself. And when he stirs himself to take impetuous action, what remains of his religious belief stands in his way. He is given an opportunity to kill Claudius but the guilty man is trying to pray and although he fails because he is unwilling to renounce either his kingdom or his marriage, he is spared, because Hamlet believes that anyone dying in that pious position may escape being sent to hell. He is also given a chance to persuade his mother to 'confess yourself to heaven' but fails because he is now entirely lacking in respect or sympathy. So what is accomplished is the unintended killing of old Polonius and the suicide of his bewildered daughter Ophelia. Evil seems to be triumphant: as Hamlet has told Ophelia while breaking her heart, she should not become 'a breeder of sinners' because 'we are all arrant knaves all', and 'it were better my mother had not borne me'.

When Laertes sees his sister moving through misery to death he cries 'Do you see this, O God?' And to the end Hamlet is not sure about the right answer. In Act 5 he seems to be superior to any emotion appropriate to a graveyard, yet leaps in a 'towering passion' to fight Laertes in Ophelia's grave. When he has escaped the plan of Claudius to kill him he declares that

> There's a divinity that shapes our ends,
> Rough-hew them how we will.

And when he is warned he may die in his duel with Laertes he remembers from the Bible that 'there's a special providence in the fall of a sparrow' – which suggests that his death may be God's way of getting him out of the mess. Yet he goes on to be agnostic. It is no great matter to leave the world, he says, since 'no man knows aught of what he leaves' and the only wisdom is 'readiness' to accept whatever 'will come'. Before the fight he tells Laertes that he is two Hamlets – which seems to be an understatement.

The play ends in great confusion. Laertes dies because he picks up the poisoned rapier intended to kill Hamlet, and the poison also intended for him is drunk by his mother. The king is then stabbed by the poisoned rapier and Hamlet dies because he too has been stabbed and because he then chooses to drink poison. It is, as is observed by Horatio, a tale of 'accidental judgments' and 'casual slaughters', and the final statement by Hamlet tells us that the world is 'harsh' and that 'the rest is silence'. But 'Providence' has established justice through this apparently total confusion, for after the dire consequences of Hamlet's sin of sloth there is the prospect of a good reign by Fortinbras, who orders the bodies to be buried decently – and in retrospect one sees that all these events which no one planned have applied a surgeon's knife to all that was rotten in Denmark.

The years 1603–04 might have been a depressing time for Shakespeare. In March the old queen's death put him into an embarrassing situation: a lingering loyalty to the imprisoned Southampton meant that he did not join the poets who lamented her passing after a mainly glorious reign of forty-five years, although he was publicly urged to do so – and in May the Globe was closed for eleven months because the plague, already serious, had begun to rage again. Yet it turned out to be a time of new opportunity, for soon after the new king's arrival in plague-stricken London it was made clear that a new era had arrived for the royal court, a time of activity, luxury and entertainment. Southampton was released from the Tower and Shakespeare and his fellow actors were renamed the King's Men and assured of protection, status and a regular income. They were to give 177 performances before King James.

Othello the Moor was one of the first new plays to be acted at the new court. Although the accident of a dropped handkerchief adds drama, essentially this is a tragedy about the effects of uncontrolled anger at the end of a spectrum where the other end is Hamlet's indecision. Iago shows cold anger (then understood as 'bile') when denied promotion in the army but the hot anger ('blood') of Othello is the main subject. It blazes and rages when he believes Iago's lie that his newly married wife, Desdemona, has been guilty of adultery with Cassio, the man promoted over Iago's head. In its emphasis on Othello the play differs from the source of its plot, one of a hundred tales told by Giraldi Cinthio in a recent book which Shakespeare must have read in the Italian. There the only person named is 'Disdemona', who has been married to 'the captain' for some time. The 'ensign' (the captain's deputy) has also been in love with her but has been rejected. So he invents a story that she has been unfaithful with a mere 'corporal' and is bribed by the captain to murder her. The captain is then murdered by her relatives.

Like Coriolanus, Shakespeare's Othello has a mind full of the 'pride, pomp and circumstance of war'. He fights furiously against the enemies of any state which hires him as a mercenary (as Venice had done nine months before) and even when he regrets that he has murdered his innocent wife he insists that he has done so 'in honour'. He captured her heart by his masculinity and by his tales of far-flung military exploits: 'she loved me', he remembers, 'for the dangers I had passed.' Now he complains that Iago's report of her infidelity has made it impossible for him to love her as he has loved her so far – 'too well'. When he is foolishly persuaded that his love must be withdrawn, 'Chaos is come again'. The only alternative to great love is now great anger: settling down to calm thought and conversation is inconceivable. He is also dismayed to think that his reputation, and with that his 'occupation' as a hired soldier, are destroyed because people will laugh at him. In the end he kills himself because he must demonstrate the strength of his honourable love and anger. He kisses her before and after killing her. He boasts that he has 'done the state some service and they know 't' and recalls that he killed a Turk who had assaulted a Venetian. As he has treated the state's enemies, so he now treats himself.

Othello the Moor is not blind to Iago's ability to use the difference in skin colours to argue that a marriage not yet consummated will never work, and Othello's colour would suggest to an English audience at that time that his passions had been heated by the sun. But this Moor is not treated as complete villain to match Aaron the Moor of *Titus*. Almost everyone in Venice admires him as a military hero and he is put in charge of the defence of Cyprus even when Desdemona defies her distinguished father and elopes after a secret marriage with this foreigner. The main contrast is not between their colours: it is between husband and wife in character and social status, to seventeenth-century Europeans a more interesting subject. She is not stupid or dumb but she loves him in entire simplicity, right up to the end, whereas he is a soldier and a mercenary who feels 'perplex'd in the extreme' when married to a Venetian lady.

Iago's character is as simple as hers: he is much cleverer than anyone else, and therefore well equipped to deceive anyone, but also icily and utterly evil. He offers no apology or excuse for being so. 'Virtue? A fig! 'tis in ourselves that we are thus and thus. Our bodies are our gardens, to which our wills are gardeners.' He is not motivated by past or present love for anyone and is not handicapped by any moral scruple or religious belief or uncertainty: he conforms to the Elizabethan idea of an Italian villain and atheist, in the tradition of Machiavelli. At the end he is led off-stage to be tortured. He, too, is a thoroughly masculine soldier. In *Othello* the good people are all women, including Iago's wife Emilia who is murdered by him after 'speaking as I think' – so courageously that she becomes in Shakespeare's mature eyes one of the greatest of his heroines. Together with the beautiful, vivacious and essentially innocent Desdemona, she redeems this tragedy.

In *King Lear* Cordelia is the woman who comes nearest to being the Redeemer, but essentially it is a story of a proud king who has exercised total power and now demands total adulation while he chooses a life of ease with continuing dignity. The comparatively innocent Cordelia is also guilty of the sin of pride, for at the abdication scene staged by her father she refuses to flatter him as her sisters have done, announcing instead that she will say 'nothing' and then saying that her love for her father will be limited to what filial duty demands since she is about to be married.

In blind fury the insulted king breaks off all relations with her and allocates the best part of Britain, intended as her dowry, to be divided between the sisters who have already been allocated their shares as a reward for their compliance with his demands. And very soon the sisters show that they have inherited pride and are determined to show who is now in charge – for although their father has selfishly rid himself of 'all cares and business' he still insists on the title of 'king' and on attendance by a hundred merrymaking knights who would strain the hospitality of a saint. Even when he is broken and mad, he is to be still in his own eyes 'every inch a king'.

Pride, its arrogance and its punishment, is at the centre of the story which now unfolds. Near to that centre is the ingratitude of Goneril and Regan to their father while Cordelia forgives him, and there is a sub-plot: the villainous bastard Edmund (another Iago) steals the inheritance due to his legitimately born half-brother, Edgar. But we have no reason to think that at this stage Shakespeare was so troubled about relationships in a family that he wanted to devote his greatest play to this theme.

He took the plot about the division of a kingdom between a king's daughters from *The True Chronicle History of King Leir*, a play performed in the Rose Theatre in 1594 and printed in 1605. There, the king abdicates because he has been devastated by his wife's death. He then finds that his two daughters plan to kill him and escapes to France where Cordelia is queen. He returns to Britain with her and a French army and reoccupies the throne. When he dies peacefully Cordelia succeeds him. And the King's Men may have felt that the old play had been better than the new version. Like *Hamlet*, Shakespeare's *Lear* is far too long to be performed as written. It is also far too gloomy to be easily popular. The bad people end up badly: Goneril poisons Regan before her own suicide, Edgar kills Edmund. But so do most of the others. One can see why it was felt that a play so verbose and so shocking had to be altered, and altered again, during its early history. In 1608 it was printed in a version so clumsy that the printer made almost 150 alterations between one copy and another; this may have been based on Shakespeare's 'foul papers', his untidy manuscript much rewritten and now used without his final revision. And when his plays were collected and printed in 1623 a hundred lines were added and three hundred were deleted. Only in 1724 were the two versions conflated, not without problems.

In Shakespeare's play as it emerged from all these revisions enough of the old plot survives to make it possible to treat it as a discussion of family problems and inevitably people wanted such problems to be solved nicely, so further changes were made when the author could no longer object. A revision which married Cordelia and Edgar, and put Lear into a retirement home, was the only version of *King Lear* acted in London between 1681 and 1838. But Shakespeare's own purpose can be seen in the crucial changes which he had made to the old *Leir*: the king is senile, he goes mad, Cordelia is hanged, only death ends the suffering. For once, he had written a play not intended to be a commercial success.

When exposed to the fury of the storm on the heath as he wanders aimlessly, at first Lear is full of self-pity: 'I stand a poor, infirm, weak and despis'd old man . . . more sinn'd against than sinning.' But gradually 'the tempest in my mind' grows as the physical storm makes him think of the plight of the 'poor naked wretches' whom he had neglected when in power. He thinks, too, of all the injustice perpetrated by hypocrites in the enforcement of laws decreed by him: when stripped of his robes a judge has no more moral authority than a dog which chases a beggar away. In the sub-plot Edgar, when banished from all that has been familiar, takes refuge in madness, but as he becomes a beggar himself he, like Lear, learns sympathy with the distressed. When Edgar appears in rags, Lear asks himself 'is Man no more than this?' And the question about humanity seems to be answered negatively when Edgar's father, the Earl of Gloucester, has his eyes torn out because he has been in contact with Lear. This old man is now in such despair that he can see no sense in anything:

> As flies to wanton boys are we to th' gods:
> They kill us for their sport.

The Duke of Albany sees that the cruelty of the gods is matched by the cruelty of humans, to which the gods are indifferent:

> Humanity must perforce prey on itself,
> Like monsters in the deep.

But the gods and humanity can also be seen in a more favourable light. When Gloucester tries to commit suicide, Edgar plays a trick designed to persuade him that the gods want him to live. When a servant has killed the Duke of Cornwall as punishment for blinding the old man, Albany now thinks that the gods arrange justice. When Lear has been appallingly cruel to Gloucester, at last he becomes human towards a fellow man's anguish, with a reminder that suffering is the human condition. When we come out of the womb we cry, when we leave 'this great stage of fools' we cry also, and the only realistic response to the inescapable is to come or go. When Lear feels 'bound upon a wheel of fire' (so much more dreadful than the wheel of fortune), at first he thinks that Cordelia has come to poison him in revenge. Then he opens his eyes and sees that she has come because she loves him; he kneels to her and she tells him that she has 'no cause' to harm him; they walk together. It is not surprising that some interpreters have gone so far as to treat *King Lear* as the story of the king's salvation, for before he dies he knows that he needs to be saved, since he too is a 'poor, bare, fork'd animal'.

He and Cordelia are arrested but he hopes that in prison, far away from any royal court,

> When thou dost ask me blessing, I'll kneel down
> And ask of thee forgiveness: so we'll live,

And pray, and sing, and tell old tales, and laugh . . .
And take upon 's the mystery of things.

This seems to imply both a recognition of the gods and a claim that they need spies if they – even they – are ever to understand 'the mystery of things'. And as he is led away to prison he expresses his loving gratitude to Cordelia for the sacrifices she has made in her love for him, and he claims that the gods can only admire humans:

Upon such sacrifices, my Cordelia,
The gods themselves throw incense.

However, Edgar reflects that his father has been thrown punishments for having also fathered Edmund:

The gods are just, and of our pleasant vices
Make instruments to plague us.

And when the wicked sisters are disgraced and dead, Albany calls it again 'the judgement of the heavens, that makes us tremble'.

Like *Hamlet*, this play ends without a clear message. When Cordelia is hanged in prison, Lear provides no obituary: he kills the slave who killed her. When he carries her on stage and he is asked whether she is dead, he gives no answer. When he is told of other deaths he says that none of them will 'come again', 'never, never, never, never, never!' And in the 1608 version his last words before his death are 'Break heart, I prithee, break!' But Shakespeare himself may have decided to add a little hope to the fatal heartbreak. In the 1623 version, just before he dies Lear thinks he sees signs of life in Cordelia's body:

Look on her, look, her lips!
Look there, look there!

We are not told what she would say if able to speak. Only, the last speaker urges honesty about reality, at any price:

The weight of this sad time we must obey;
Speak what we feel, not what we ought to say.

That misery was caused by a king's pride and *Macbeth* is a tragedy about a man who has been a brave general like Othello but who, spurred on by his wife, covets the throne. Their 'vaulting ambition' leads to many more than one murder and is punished by her madness and suicide and by the death in battle of 'this dead butcher'. Shakespeare, too, was driven by an ambition – but it was this, in Sonnet 55:

Not marble nor the gilded monuments
Of princes shall outlive this pow'rful rhyme;

But you shall shine more bright in these contents
Than unswept stone, besmear'd with sluttish time.

And by now, after many experiments, he had the power to raise a monument in words to a king and queen of the kingdom of darkness. *Macbeth* intensifies the cry of Othello before his own deed of darkness: 'Put out the light; and then put out the light.'

The contrast with this terrible darkness is made clear by Malcolm, who lives in the light. He is human and candid, and so he confesses that he is tempted to a 'staunchless avarice' as he contemplates the wealth that a king can enjoy, but he resists that temptation because he knows what are the 'king-becoming' graces,

As justice, verity, temperance, stableness,
Bounty, perseverance, mercy, lowliness,
Devotion, patience, courage, fortitude . . .

And when he is acclaimed as king he announces that he hopes to meet every challenge 'that calls upon us, by the grace of Grace'.

The most obvious message of *Macbeth* is that it is wrong to kill a good king, but (more clearly than *Julius Caesar*) the play also says that it is right to kill a tyrant – a message which makes it more than a piece of flattery offered by the King's Men to James VI of Scotland and I of England. The plot is very different from what was told about Macbeth in the old histories: there, he murdered the tyrannical Duncan and reigned satisfactorily until murdered himself in 1054. Here, he murders Duncan while the good king is his guest, kills the king's servants and then arranges the murders of Banquo and of Macduff's family. He reigns as a tyrant but is controlled by his even more wicked wife, whereas Duncan's queen has been 'oft'ner upon her knees than on her feet'. And he dies as all tyrants should die.

The play was almost certainly performed at court during a visit by the (drunken) King of Denmark during the summer of 1606. It would have interested James: his father had been murdered, his mother had been executed, and he had himself been a target in the Gunpowder Plot to blow up Parliament in November 1605. It would also have pleased him by being short and flattering. The belief that a king could cure the sick by touching them is praised by a doctor; the practice of 'equivocation', used by Jesuits when accused of treasonable plotting against the king, is mocked; witchcraft, about which James wrote a book, is prominent, although the predictions chanted by the witches are misleading. James spread the idea of 'Great Britain' when he had united the kingdoms of Scotland and England in his own person, and the army which saves Scotland from misrule by Macbeth comes from England. He shared the belief of the Stuart dynasty that it was descended from Banquo, so when Banquo is murdered in the play his son escapes and when his ghost appears it is followed by the spirits of a long line of kings. And the strongest tribute to James, whose proudest boast was to be *Rex Pacificus*, is the presentation of Malcolm as the king who replaces violence and darkness by a good tomorrow; his vision of kingship is inspired by James's published book of advice to his son, *Basilikon Doron*.

Thus the King's Men did their loyal duty at court. But the play enters a darkness which is deadly when Lady Macbeth's death offstage causes the death of hope in her husband's heart. It is not that he has always been dependent on her or close to her. Before his first murder he had to be persuaded by her to do it, but that has changed: he did not tell her before his other murders. The two have become isolated from each other and from God – which, we may think, is a good definition of hell. Before murdering Duncan he told himself to risk punishment in 'the life to come' because that possibility, although real, seemed remote. Now he thinks that the darkness closing in will be followed by an everlasting night because there is no God and no 'life to come', and he draws the conclusion that there is no meaning in life before death:

> Tomorrow, and tomorrow, and tomorrow,
> Creeps in this petty pace from day to day,
> To the last syllable of recorded time;
> And all our yesterdays have lighted fools
> The way to dusty death. Out, out, brief candle!
> Life's but a walking shadow, a poor player
> That struts and frets his hour upon the stage,
> And then is heard no more; it is a tale
> Told by an idiot, full of sound and fury
> Signifying nothing.

But in the play the last word belongs to Malcolm, the good Christian who will be a good king.

Based on Plutarch's *Lives* even more closely than *Julius Caesar* had been, *Antony and Cleopatra* explores a thought already expressed by Malcolm: he confesses that he is so tempted by 'voluptuousness' that no woman would be safe were he to be king. Macduff dismisses lust as 'summer-seeming' and tells him that the wintry sun of 'avarice' or ambition is far worse: 'it hath been the sword of our slain kings'. But Malcolm was being honest.

Shakespeare now treats lust as a sin which does not merely come and go like summer. He creates the last of his great tragedies around the passionate lust of a man who in *Julius Caesar* had mastered the people of

Rome by oratory, who had been the most successful general amid the competition of his age, and who was now the ruler of the richer half of a great empire – and, matching this, the equally intense sexuality of the queen of Egypt who was a 'lass unparall'd'. But the play is not sentimental: Antony has become self-indulgent and Cleopatra histrionic, they conquer and destroy each other, and the world which they lose in their lust is described with soaring rhetoric about its wealth, its power and its glory. With all his head Shakespeare knows that Octavius the present master of Rome must rule that world. Jesus Christ is about to be born, when Octavius is to be the emperor Augustus; Paul is about to take the gospel to the empire, using the empire's roads and ships; Constantine will before too long make the empire Christian; he, William Shakespeare, will be educated as a Christian in Latin. Yet his heart is soft on love and therefore on lust if it is more than a rapist's violence, and these middle-aged lovers are allowed to die in a blaze of a glory greater even than *Romeo and Juliet.* Antony has not forgotten that he has been 'the greatest prince o' the world' but what he now wants is something better than the world: the last of 'many thousand kisses'. When he dies after a pathetically bungled suicide begun when he hears false news of her death, she says:

> The crown o' the earth doth melt. My lord . . .
> And there is left nothing remarkable
> Beneath the visiting moon.

And now the genuineness of her love, previously in some doubt, is proved: they marry in death. She has 'immortal longings' which are fulfilled sumptuously although it takes the whole of Act 5: 'Husband, I come . . . I am fire, and air . . . O Antony!'

So at its end *Antony and Cleopatra* is not a tragedy like the others. Their story is about a disaster which is not a defeat (as it was in Plutarch's *Lives*). Their love reveals the 'nobleness of life' and in comparison with it 'kingdoms are clay'. And on their way to that victory and that glory, the lovers can enjoy life at a lower level. In Act 3 Cleopatra bewitches not only by being a queen of sex but also by her Falstaffian lust for life in general. She loves billiards and fishing, she laughs a sulky man into bed and in the morning they collapse into bed again after more drinks. It does not sound as if the writer who had recently given birth to the greatest tragedies ever written was in a mood of paralysed despair.

What, then, was his predominant mood in this period when he wrote these tragedies but also the 'problem' plays? It is a bold question, but like the question about the significance of the sonnets it must be asked in any serious attempt to understand a person to whom we owe so much.

He can sound so depressed as to be ill and it has been suggested that he had to endure what might now be called a nervous breakdown, but no evidence survives that these years brought him any personal disaster after his son's death. We seem to be left with the rather dull explanation that like Chaucer he became more serious about life and death, and more conscious of human frailty, as he entered middle age. Again like Chaucer, he could still be gloriously creative but his energy was not now inexhaustible: some of his work was like Chaucer's *Troilus* but his own time around Troy was more dismal, like Chaucer's *Legend.* He let three or four years pass between *Hamlet* and *Othello* and although he could still breathe pulsating life into imagined people he could be less successful when a character was utterly different from his own. Thus he could imagine Antony as orator in Rome or lover in Alexandria, but Bertram's sullen refusal to embrace his bride left him cold. He could fully understand Macbeth's ambition but not the semi-abdication of the Duke of Vienna. He could feel with Othello's passion to win battles and to control a wife, but not with the futility of the Greek and Trojan commanders. He shared both the majestic pride of Lear and the intellectual hesitations of Prince Hamlet, but he could not hate humanity like Timon or Coriolanus.

After these triumphs and comparative failures he again resembled Chaucer, for he still had the energy to work on plays of a new kind. In a sense they are comedies: the plots are elaborate, many people are in disguise, many misfortunes or misunderstandings are cleared up in happy endings. But now the plots are to be so improbable, so obviously mythical, that they will need large doses of magic. They will be like fairy stories, not least because they will be about a world in which people do live happily ever after. And through the myths, the magic and the make-believe these romances will deliver a message: when seen as a whole, human life is not tragic.

Officially Protestantism was fighting against magic as the Catholic Church had fought in Chaucer's day against the alchemy which could fascinate the elite and the pagan superstitions which could be inherited by the people. But whatever Shakespeare may have thought about magic privately, he knew that most people would not object to its use in a play as a substitute for miracles which might lead to fines or prison for talking on a stage about 'God' or 'Christ'. Nor would they object to references to the gods as a way of avoiding any open reference to the Christians' God. And in this use of magic and paganism there can be music, for music can speak about what *Lear* called the 'mystery of things'. Indeed, music can be needed because after achieving so much, Shakespeare's power with words is failing. Some of the speech is now very simple but some is so dense as to be difficult to grasp even when it is printed in a book instead of being heard in a theatre. What will really matter, however, will be the story itself, a story about magical events which will be hints about the meaning of all events.

On a practical point: most of these plays were not written primarily for performance in the Globe. That theatre was kept open from May to September but from the winter of 1609–10 the King's Men were able to use the hall of Blackfriars, the former Dominican priory on the north bank of the Thames, during the wetter and colder months. There, plays could be profitable if they could attract an audience of as few as a hundred, all seated and all paying more than at the Globe. Candles could shed a romantic light; softer music could be effective; more ambitious stage-effects could be attempted.

The first play in the new series did not rely on the new setting, however: according to the title page when it was printed in 1609 it was performed mainly in the Globe. It was *Pericles, Prince of Tyre*, a non-stop adventure story with a plot taken from Chaucer's contemporary John Gower and links between the acts spoken by Gower. The first two acts were written by George Wilkins, who also used the story in a printed novel. Shakespeare supplied the rest, telling how Pericles met his wife and daughter and slowly recognised them. Thaisa, now the high priestess of Diana in Ephesus, had last been seen sixteen years ago, in a coffin put out to sea after her death in childbirth, but she had been resurrected by magic. Her child Marina had been kidnapped by pirates and sold into sex-slavery in a brothel, but had remained a virgin and had changed a prince from would-be customer to husband. If we take this tale seriously we can treat *Pericles* as the start of a journey, an Odyssey, which will end on the island of *The Tempest* – a voyage to the mingled sound of storms and music which will result in magical meetings, tearful reconciliations, a new life. But it is not easy to be serious about a romance written partly by George Wilkins, who ran a brothel.

Ben Jonson scorned *Pericles* as a 'mouldy tale' and Samuel Johnson called the plot of its successor, *Cymbeline*, 'imbicilic'. It may be asked what such tales have to do with Shakespeare's religion, but in both there are many references to the gods who, bring about reconciliations and in *Cymbeline* no lesser god than Jupiter, mounted on an eagle, descends with thunder to the sleeping Posthumus in prison, promising release and happiness since

> Whom I best love, I cross; to make my gift,
> The more delay'd, delighted.

And it is unlikely that the word 'cross' got there by accident. Modern-minded Christians would not be comfortable with this story of one miracle after another, and sophisticated moderns would laugh at Jupiter's descent on a clumsy machine, but these would probably not be the reactions of most theatregoers in 1609, when this play set partly in Wales was probably written to celebrate the installation of Henry, Prince of Wales. People would see 'the fingers of the Powers above which do tune the harmony of this Peace'.

The Winter's Tale suggests by its title that it is a fireside tale. It is based, although not very closely, on a novel by Shakespeare's former enemy Robert Greene.

In the first three acts all is tragedy and we seem to be near *Othello.* Leontes rants and raves when mistakenly convinced that the child in the womb of his wife Hermione has been put there by Polixenes, his friend from boyhood. She responds with the dignified innocence of Desdemona but 'dies' in prison. Then the mood changes, helped by Shakespeare's loveliest poetry about flower-filled nature and innocent love. The child, Perdita, is landed by shipwreck on the coast of Bohemia(!) where Polixenes is king and Florizel is his son and heir. Of course Florizel and Perdita fall in love (in disguise). Polixenes objects to their marriage but they are welcomed back to Sicilia by Leontes, who in penitence has said many prayers on Hermione's grave. Polixenes arrives from Bohemia and blesses the couple; Hermione arrives from mystery when her statue comes to life; she forgives Leontes. So the gods pour down their 'graces upon you precious winners all'. To Christians this would be a theatrical equivalent to the mystery of Easter and as Paulina says before summoning music and magic: 'It is requir'd you do awake your faith. Then, all stand still.' But did Hermoine really die? The text leaves it as a question.

The Tempest is also full of magic or miracles and music. First acted in the Banqueting House in Whitehall in November 1611, it is the last play known to be entirely Shakespeare's work. It owed a little to the wreck of the *Sea Venture* on an island of Bermuda during a voyage to the new little English colony of Virginia, and it included a reference to 'the still-vexed Bermoothes', but the plot had no close connection with the pamphlet written by a member of the crew about their escape from 'the Bermudas, otherwise called the Isle of Devils'. No doubt Shakespeare read the pamphlet, which caused a minor sensation, but for his own purpose he moved the island to the Mediterranean in order that it might be reasonably near Milan, itself said to be not far from the Italian coast. And he made it an 'isle full of noises, sounds and sweet airs that give delight and hurt not' – at least in the ears of Caliban and Ferdinand. It is an island remote from the real world yet also a fitting place for a further drama of reconciliation between humans, achieved by more than human means.

Prospero is a magician who while Duke of Milan had been so absorbed in his library that he had allowed his brother Antonio to run the duchy, with the result that this deputy seized the opportunity to become duke by sacrificing Milan's independence in exchange for support from Alonso, King of Naples. Twelve years ago Prospero and his daughter Miranda had been put on a leaky boat without oars or sail which somehow reached an island inhabited only by Caliban, the son of an Algerian witch. The play opens in a storm which brings Antonio and Alonso to the island along with Alonso's son Ferdinand, who is heir to Milan and Naples; they are all wedding guests trying to get back to Naples from Tunis. Within a few hours Ferdinand has shown that he has survived; he and Miranda have fallen in love and are playing chess like a married couple; Alonso has repented and been forgiven; Antonio has not repented but has also been forgiven; Caliban has been freed from slavery; and Prospero has renounced his magical powers before embarking for Italy.

The plot is therefore close to other plays in this last period: the older generation has got into a mess but the hope for the future lies in love between the young. But among the passengers on that boat back to Naples the one who has interested many generations most is Prospero, for he seems to be Shakespeare who has buried his magician's staff and drowned his book of magic. And there is a hint that we are encouraged to believe this, for Prospero boasts that

> Graves at my command
> Have wak'd their sleepers, op'd and let 'em forth,
> By my so potent art.

Resurrections of the dead have been achieved by Shakespeare's imaginative art in other plays, but not so far as we know by Prospero's magic. Also, when writing Prospero's speech of renunciation, this product of the grammar school in Stratford has allowed himself a last, long quotation from the Roman poet who had meant most to him there, Ovid. So if *The Tempest* is in some sense a playwright's farewell, it is worth seeing whether it contains some message about the play's ultimate significance.

Inevitably, some twentieth-century interpreters treated it as a play about colonialism, and it is indeed a marvel that Shakespeare articulated themes which were scarcely beginning to be heard in his time. On the one hand, Prospero is firmly in charge and has brought from Milan some of the apparatus of European civilisation: books, clothes, apparently magical technology, a language which can describe and use the world. He feels so superior to Caliban, a 'thing of darkness', that he repeatedly postpones the promised release from slavery, but his biggest worries are that Caliban wants to rape Miranda and to murder him. On the other hand, Caliban knows the island as his master does not; he knows how to feed off the land; he does the hard work; he thinks his own thoughts and uses the language brought by Prospero to curse him. An idealist among the visiting Europeans, Gonzalo, can see the island as a kind of primitive Utopia, free of Europe's woes, but Caliban is delighted to see the back of Prospero, leaving him free to live his own life in his own land – and with his own aspirations: 'I'll be wise hereafter and seek for grace.'

However, so far from being excited about an English colony in the New World, Shakespeare did not locate his island in the Atlantic, and so far from being determined to explore the ambiguities of colonialism he never wrote a play about the British in Ireland, and so far from being fascinated by Caliban he confined him to a tenth of this play. Reports of voyages making discoveries were stirring stuff but settlements by the English overseas were still marginal. So perhaps *The Tempest* says something through its mythology about religion, which in the 1610s was fast becoming England's central interest?

We must be cautious. The tempest need not be understood in direct connection with biblical images of creation out of water, exodus over a sea or new birth from water, since in the play its force is attributed not to God but to Prospero's agent Ariel, a spirit rescued from imprisonment in a tree. Later it is also said to have been the work of Destiny, Fortune or Fate. The preservation of all on board need not have been an answer to the sailors' panic-stricken prayers. Ferdinand is led towards Miranda by what he calls 'immortal Providence' but also by magical music. His father begins to experience 'heart sorrow' about his earlier treatment of Prospero when he is told by Ariel that a storm can be aroused by 'the powers, delaying not forgetting' as they punish sin, but these 'powers' cannot turn 'heart sorrow' into full repentance. Prospero is first moved to consider forgiving the impenitent Antonio not by 'the powers' but by Ariel's hope that his affections would become tender if only he could see the miserable humans. Prospero replies as a humanist:

> Hast thou, which art but air, a touch, a feeling
> Of their afflictions, and shall not myself,
> One of their kind, that relish all as sharply
> Passion as they, be kindlier moved than thou art?

However, Prospero is not blind to human faults. When Miranda sees the ignoble nobles in her father's company she exclaims

> How beauteous mankind is! O brave new world
> That has such people in 't!

But her father comments more realistically: ''Tis new to thee.' And in fact the people who have landed on the island include a perpetually drunken butler and a really foolish fool, who dance in a polluted lake and plan to join Caliban in murdering Prospero. At an earlier stage Antonio and his son had intended to murder Alonso and Gonzalo. Prospero may be kind to his own kind but has no illusions about human nature. And when a vision of the truly beautiful English countryside is created on this barren island, that too is an illusion, to be forgotten like a dream followed by sleep.

So when the vision fades, and such 'revels' are ended, and Prospero says that

> We are such stuff
> As dreams are made on, and our little life
> Is rounded with a sleep

– is that all that is finally said about the human condition? It is not. Prospero has told Miranda that they owed their safe arrival on the island after their expulsion from Milan to 'Providence divine'. Now Alonso adds 'Amen' to what Gonzalo prays about the marriage of Ferdinand with Miranda:

> Look down, you gods,
> And on this couple drop a blessed crown;
> For it is you that have chalk'd forth the way
> Which brought us hither.

And in his epilogue to the play Prospero adds a request for the audience's prayers as he enters his future:

> And my ending is despair
> Unless I be reliev'd by prayer,
> Which pierces so that it assaults
> Mercy itself and frees all faults.

Such references to religion can be linked with what the actor playing John Gower says at the end of the first of these four romances, claiming that 'Pericles, his queen and daughter', were 'led on by heaven'; and with what Cymbeline says in his farewell, 'Laud we the gods'; and with what Leontes says at the end of *The Winter's Tale*, about 'heavens directing'. To dismiss those epilogues as nothing more than touches of piety to adorn a request for applause seems no more fair than the claim that they are explicitly Christian climaxes. Within the terms accepted by all who wrote for, or went to, theatres in the early 1600s they were Shakespeare's references to 'Mercy itself', to the 'Providence' which guides those who are willing to follow its leading to a good end.

There was, however, at least one big difference between Prospero and Shakespeare: the dramatist who was to live mainly in Stratford after *The Tempest* had not used magic to resurrect kings and queens in his history plays, to unite lovers and families in the comedies and 'problem' plays, and to confront what could be seen as the tragedy of the human condition. He has used his imagination to make experiment after experiment. That life of hard labour had taken its toll and although still in his mid-forties he saw that he could never achieve another first-class play single-handed. But the theatres had been his real life and he was not willing to retire completely into the life of a country gentleman. An able youngster who was the son of a Bishop of London was now the chief script-writer for the King's Men and he was willing to collaborate with the master. So three more plays proved possible, co-authored by William Shakespeare and John Fletcher.

One has been lost and the fact that we know scarcely anything about *Cardenio* apart from its title is a reminder that Shakespeare took no trouble to make sure that his scripts were all preserved and tidied up for the printer. Such work would not have been unthinkable. Ben Jonson, who was eight years his junior, collected and revised his poetic and dramatic *Works* and in the year of Shakespeare's death had them published in an impressive folio (large) volume which earned him a royal pension. But what had been written between *Titus* and *The Tempest* was, it seems, regarded by its author as written for performances which now belonged to history and he had no wish to enable other actors' companies to use printed versions. He was content to leave it all in the hands of the King's Men for possible revivals, never mentioning his plays in his will: they were not his property. After his death seven years passed before they were put on record for posterity. Their editors then expressed a diplomatic regret that the author had not lived to do the job himself, but in fact he had been given plenty of time. Had they not been printed for the first time in 1623, half of his plays might have been lost for ever.

We who would like to hear a final, definitive message cannot get it through the two co-authored plays which survive – not only because we cannot be absolutely sure which collaborator wrote which words, but also because *Henry VIII* (originally called *All Is True*) and *The Two Noble Kinsmen* are so different in tone.

Everyone who admires Shakespeare would like to agree with the scholars who think that he was responsible for almost the whole of *Henry VIII*, for what a contemporary wrote after seeing a performance at the Globe catches the excitement. The rich costumes were part of 'many extraordinary circumstances of pomp and majesty', yet the richly presented characters made 'greatness very familiar, if not ridiculous'. But that last word was insensitive. In the prologue the audience is told that the play is not intended 'to make you laugh'. This King Henry is treated as a tyrant and Cardinal Wolsey as a proud priest who deserves his fall, but when he has fallen Wolsey is to be pitied. As Henry's victim Queen Katherine is the last of Shakespeare's tragic heroines, and one of the most saintly. And then Act 5 moves well beyond that defence of Katherine, which can be interpreted as an attack on the Protestant Reformation. The baptism of the infant Elizabeth enables Archbishop Cranmer to pay a tribute to the great queen which Shakespeare had not offered when she died – a prediction about the greatness of her reign which, however, ends with a prophecy about King James whose own greatness will be equal to her 'wonder'. Now Protestantism is endorsed without qualification: 'truth shall nurse her, holy and heavenly thoughts shall counsel her' and in her reign 'God shall be truly known'. The original context of the performance of this play by the King's Men in 1613 (accompanied by *The Tempest*) was the hope surrounding the marriage of another Elizabeth, the king's daughter, to the ruler of Bohemia and leader of the Protestant cause in Germany: for a time Britain seemed to be taking its place at the head of a revival of the Protestant Reformation against the Catholic recovery. That time of hope was, however, soon destroyed by events – and so was the Globe.

One of the stage effects during a performance of *Henry VIII* during June 1613 was the discharge of a cannon, which produced a fire and the theatre's destruction; its roof had been thatched. We also know that the theatre's shareholders had to pay for the expensive rebuilding and that like the plays his shares go unmentioned in Shakespeare's will, so that it seems probable that he had disposed of them. It would have been a wrench: in March he had bought the first property that he is known to have owned in London, a large house above the gateway to old Blackfriars priory and only a few steps from the hall used as a theatre. It seems to have been intended both as a lodging and as an investment, and co-trustees were appointed, presumably to make sure that no one of whom the new owner would have disapproved got hold of it after his death. And although his own property escaped, another disaster was the fire which destroyed half the houses in Stratford a month after the Globe's fire.

It seems that after, or even before, those disasters some inner fire consumed, at least for a time, the feelings of benevolence and hopefulness which make *Henry VIII* watchable and enjoyable, for *The Two Noble Kinsmen* is different. The central part seems to be Fletcher's and it adds dramatic touches to Chaucer's knight's tale: for example, the maid who helps Arcite to escape from prison is in love with him and goes mad when he escapes from her. But in the two acts (1 and 5) which seem to be Shakespeare's the mood is definitely unromantic. What is left is disillusionment with the loves and glories of the world: now all that is needed is patient courage in preparation for death.

In the first act three widows speak about the corpses of their husbands, left to rot or be devoured outside the walls of Thebes: such is the end of princes as of lesser mortals. Theseus and his cousin Pirithous then go to war against Thebes, expecting further horrors, and Queen Hippolyta the Amazon talks with her equally thick-skinned sister, Emilia. The queen accepts that his marriage will never mean as much to Theseus as does his friendship with Pirithous, and in equal gloom Emilia accepts that any marriage she may be made to make will never mean as much to her as her childhood friendship with Flavinia, dead at the age of eleven.

Shakespeare also seems to have been responsible for the first scene of Act 3, where Arcite and Palamon put on their armour for their duel-to-the-death; they are determined on this crazy fight because they are 'gentlemen'. In the last act the tournament on which Theseus insists is preceded by prayers in the three chapels: not only does Emilia pray against marriage (as in Chaucer) but the men address Mars and Venus expecting to receive from divinity nothing but suffering. When Arcite has been killed by sheer chance, Theseus makes a speech very different in tone from the edifying speech written for him by Chaucer, or from the speech of wise blessing which Shakespeare wrote for him at the end of the *Dream*. He has been preparing to execute Palamon and his knights as the promised sequel to defeat in battle but now they must 'look sadly' as they prepare for the funeral of Arcite, before smiling for the wedding of Palamon.

He neither curses nor thanks any gods and neither rejects nor accepts their decrees. He merely says

O you heavenly charmers,
What things you make of us!

And he adds that human life is neither to be celebrated nor lamented. We are still 'children in some kind' with passing moods; even when we lack something we can laugh, even when we have something we can be sorry. So 'let us be thankful for what is', whatever it is, and let us leave to the gods mysteries 'that are above our question'. 'Let's go off' and 'bear' the time before death. And it seems that Shakespeare did then go off: so far as we know, he neither wrote nor edited a play during the last two and a half years of his life. In 'retirement' (one of the many words he had invented) perhaps he died of boredom?

However, it does not follow that he was always utterly depressed during these years. On the contrary, it seems that his last illness was traceable to a chill caught after getting too hot while drinking too much in the company of friends including Ben Jonson. The end of *The Two Noble Kinsmen* is indeed grim in comparison with the four previous plays, as *Troilus and Cressida* or *Coriolanus* had deflated the heroics of *Henry V*, but the end of *Antony and Cleopatra* had signalled a return of cheerfulness after the tragedies. Being human, Shakespeare was a man of moods; being intelligent, he had some moods in which his sympathy lay with those who denied the loving purpose of Providence; but if we are to see his vision of life as a whole, we must look at the man as a whole.

Our knowledge of his final years is almost entirely confined to his financial arrangements. Some of his time was taken up by the controversy about the 'enclosure' of fields in the neighbourhood from which he derived profits in the shape of tithes. Landowners were putting ditches and hedges around large areas of fields which tenants had cultivated in strips or used as pasture for their own cattle. It was modernisation and most of Shakespeare's neighbours were against it, filling in one ditch amid disorder, but he refused to join the protest, preferring to make a private agreement that his profits would not be affected.

It is clear both from this action or inaction and from the arrangement over the London house that his mind was on the future in the sense that he was determined that his hard-earned estate should continue to support whomever he wanted after the death which he saw approaching. His two remaining brothers, both younger than him, had died in 1612 and 1613.

In January 1616 he dictated the first draft of his will, and then a domestic problem hit him. On 10 February his younger daughter, Judith, married Thomas Quiney, but this was considerably less happy than the many weddings which had been climaxes in his comedies. This, it seems, was the occasion on which he caught the chill which turned into pneumonia – but the marriage itself was also bad news. She was aged 31 and the unkind may attribute the lateness of her marriage to her looks, but she left no explanation to posterity because she was unable to sign her name – a fact which reflects discredit on her father. Worse, her husband was a Stratford tradesman who turned out to be the father when Margaret Wheeler died in childbirth a month after his marriage to Judith. The records show that he could offend in other ways, including the sale of unpleasant wine in his little shop. And so on 25 March his angry father-in-law dictated a revised version of his will, leaving very little to Judith and thus making sure that Thomas Quiney (not named) had no access to the estate. There was a great contrast with the splendid house bought for Judith's sister as her dowry in 1607. If we ask whether Judith was so deeply hurt that she wanted to forget her father, she has given us the answer: her first child was christened Shakespeare. It seems that much later she had the fact that Susanna was only 'co-heir' to their father added to the epitaph carved on this envied sister's grave. But although she lived until 1662 she probably never knew quite what her father had done in London, any more than her mother did.

In his will he remembered his 'fellows' from the London years with little gifts including a mourning ring for Richard Burbage who had played the leading roles for men in the great tragedies. He also remembered some of his relatives or neighbours in or near Stratford, but to the poor he bequeathed less than the fee reserved for his lawyer; like many others who have struggled to make their way in the world, he was proud of what he had made and willing to leave financial generosity to the noble-minded. And when he revised the will he added a legacy to someone previously ignored.

To his wife, then aged sixty after a marriage of 33 years, he bequeathed no more than 'my second best bed with the furniture' meaning its fabrics. Since he had written at least as beautifully as anyone else about love and marriage, of course this action can seem scandalous and the now usual explanation, that this was the bed she had shared with her husband while the best bed was reserved for guests, is not a completely convincing defence. Since Judith was the last of their children they may not have shared a bed recently, and since the will spoke of 'my', not 'our,' bed we cannot be sure that this legacy expressed devoted affection. Nor can we sure that the best bed was reserved for guests; Shakespeare may have used it himself and intended it for use by the Halls. Certainly they would own it and the rest of the house and it is difficult to believe that there was nothing that poor Anne would have liked to be definitely her own, had her husband been feeling sentimental. Friction between her and her adult daughter was possible.

The only mystery about Susanna, described on her memorial as 'witty above her sex', and 'wise to salvation', is why she had been summoned by the vicar along with 22 other townspeople for missing her Easter communion in 1606. But she had demonstrated that she was not a convinced Roman Catholic, the affair had been closed, and next year she had further demonstrated her respectability by marrying John Hall, the leading doctor of the district who was to become an active churchwarden and was to refuse a knighthood. He also refused to attend the town council, with the explanation that he was too busy visiting his patients. His notes about some of the cases were published and presumably he could be trusted to take care of his mother-in-law until her death (in 1623). Had this arrangement not been made, Anne would almost certainly have been entitled to claim a third of all the estate, which was the law protecting widows although it does not seem to have been observed always.

Nevertheless, it is sad that this was the only mention he made of his wife in his will. An expression of love would not have been inappropriate and a legal recording of an arrangement to ease her widowhood would not have been redundant. Nor does it make us happy about their relationship to be told by a modern researcher that in 1601 a former shepherd on the Hathaways' farm had made a will directing that forty shillings which he had loaned to Anne were to be repaid by 'Master William Shakespeare' but given to 'the poor people of Stratford'. This seems to imply a criticism of the great man both for leaving his wife short of cash (occasionally?) and for being mean in his charitable gifts (habitually?), and if that is so the defence (unconvincing?) has to be that he had other things on his mind. It seems that their marriage brought disappointment to them both, but at least he had provided security for her all the years since he had been told that she was pregnant – which was more than Thomas Quiney had done for Margaret Wheeler.

He died on 23 April 1616. He had written a song for the two sons of Cymbeline. They were to use it at the funeral of their half-brother Cloten whom one of them has beheaded, and if Shakespeare wants that lout to be treated as a prince we can use it about him:

> Thou thy worldly task hast done,
> Home art gone and ta'en thy wages.
> Golden lads and girls all must,
> As chimney-sweepers, come to dust . . .
>
> The sceptre, learning, physic, must
> All follow this and come to dust . . .
>
> Quiet consummation have;
> And renownèd be thy grave!

His last years in Stratford had made him a bit of a schoolboy again – not least because his grand house was very near his school. Very hard work at the Latin and English languages had given him access to a world which had often seemed golden but now it had disappeared, so he must go back to a world which in comparison was made of dust and often of dirt, Thomas Quiney's world, not the miracles and music of *The Tempest.* He could not know that some study of what he had written would become a part of education around the modern world. He could not be sure that his plays would have any future at all, let alone frequent performances in many languages. For himself as he moved towards death there might be the 'hoping and surely believing' to which he assented when he signed his will, but his own future was not going to be decided by his will: neither hope nor trust could be certainty and the benevolent power of Providence might be absent at the last, with the end 'mere oblivion' as is expected by Jaques in *As You Like It*, 'eased by being nothing' as is said by Richard II. However, he made a modest request about the future treatment of the body in which he had done his earthly task, and the homage which he was to receive could begin by honouring this request. Over his renowned grave was placed a simple stone inscribed with a plea (almost certainly his own) that his dust should never be disturbed and his bones never moved to the adjacent charnel-house. A man, he had once written, is 'this quintessence of dust' – yet under 'this majestical roof fretted with golden fire . . . what a piece of work is a man!' That was true about this man, the greatest of all the English. Now his last word was a plea from one Christian to another, the favour about his own dust being begged FOR JESUS SAKE.

THREE

HERBERT

During George Herbert's life it would have been impossible to imagine that one day he would be loved internationally as a revealer of depths in spirituality, studied intensively as a technically brilliant poet, and admired as a model pastor. Not many people knew that he existed. Probably no one knew at all fully how extraordinary was his relationship with Christ – for many years like a lover unable to abandon a difficult courtship, then like a courtier serving his invisible king in a village.

Born in 1593, he was the fifth son in a family connected with the rich earls of Pembroke and Montgomery but not itself wealthy. Among his brothers only one became a priest – Charles, an Oxford scholar who died young. The eldest was Edward who was a diplomat and, after being sacked, a writer, the author of an undiplomatic book about religion. Sir Henry was also in the service of the government, as Master of the Revels who censored plays, but he lost that job when the theatres were closed. Two brothers met early deaths as army officers and Thomas had a naval career but, when shipless, a disgruntled old age. So all the brothers had to earn their living in the world and found that the world could be tough. They had a mother who was greatly admired as a very good woman and a very attractive Christian; on her death John Donne preached one of his most magnificent sermons and George wrote Latin poems saying that he was now exposed to the world's storms. His father had died when he was aged three.

For some years his career seemed about to take off. After education in the school attached to Westminster Abbey, in 1609 he began almost twenty years as a student or fellow of Trinity College, Cambridge. He became MA in the year of Shakespeare's death and was elected Public Orator of the university in 1619. His two predecessors had moved on to senior positions in the civil service and for the next five years his brother Edward was the British ambassador in Paris. He was paid (but not well) to flatter distinguished visitors or benefactors, and since King James never thought any flattery excessive he seemed likely to earn the vitally necessary royal favour. But he also impressed a major intellectual figure, Francis Bacon, then England's leading lawyer and the world's first systematic advocate of the experimental method in science. He helped to translate *The Advancement of Learning* from Latin and the great man dedicated his own translation of psalms to him as 'my very good friend'.

But the position of Public Orator, initially sought eagerly and written about as one of the 'gaynesses which please a young man well', became a bore. It did not lead to any quick promotion and when he served as a member of the Parliament of 1624, representing a small Welsh constituency controlled by the Earl of Pembroke, that was his last involvement in politics. After that year he arranged his ordination as a deacon, which in that age was a step which fellows of his college were expected to take at this time in their careers. Before becoming Orator he had begun to equip himself as a theologian, but now he did not resume intensive studies. Nor did he qualify himself as a pastor or dignitary in the Church by becoming a priest. He remained a deacon, which disqualified him from returning to the House of Commons and made it all the more unlikely that he would be offered a desirable position in the service of the Crown normally filled by a layman. His friend Nicholas Ferrar, who had sat with him in that Parliament, retired to his own estate to live like a monk but with his family joining his devotions, but Herbert had no such estate or family.

It seems that he was cautious in his movement into the life of the Church because with a rare honesty he acknowledged to himself that he was neither fit nor called to be a priest, however convenient that further ordination might have been. His patron in the Church was a Welshman, John Williams, who made him a deacon and gave him an income attached to Lincoln Cathedral and derived from a small estate deep in the countryside. The church on this estate was in ruins and Herbert rebuilt it at his own expense and after some fund-raising from rich friends, but his conscience did not tell him to minister there.

He did not reside in Cambridge either: a deputy performed his duties. One of his poems about his mother mentions a country cottage, but he also seems to have stayed with family or friends. After his mother's death he resigned his academic positions but still had no clear direction in his life, partly because he was not strong in health. A severe illness, probably tuberculosis, was followed by convalescence first with his brother Henry and then with the Earl of Danby, his stepfather's brother. During this time he seems to have resolved to put purpose into his life. While recovering his health in Wiltshire he was introduced to Jane, a cousin and neighbour of his host's. His first biographer, Izaak Walton, was to report that the two were engaged to marry within three days of meeting. Marriage seemed possible because he had at last been given a financial grant by the Crown – a third of the value of a small estate. (A similar grant was given to console Edward for spending his own money while ambassador, but he was also made a lord.) And one of Jane's attractions was that she was willing to be the wife of a priest.

On the surface he had reached the spring of 1629 without achieving anything except the repair of a small church, some academic exercises in flattery and Latin poems celebrating the royal family or defending the Church of England against a Presbyterian critic. Any political hopes had been forgotten when King James had died in 1625. King Charles was intent on securing, and deeply loving, a Catholic princess as his queen and Edward Herbert had been recalled from Paris as being an indiscreet Protestant. The Herberts' lay patron was William, Earl of Pembroke, the leader of the Protestant opposition to negotiations with France (and previously with Spain) at a time when European Protestantism was being rolled back by the military and spiritual forces of the Counter-Reformation. Another reason for disillusionment was the fall of Francis Bacon, rightly or falsely convicted of corruption at a time when that practice was general. But for twelve months after his marriage George Herbert still contemplated the possibility of the priesthood without making a decisive move. His poem on 'The Priesthood' expresses a deep respect for the 'sacred and hallowed fire' which purifies those who 'convey my God to me', but it is clear that 'my time' for joining the priests is not yet.

In poems which he did not publish but which also seem to belong to his time as a layman or deacon his loyalty to the Church of England was either superficial or critical.

'The Church-Porch' is a long poem of advice to a young gentleman (a 'sweet youth') which may have been offered to his younger brother Henry, sent to improve his French in Paris. He is to be charming to everyone but steadily ambitious. When he enters a church he must be metaphorically barefoot but on the way there he must always calculate what are his interests in the world where he must rise, whenever possible turning an acquaintance into a friend. He must avoid bad company, which will get him nowhere either morally or in terms of a career. If he becomes a soldier he must 'chase brave employments with a naked sword' but there is of course no suggestion that he might go into business or trade. Although this 'Church-Porch' has the interesting feature of three rhymes in each of its 77 stanzas, the advice given is unoriginal and not unlike the wisdom conveyed to his son by old Polonius in *Hamlet*. In the same vein, Herbert has developed a habit of collecting proverbs and he also translates from the Latin a *Treatise of Temperance and Sobriety*.

Another early poem praises 'The British Church' without mentioning what it believes: he concentrates on what it wears. If Anglican dress is 'neither too mean, nor yet too gay', the Catholic Church of Rome has become 'painted' like a 'wanton' harlot through her habit of kissing 'painted shrines'; the Calvinist Church of Geneva does not bother to tidy her hair and 'nothing wears'. On this flimsy basis it is claimed that God has given his grace to 'none but thee'.

A later poem, 'The Church Militant', is more critical. Its strange theme is that in church history the 'course' has been 'westward'. Christianity, originating in the Holy Land, moved to Egypt, to Greece, to Rome, to Germany and to England, always pursued not only by the travelling sun but also by Sin. In lines which so alarmed the authorities in Cambridge that they almost vetoed the publication of his poems by the university press, Herbert then glanced at the spread of Catholicism to Latin America and of Protestantism to the little colony planted by the Virginia Company which the Crown dissolved in 1624. He wrote:

> Religion stands on tip-toe in our land,
> Ready to pass to the American strand.

Yet America's 'times of Gospel' will also pass when Sin has caught up, until after the Gospel's journey through Asia (Africa is out of the picture) 'judgement shall appear' as Christ comes back to the Holy Land, completing the circle. Thus if the Church of England is the best church available at present, it will soon be bettered across the Atlantic and not totally admired at the Last Judgement.

Even before that verdict, Herbert condemns 'Church-Rents and Schisms' in a poem of uncertain date, about 'debates and fretting jealousies' which are as disagreeable as the conflicts and intrigues of politics. He calls the Church 'my mother' and compares her with a rose – but with a rose now in shreds because destroyed by a hairy worm with 'many feet'. Seeing how internal disputes can 'unloose' the 'sev'ral parts' of the rose, neighbours can rush in like a 'north-wind' and throw it 'in the dirt'. It is an uncanny prediction of what will become of the Church of England when an army of Presbyterians from Scotland invades as the 1640s begin.

But his substantial essay called *The Country Parson: His Character and Rule of Holy Life* is utterly different in tone: instead of boasting or lamentation about the Church in general, it sets out an ideal of what a parish priest could be and do. It was published in 1652, when the reputation and morale of the Anglican clergy needed a big boost since Church and King had been overthrown together in the civil war. By now his poems published as *The Temple* had made him quite well known, so the book in which *The Country Parson* was included was called simply

Herbert's Remains. It is a very personal piece of prose, written as 'a mark to aim at' before he began the work of a parish priest at the age of 38. It was never intended as a plan to be followed by all the clergy; it was a confession of his own ambition in a new life – an ambition totally different from the worldly wisdom of the advice to a young gentleman in 'The Church-Porch'.

Probably it was written in the interval between his installation as the rector of Fugglestone-with-Bemerton in Wiltshire in April 1630 and his ordination as a priest in nearby Salisbury Cathedral five months later. The main reason for this delay was no doubt the need to rebuild the rectory before he could reside in the parish but he must have used the time for prayer and thought about the work which lay ahead and in the same period he may have written his poem 'Aaron', meditating with awe on the continuity with the Old Testament's priesthood but confessing that the 'old man', the sinner, will still be present:

Profaneness in my head,
Defects and darkness in my breast,
A noise of passions ringing me for dead
Unto a place where is no rest.
Poor priest thus am I dressed . . .

Christ is my only head,
My alone only heart and breast,
My only music, making live not dead,
That to the old man I may rest,
And be in him new dressed.

Almost four hundred years later *The Country Parson* is likely to seem even stranger than 'Aaron' because inevitably the circumstances in which the clergy must work are almost totally different, around the world and even in rural England. The reason why Herbert was in this rural parish of some four hundred inhabitants was that he had been appointed by William, Earl of Pembroke, who lived not far away in the grandeur of Wilton House. That earl, who had admired Shakespeare, died before Herbert moved in, but his son Philip seems to have welcomed the poet as cousin and chaplain while extending the house and creating a great garden. For this reason alone his parishioners would have been aware of who their new rector was, but even without his connection with the local great landowner he would soon have been recognised as a man far better educated, and more highly motivated, than the average clergyman.

He lived in the tiny hamlet of Bemerton, next to a chapel which held forty people at the most; the parish church in Fugglestone was some distance away, further from Salisbury to which Herbert walked twice a week, to hear and make music. He had to rebuild the medieval chapel as well as the rectory where he, his wife and two nieces of hers were served by four maids and two men, with an assistant curate serving in the parish. A famous poem, 'The Elixir', was originally called 'Perfection' because it is about a servant sweeping a room: if done for God's sake, in his service, that humble action is as 'fine' as the room will be and the sweeper will be perfect. But when admiring Herbert's attitude we are disconcerted to read in *The Country Parson* his resolution to show 'more terror than love' to his servants. In his parish, where his predecessor had not even resided, he regarded himself as 'the deputy of Christ for the reducing of Man to the obedience of God'. Therefore 'a priest may do what Christ did, and by his authority', and 'there is nothing done, either well or ill, whereof he is not the rewarder or punisher'. We shall see that John Milton was among the lay people who very strongly objected to such patronising clericalism.

This somewhat lordly role must, however, involve self-discipline and self-sacrifice, for a priest's life must be like his clothes, without spots, dust or smell. 'The country parson is exceeding exact in his life, being holy, just, prudent, temperate, bold, grave in all his ways.' Every day he and his family must go twice to church; every Sunday he and his parishioners ought to be in church four times; every Friday he must 'eat little and that unpleasant'. He must invite all his parishioners into his home for a meal at least once a year. As he moves around his parish he must comfort or reprove; he must know enough law to be the local judge, and enough medicine to be the local doctor, and he must set an example of tireless work because 'the great and national sin of this land' is idleness. If parishioners experience some disaster, they must be told that it is God's warning to them about this or some other sin – but they must know that their pastor does care, 'as if he had begot his whole parish'.

In church the priest must be 'God's courtier' (the title of Marion Singleton's study of Herbert in 1987). His behaviour, there as elsewhere, will be more influential than his preaching. So he must show that he is 'amazed with the majesty of God'; he must stop any uncivilised behaviour in the congregation; while he preaches he must interject prayers for inspiration but also keep his eyes sharply on his hearers, for 'country people are thick and heavy' (and, no doubt, tired). His sermons must be brief and full of references to country life, like his Master's parables. He must not 'crumble' a text with learned eloquence like preachers to the royal court. His aim must be to arouse holiness, not controversy or applause; what comes out of his mouth must come from his heart; and his heart must be ardent with love for the people entrusted to his care.

If people look around in church they must see that everything is clean, and decorated and perfumed at festivals. At the communion table they must all kneel, humbly receiving the sacrament at least five times a year. About the sacrament he is not specific, but any child who understands that it is not an ordinary meal is welcome. Such practical arrangements do not reflect the extent of the commitment to the Eucharist in his poems: perhaps the absence of a daily celebration made it all the more solemn and precious when it came and Herbert had no wish to arouse controversy by high church innovations. In his century blood as well as ink was being spent in controversies about the doctrine that during this service the substance of the consecrated bread changes into Christ's flesh, but Herbert did not trouble his parishioners with such questions. In 'The Holy Communion' he wrote dismissively:

First I am sure, whether bread stay
Or whether bread do fly away
    Concerneth bread, not me . . .

Then of this also I am sure,
That thou didst all those pains endure
    To abolish sin, not wheat.

He did not live long enough to put on record any reflections on his experience in that parish but about five months before his death he was sent a manuscript, the translation by Nicholas Ferrar of *110 Considerations* by a Catholic reformer, Juan de Valdes. Ferrar's own semi-monastic but family-based community at Little Gidding normally preferred Anglo-Catholic practices but he was an enthusiast for any sign of spiritual renewal anywhere. Herbert encouraged his friend to publish and when the book appeared five years later this English edition included a letter and notes by him, but his reaction was cautious. As translated, Valdes had written that the liberty of a Christian 'consisteth in this, that a Christian shall not be chastised for his evil living, nor shall he be rewarded for his well living: all that is needed is faith in Christ'. But Herbert wanted some sign accessible to others, 'otherwise any malefactor may pretend motions, which is insufferable in a commonwealth'. 'Things good, as to relieve my neighbour', he insisted, 'God hath already revealed his will about it.' He was shocked that Valdes 'opposeth the teaching of the Spirit to the teaching of Scripture'.

His parishioners would also have been shocked, had they known that their authoritarian pastor, a holy man who was impeccably orthodox, had written a series of poems full of self-accusation and of anguished doubt or despair. Yet without that Good Friday, would Herbert have known Easter? His pilgrim's poems were to be called *The Temple*.

During his last illness, in 1632, he asked that the revised manuscript of these poems should be taken to Ferrar, who may well have had no earlier knowledge of its existence. According to his biographer Izaak Walton, it was to be explained as 'a picture of the many spiritual conflicts that have passed betwixt God and my soul, before I could subject my will to the will of Jesus my Master, in whose service I have now found perfect freedom'. Ferrar was to burn it if he did not think that 'it may turn to the advantage of any dejected poor soul', but he did not. The pastorate in Bemerton had lasted for a little less than three years and most of Herbert's papers, and his library, were to be burned during the civil war. But the poems were copied out, given a title and printed.

He inherited three traditions in English poetry. One was of devotion to Christ in images originating in Scripture (in both Testaments) and used lovingly over the centuries. This was the medievalist emphasis in Rosemond Tuve's *Reading of George Herbert* (1952) but more recent scholarship has tended to put him among the 'metaphysical' poets of his own time, celebrating beauty, natural, human or divine, in a new brilliance which was sharp both in its sensuality and in its wit. And his time was also one of new eloquence about an intensely emotional relationship with Christ, taking a Catholic or Protestant form. But how was he to combine all three traditions?

What he did was to reinvent them, developing a style not completely unlike the experimental science advocated by Bacon (whether or not he was conscious of this). He would record his experiments in his relationship with his Maker and his Saviour, a relationship as passionate as sexual love at its most ardent, and he would be honest about every emotion – about his longing for union with God, about his delighted love for Christ crucified and crowned, but also about his dejection when he felt unloved. Yet always he must speak to God as a gentleman, and he must write about God as a poet, of his period. He was therefore doomed to go out of fashion: the Victorian *Dictionary of National Biography* was to classify him as a 'literary workman' whose work merits 'no lofty praise'. Another Anglican priest and scholar, F. E. Hutchinson, was to bring out a proper edition of his *Works* in 1941 (still the standard text), but until Helen Vendler's close reading of *The Poetry of George Herbert* (1975) it was not appreciated just how skilled his work was, to be admired and enjoyed even by readers who (like her) do not share his religious beliefs. Devout meditation and visualisation, intellectual energy, moral vision and humble revision – all had to go into the making of poems, many of which have the character of a raging storm which has been poured into a decanter of cut glass.

In *The Temple* 'Jordan (2)' gives us a glimpse of the work involved. 'Quaint words and trim invention', when he had been 'curling with words' like a hairdresser, had to be 'blotted' and cancelled, not because they had been too elaborate but because he must try again in the same style, for 'nothing could seem too rich to clothe the sun'. But then he had seemed to hear a voice urging him to be plainer, since

> There is in love a sweetness ready penned:
> Copy out only that, and save expense.

So in 'The Forerunners' he bids farewell to 'lovely enchanting language, sugar-cane, honey of roses' – yet he still feels that 'beauty and beauteous words should go together'. In 'The Quiddity' he claims that 'a verse' need not belong to the world of crowns, honours, rich dress, sports, banquets, fame, music, travel, politics, business: it can be about God and, please God, it can sometimes be successful. So he ends with the conviction that when writing his kind of poetry he can be close to God and he uses the cry of a lucky gambler at cards: 'most take all!' In *The Temple* can be found more than a hundred different forms of rhyming verse, all turned towards God.

In the book may also be found many different moods, including times of deep distress. These must have been connected with his poor health over many years but one of the difficulties honestly confronted by this poet is that God is not always pleasantly simple to understand. The heart which he tries to lift up is 'broken' but 'cemented with tears'. In the next poem this Saviour speaks from the cross, for here is the sacrifice by God the Son to God the Father ('Was ever grief like mine?') which is needed before any human life, or work such as poetry, can be acceptable. And the central theme emerging from *The Temple* is the poet's struggle to find, to experience and to keep a faith which will really assure him that through this Saviour he has been accepted, as a poet and as a man, by a Creator who often seems absent, remote or hostile.

His spiritual pilgrimage has to be along a path not taken by Baconian scientists. From their road it can be seen (in 'Man') that Man can shoot down ('dismount') 'the furthest star' and use everything on earth for food or pleasure – but get no nearer to the Creator. Nor will it be the way of 'the merry world' (in 'The Quip'), a world of beauty, money, music, glory, wit – but not of union with God. His 'Pilgrimage' looks back on a spiritual journey which has been both arduous and solitary. He has avoided imprisonment in the dark cave of Desperation but has not avoided much else, moving through the flowery meadow of Fancy to the wood of Care, then through the wild country of Passion to a 'gladsome hill', only to find at its summit 'a lake of brackish waters'. At the end of 'so foul a journey' he asks 'can both the way and the end be tears?'

In 'Affliction' he is clearly autobiographical. Early years were full of 'flow'rs and happiness' but he found himself wrapped in a boring academic gown instead of being welcomed to the glamorous 'way that takes the town'. And he has been devastated by physical 'sicknesses' to add that kind of pain, so that now 'I read, and sigh, and wish I were a tree'. In that poem he envies a tree because it can bear fruit, and 'Employment (1)' is a lament to God about unemployment: throughout the creation 'all things are busy', yet he is 'no link of thy great chain'. In 'Employment (2)' he complains that God has not enabled him to produce fruit: he never gives him the right weather, he disappears when he is needed, he leaves him to face a fruitless winter. So this is his self-pitying lament:

> O that I were an Orange-tree,
> That busy plant!
> Then should I ever laden be,
> And never want
> Some fruit for him that dressed me.
>
> But we are still too young or old;
> The man is gone,
> Before we do our wares unfold:
> So we freeze on,
> Until the grave increase our cold.

In 'The Pearl' he looks back on his university, but this time on its intellectual and other excitements. 'I know the ways of learning', both the investigation of nature by reason and the shaping of 'laws and policy' after the examination of 'cause and history'. He had explored 'both th' old discoveries, and the new-found seas'. He also remembers his hopes of success at court through the exercise in Cambridge of the 'quick returns of courtesy and wit'. And he has not forgotten the fun:

> The propositions of hot blood and brains,
> What mirth and music mean . . .

But what he wants now is a 'silk twist' let down from heaven to rescue him from 'the labyrinths'.

In 'The Collar' he has heard one word which promises rescue from this dispiriting pilgrimage. 'There was wine' before his tears drowned it and there might yet be 'fruit' if he could use his hands to grab it. So 'forsake thy cage!' But 'as I raved' one word reached him: '*Child*, and I replied, *My Lord*'. 'The Pulley' suggests that even if he had enjoyed a greater success in the world he would still have been open to hearing his Lord's summons, for he hears God saying

Let him be rich and weary, that at least,
If goodness lead him not, yet weariness
May toss him to my breast.

But he really did rave, and he really became tired, and in 'Perseverance' (omitted from *The Temple*, probably as being too pessimistic) he is left 'clinging and crying, crying without cease', on the breast of the mother-like God.

To him God was often more like a remote king than like a reliable father (did he ever fully recover from his own father's death?). He could say that 'thy absence doth excell all distance known'. At first a glimpse of a glance by God made him feel 'a sug'red strange delight' but that proved to be 'a mirth but open'd and seal'd up again', and now he longs to see God face to face, that he may know 'full-ey'd love'. And in 'The Glance' the memory of that brief joy is all that he has: God sees him but he does not see God. In 'Misery' he says that 'Man is a foolish thing' and that God can see this: Man cannot escape the divine investigation by retreating 'into his head' or by hiding behind the curtains in his dark bed. And he finds it quite easy to write cleverly like this about the human condition of being in the dark – but then he breaks off: 'My God, I mean myself'.

When he looks into himself during this serious game of hide-and-seek with God, he sees that his emotions are chaotic, as in 'Bitter-Sweet':

Ah my dear angry Lord,
Since thou dost love, yet strike;
Cast down, yet help afford;
Sure I will do the like.

I will complain, yet praise;
I will bewail, approve:
And all my sour-sweet days
I will lament, and love.

In several poems he feels that God is not merely the great Absentee; he is the almighty Torturer. If he has hopes, God is able 'to make my hopes my torture'. Using images drawn from the savage justice of seventeenth-century England, he feels 'tortur'd in the space between this world and that of grace', racked or crushed, 'broken in pieces'. In 'The Temper (1)' he pleads that God does not remember how small and fragile he is – and how distant from heaven:

O rack me not to such a vast extent!
Those distances belong to thee.

But in 'Confession' he protests that God knows better than any human torturer how to break a man down – that

No screw, no piercer can
Into a piece of timber work and wind,
As God's afflictions into man,
When he a torture hath designed.

In 'Sighs and Groans' the poet is the victim who cries 'Do not bruise . . . scourge . . . grind . . . kill me!' But the worst pain is knowing that he is the criminal, that he deserves the punishment, that he is a 'crumble of dust' being blown 'from heav'n to hell'. He has no valid excuse: he can look back on an education in 'laws, rules of reason', on what he has been taught by 'pulpits and Sundays', by 'Bibles laid open', by the instructive combination of 'anguish' on earth with 'the sound of glory ringing in our ears'. But all these good influences can be blown away by a single temptation, by a wind which will blow him to death. In 'Mortification' he sees his boyhood, the time when all those good influences were strongest, as nothing more than a preparation for death as punishment. An infant is wrapped up like a corpse; a boy's bed is like a grave; a young man who calls for music hears the church bell tolling at his funeral.

He has found that the study of theology is no cure for such depression. 'None of my books will show' what God will do with him. In 'Divinity' that semi-science is dismissed as 'definitions' which attempt to apply reason to what is 'transcendent'. It only results in 'divisions' about the correct answers to questions which are merely 'curious'. The best guide to life is Scripture but he finds it difficult to know how 'all thy lights combine'. Only after an earnest search does he find that here is a 'book of stars' which 'lights to eternal bliss'. Its brightest part is the teaching of Christ himself, as 'clear as heav'n, from whence it came'. The right response to Christ is also simple, for it is faith in him – faith which humbles the grandest of men to the level of Bethlehem's stable but which enables a peasant to reach 'the highest stature'.

But while that response must be simple trust, this poet must still use his 'utmost art', as in 'Praise (2)':

King of Glory, King of Peace,
I will love thee;
And that love may never cease
I will move thee.

Thou hast granted my request,
Thou hast heard me:

Thou didst note my working breast,
Thou hast spared me . . .

Though my sins against me cried,
Thou didst clear me;
And alone, when they replied,
Thou didst hear me.

The glory and peace of that poem may come from the mood recorded in 'The Flower':

How fresh, O Lord, how sweet and clean
Are thy returns! ev'n as the flowers in spring . . .

And now in age I bud again,
After so many deaths I live and write;
I once more smell the dew and rain,
And relish versing: O my only light,
It cannot be
That I am he
On whom thy tempests fell all night.

The tempests have become dew because he has had the experience which inspires 'A True Hymn':

As when th' heart says (sighing to be approved)
O, could I love! and stops: God writeth, *Loved.*

In modern and prosaic terms, the idea of 'God' or 'Christ' has previously aroused guilt through the conscience, through the superego which condemns, to use the Freudian terminology – but now it arouses love because it is the idea of the Holy One who loves him even during the tempests of his emotions. In 'Affliction (3)' he adds an insight seldom seen in the theology of his age, although it is Pauline: Christ still suffers 'daily' in the sufferings of Christians. So his Master had been with him throughout his spiritual journey and in 'The Odour' the perfume which now fills his mind is the thought of 'my Master'. It is reported that he had developed the habit of always adding 'my Master' when he spoke the name of Jesus.

That may imply that he acknowledges no other master, in society or in theology. Certainly it is striking how many Christians in different traditions have thought that in the final analysis his one and only Master is not ultimately different from theirs. In his own century Charles I used his poetry while praying in prison (he also read Shakespeare), yet Richard Baxter, the most truly distinguished of the

Dissenters who were excluded from the Church of England, praised this poet for all Christians: 'Herbert speaks to God like one that really believeth a God, and whose whole business in the world is most with God.' John Wesley was to love his poetry, like the high church T. S. Eliot. Louis Martz was to link him with 'devout humanism' in the Catholic tradition and Richard Strier with the very different faith of Martin Luther.

The nearest he gets to what is called in theology the 'scheme of salvation' is the poem about 'Redemption'. It is a parable. A tenant wants his rent to be reduced, so he tries to see his 'rich Lord' in his manor-house, only to be told that he is away. So he seeks him 'in cities, theatres, gardens, parks and courts' before

> At length I heard a ragged noise and mirth
> Of thieves and murderers: then I him espied . . .

And since this crucified Lord is divine, he foreknows what his tenant wants. But what he says is simply a new covenant or 'testament':

> Who straight, *Your suit is granted*, said, and died.

In 'Obedience' all that is clear about the agreement reached between God and Man on Calvary is that it is not about a mere gift from God; it is about an unspeakably expensive purchase by God. In 'Good Friday' the poet feels that he would need to write in blood about Christ's sorrows. In 'The Thanksgiving' he contemplates the cross and asks how he can describe 'such a grief' in the poetic style to which he has become accustomed:

> Shall thy strokes be my stroking? thorns, my flower?
> Thy rod, my posy? cross, my bower?

He thinks of all the sacrifices he can make in response to Christ's death but ends speechless in gratitude:

> Then for thy passion – I will do for that –
> Alas, my God, I know not what.

It might be expected that after his acceptance of God's love as communicated in Christ he would experience nothing but peace, yet the order in which he placed his poems suggests otherwise: there is no undeviating progress to the Celestial City. Both the earlier 'Williams' manuscript now in London, and a manuscript now in Oxford which is a fair copy of what Herbert handed over on his deathbed, mix up his emotions, so that his modern biographer, Amy Charles, wrote: 'I very much doubt that anyone can now discern the precise reasons for the order.' But the lack of any obvious order was deliberate, to show that the assurance given by his full conversion could survive more tempests raging 'all night'. In 'The Call' he experiences a time when again Christ seems to need to be asked to 'come', but now he already knows that this Lord is 'my Way, my Truth, my Life . . . my Light, my Feast, my Strength . . . my Joy, my Love, my Heart'. And in 'Clasping of Hands' he can dare to pray that one day there will be no more times of apparent separation, that 'Thine and Mine' will no longer be different. This touch of mysticism may be contrasted with 'Home':

> Come Lord, my head doth burn, my heart is sick . . .
> O show thyself to me.
> Or take me up to thee!

The event which has made this difference is Christ's resurrection as its power has reached him. In 'Easter' he finds cheerful music in the most dreadful of places:

> His stretched sinews taught all strings, what key
> Is best to celebrate this most high day . . .

– with 'a song pleasant and long'. And he knows that the song is needed by Man, not by God, for at Easter

> I got me flowers to straw thy way;
> I got me boughs off many a tree:
> But thou wast up at break of day
> And brought'st thy sweets along with thee.

After that, the poems in *The Temple* about the Church – the 'Easter people' as it was to be called – are disappointing, probably because they come from his time before he got to know the Church as a priest. It is a pity that he never wrote either prose or poetry celebrating his parishioners, the living Church.

A poem on 'Church-Lock and Key' speaks about a sinner's cold hands as he (it is he himself) enters. Inside, he may meditate on monuments which remind him that all flesh ends as dust, and if he looks at the marble floor he may reflect that its differently coloured stones teach different virtues. The coloured windows may suggest to him that their biblical pictures are better than speech that 'doth vanish', but also that the preacher is challenged to let the people see 'colours and light' in his life. The seasons in the Church's year are observed – even Lent when 'let's do our best'. But what caught Herbert's imagination was the little chapel in Bemerton which had neither monuments nor marble, neither coloured windows nor a colourful orator. What it had was prayer, and welcoming love, and these are celebrated in his two best poems.

'Prayer (1)' piles up 26 images suggesting prayer in the light of Easter.

Some of these are close to the ground. Prayer is 'the Church's banquet', the corporate Eucharist, and for the individual the 'heart in pilgrimage'. For the afflicted Christian who protests to God it is 'Engine against th'Almighty', 'Christ-side-piercing spear', and so the sufferer may eventually hear 'a kind of tune' which makes sense of everything. Prayer is 'thunder' demanding to be heard. But prayer is also 'softness, and peace, and joy, and love, and bliss', a 'tower' raised above all the dirt, 'Church-bells beyond the stars heard'. And most simply and most importantly, it is 'something understood' – not by the Christian only, but also by God.

Through such prayer we come to 'Love (3)', the climax of the main part of *The Temple.* Modern scholars – especially Michael Schoenfeldt in *Prayer and Power* (1991) – have illuminated the background, found partly in books about courtesy as understood in the Renaissance and partly in poetry which is openly erotic. That study helps us to understand the polite and nervous way in which 'I' respond to Love's welcome which is admission to Paradise. I am like a courtier covered in dust, like a lover who has grown 'slack' in Love's absence. I cannot look Love in the eye when invited to be his guest. When Love takes me by the hand and reminds me that he made my eyes, I still feel ashamed. Then Love reminds me about the cross: 'Know you not who bore the blame?' So I offer to serve Love although he needs no servants, only to be told to 'sit down and taste my meat' – according to John's gospel the flesh of Love. 'So I did sit and eat.'

Edward, Lord Herbert of Cherbury, remembered that as a boy this brother who was now regarded as a saint had not always suppressed his anger, but he left no report of how George reacted to the manuscript of his *De Veritate* when it arrived during 1622. It was sent before being printed in Paris in order to avoid the censorship in England. George was one of the two men to whom it was dedicated and presumably the request that he should delete any passage thought to be contrary to good morals or the Catholic faith was not meant very seriously. Almost the whole of the book was contemptuous about almost the whole of what George Herbert believed or wanted to believe.

Edward was an action-man who in his autobiography boasted of the women he had seduced and of the men he had challenged in duels, and his theology was manly and blunt. His book asked: what is the essence of religion? Is it, as George's poems suggest, fascination with the mystery of God, with his apparent absence and hostility, with his love revealed on the cross, with his call to the priesthood? That was not true religion to Edward. On the contrary, *De Veritate* summed the 'truth' up very concisely. There are five 'common notions' or natural instincts and they are correct. There obviously is a Supreme God; he is to be worshipped; the best worship is the practice of virtue; vices and crimes can be expiated by repentance which needs no mediator; virtues or unrepented vices will be rewarded or punished after this life. Believers in this simple creed constitute the true Catholic Church which cannot err and those who thus believe are saved without any further belief. Indeed, all other beliefs are dangerous even when an individual claims a private revelation and there is evil, not merely danger, in a religion of superstition, of miracles and mysteries, organised and exploited by priests, 'a crafty and deceitful tribe, prone to avarice'. Edward asked: 'how can anyone who believes more than is necessary, and does less than he ought, be saved?' He also asked how a religion which sends 'the far greatest part of mankind' to eternal punishment can be either true or moral. He was not impressed either by the Catholicism or by the Protestantism whose adherents were ruining central Europe in the Thirty Years' War (1618–48), as they had previously fought in a long civil war in France, bringing hell to earth.

Later writers have addressed questions to him. How has it happened that no group known to history has held precisely these beliefs, no less and no more, if these beliefs were instinctive and universal before crafty priests corrupted them? When Edward claims that the believers of whom he approves are 'normal', is he not defining 'normal' as those who accept his controversial position, which was to be known as Deism? But here it is necessary only to note that Edward's religion was not the same as his brother's.

The God who fascinated George Herbert was the God of the Hebrew Bible, hidden in a cloud of glory and thundering in demands and rebukes, but also the God of the New Testament, dying 'for me' and rising so that the heart leaps to adore the victorious Christ. The God who was obvious to Edward Herbert was never likely to turn a man such as he was into a poet. But could a great poet write a great poem about a vision of God not entirely unlike Edward's? We shall see.

FOUR

MILTON

LIKE CHAUCER, JOHN MILTON (born in 1608) grew up in a London which before the great fire of 1666 looked, sounded and smelt medieval. Yet much had changed. In Chaucer's time usury, the charging of interest on loans, had been prohibited to Christians. Shakespeare's father had been both a nostalgic Catholic (it seems) and a small-time money-lender (we know), but Milton's father left the family farm, added himself to London's expanding population, identified himself as a devout Puritan, and learned the business of a scrivener. This meant that he received money to be lent out at a high rate of interest and arranged and supervised the loans. He also dealt in the selling and buying of property. In the process he built a comfortable fortune although he does not seem to have been dishonest or grasping; he retired early.

John Milton was therefore able to depend on his father's money all through an exceptionally prolonged period of full-time study and, more subtly, could depend on his family's respectability for a lifelong assurance that he was at least the equal of almost everyone he met. In particular he was able to think that the group to which he belonged was morally superior to bishops and to kings and their courtiers. The court of James I was viewed as a scene of extravagance, of corruption and of coarser forms of immorality. The court of Charles I was not so open to those charges but was believed to be out of touch with the most solid part of the country – not the landowning nobility, or the rich who owed their wealth to royal patronage, or the old-fashioned gentry whose loyalty to the Crown was instinctive, but the Godfearing but modern-minded businessmen of London, their respectable wives, and the rest of the 'middle sort' who had been raised above the common people by their Protestant piety, their industrious enterprise and their belief in education.

In some ways his own education was the same as Shakespeare's or Herbert's: he was made familiar with the classics of Greece and Rome and trained to be confident in the use of Latin. But he was privileged, more so than George among the orphaned Herbert boys, and almost beyond comparison with the glovemaker's son in Stratford. He was treasured: a portrait of him at the age of ten shows a boy dressed soberly but expensively, with an expression which is thoughtful but not shy. He was educated by a private tutor and then sent to the first-class grammar school which had been founded in 1512 by drastically improving the school attached to St Paul's Cathedral which Chaucer had probably attended. Some private tuition supplemented St Paul's School and the result was fluency in Latin, Greek, French and Italian, with some knowledge of Hebrew – plus a definitely Protestant faith and a lifelong love of learning.

While Shakespeare seems to have taught himself how to write English poetry, Milton wrote verse (from the age of ten, we are told) which owed much to a cultured and highly musical father, an amateur composer with friends who were professional musicians. London's medieval cathedral had developed a musical tradition almost as fine as the oratory of its poetical dean, John Donne, who began to preach there soon after the boy's admission to the school. The music of St Paul's Cathedral – or is it of King's College Chapel in Cambridge? – is remembered in a poem written by Milton in his early twenties: it resounds with love for the high vaulted roof and the richly 'storied' coloured windows, but supremely for the anthems whose 'sweetness' dissolves him into ecstasies. In 'At a Solemn Music', written later, 'Voice' and 'Verse' are in a harmony which can raise the listener to hopes of singing 'in endless morning light'

> Where the bright Seraphim in burning row
> Their loud uplifted angel-trumpets below.

Stronger than his love of music, however, was the young Milton's appetite for printed words in a number of languages. He was to recall that from the age of twelve he scarcely ever went to bed before midnight, although he had inherited weak eyesight from his mother and the hours of reading by candlelight began the eyes' decline into blindness. At the age of sixteen he matriculated in Christ's College, Cambridge, apparently with the intention of becoming a highly literate preacher in the Church of England. This would have made him a successor to Lancelot Andrewes, bishop and saint, to whom he paid tribute in a poem on his death, but he cannot have seen much – if anything – of Herbert in Cambridge. In 1646 he was to publish a collection of his early poetry in Latin or English and although the small edition received little attention it enables us to know his young mind. Later he was to say that a man who hoped 'to write well hereafter ought himself to be a poem, that is, a composition and pattern of the best and honourablest things'. The trouble was that when young he did not keep this thought to himself.

A letter in Latin to his one intimate friend, Charles Diodati, is revealing. Diodati had been with him in St Paul's School and was equally clever. Milton tells him that because of disagreements with his tutor he had been expelled from his college after a year. He makes light of it: his banishment will not last, in London he is enjoying his books and the sight of pretty girls. But his first tutor in Cambridge had evidently found his conceit insufferable and it was only because of his ability that the college found another tutor for him on his readmission.

He conformed to some extent, as is evident in non-controversial poems on unoriginal subjects or university personages, but a speech made at college festivities in 1628 has also been preserved. There he admits that his nickname was 'the Lady' but he makes no apology for his unusual personality. He says that he has not dirtied his hands in the fields or at sport, that he has lived a clean life and that he intends to write poems about the gods of the classics, kings and queens, and heroes of old. From downward looks at his fellow students he passes to complaints about the curriculum: instead of being compelled to learn logic according to Aristotle and then use it in unreal disputations, he ought to have been helped to reason on the basis of up-to-date knowledge. We can understand why the fellows of the college did not invite him to join their small circle when he became MA in 1632.

After those seven uneasy years of involvement in Cambridge he lived with his parents in the countryside quite near to London. He seems to have been happy to combine being with them in their retirement with his own reading of Greek, Roman and medieval history and of the ancient Fathers of the Church. The books disappointed: the history was found to be full of boring battles, the Fathers to be empty of true religion, and working through a library did not get him nearer to becoming a great poet. However, no disappointment deterred him from storing up careful notes for future use and a notebook begun in this period came to light in 1874.

At home as in Cambridge he was usually at his books – but not always. His country walks were to be remembered, it seems, when he wrote about the Garden of Eden in *Paradise Lost* and two early poems allow us to overhear the walker's thoughts. 'L'Allegro' is light and warm on a summer's day and he is cheered by the jollity of the country folk observed at a distance, but 'Il Penseroso' is clearly his favourite: the countryside in moonlight both evokes and consoles his self-absorbed melancholy. And the Italian in the titles suggests that when out walking if he was not thinking about himself he was thinking about the culture of Europe.

He hoped and dreamed that one day he would be able to write at length and greatly about 'some graver matter' as he had promised his fellow students, but he had not yet found that matter. When inspired at dawn on Christmas Day 1629 he had begun his ode *On the Morning of Christ's Nativity*. The 'infant God' has come down from 'heav'n's high council table' where he had sat with the rest of the Holy Trinity, and to welcome him to earth both nature and the political world are for once at peace (all these ideas were traditional). But there is also a religious reformation: in the pagan shrines their oracles fall silent and their deities depart to 'profoundest hell'. At the end the poet is in the 'courtly stable', silent in adoration among the 'bright harnessed angels'. But he cannot conceal the fact that he is also very interested in himself. He has been eager to overtake the 'star-led wizards' so that he may offer his poem before they arrive, and he has not joined the shepherds. Before they were silenced by the celestial concert they had been 'chatting' with 'silly thoughts' about 'their loves or else their sheep' and they would not have been fit company for him.

He knows that the 'age of gold' which seems to begin at this first Christmas is not yet: 'wise infancy' must 'redeem our loss' by glorifying both 'himself and us' by his death on 'the bitter cross'. But the brief reference to the crucifixion was not expanded either in this ode or in a poem intended as a companion piece, on the passion of Christ. That was abandoned after eight stanzas which managed to avoid the subject because, as he explained in a note added later, an understanding of the cross was 'above the years he had when he wrote it'.

In 1632 his first poem to be printed was an introduction to the second edition of Shakespeare's collected plays. It was anonymous and it is not clear why an unknown young admirer had been asked. A poem of homage and envy, it expresses 'wonder and astonishment' that 'to th' shame of slow-endeavouring art' (his own) the master's 'easy numbers flow'. In 'L'Allegro' a reference to 'sweetest Shakespeare' suggests that 'Fancy's child' needed no preparation at all before he could produce 'native wood-notes wild'. Knowing that he was in another category, on his twenty-fourth birthday Milton wrote a sonnet about his own slow-endeavouring development. Time, 'the subtle thief of youth', had stolen his life up to this point without producing much 'inward ripeness' or any outward fruit. He would only cling to the faith that time was leading him on to some work, 'however mean or high', and that meanwhile he must continue to prepare, 'as ever in my great Task-Master's eye' – a somewhat cool reference to God, like his earlier reference to 'wisest Fate'. But in what seems to be his next poem he is in despair about ever accomplishing his task. Now all life is 'false and vain' and 'merely mortal', and his only hope is that eternity shall 'overtake us like a flood'.

In a long Latin poem he entreated his father to be patient. The father loves music, poets add words to music, and even without music his own words may yet make the old man famous in a distant age. One thing he can promise: come what may, he has no intention of walking unknown in a crowd which is worse than dull: the common people are 'loathsome'.

Any parent would be disappointed that an adult son held himself so aloof not only from people such as shepherds but also from any job, clinging to a dream of becoming a great poet without producing any substantial evidence that he had the capacity – and this father was a businessman who had made his son (in Kermode's phrase) his 'chief investment'. But he responded tolerantly and generously. Almost certainly he recommended this strange son of his to one of his friends, Henry Lawes, who had been commissioned to provide music for masques to be performed by the children of two aristocratic families. Masques had come into fashion because they were the favourite entertainments at the court of James I or of Charles I: they provided an opportunity to dress up and dance amid elaborate scenery, with women acting(!) and the queen often taking a leading role. Even the king, to whom such flattery was submitted, could consent to be among the dancers. Words would be needed as well as music and Ben Jonson among others had been happy to be paid for a supply. But Lawes, although a court musician, had been hired for masques intended to be more modest.

A short script by Milton enabled the grandchildren of the Dowager Countess of Derby to honour her as she entered her seventies, but innocent young voices, praising her great generosity and the delights of her estate, had to purify the air after an unmentionable scandal. One of her daughters had been married to the Earl of Castlehaven, recently executed after a series of brutally sexual crimes against her, their daughter and the servants. The success of Milton's healing words on that occasion led to an invitation from another daughter, married to the solidly respectable Earl of Bridgewater, Lord President of the council which administered Wales. In 1634 the poet supplied words to be recited at a masque in Ludlow Castle by the children of that happy marriage.

Two sons, aged eleven and nine, are made to exchange thoughts as they are lost in a wood by night and separated from their sister aged fourteen. The elder brother is confident that she is safe, being 'clad in complete steel': ''Tis chastity, my brother, chastity'. The younger boy admits 'how charming is divine philosophy' but cannot help being worried – sensibly, because she is confronted by a satanic tempter, Comus. He advocates sensuality and revelry: when Nature is so bountiful, why should we restrain our instincts? He offers her a drink and it seems that something nasty is about to happen since she is imprisoned in a chair by his magic. But she rejects the cup, explaining that she accepts such offers only from good men, and gives him a sermon of icy contempt. She is liberated by Sabrina, the good spirit of the river Severn on the border of Wales, and the children are presented to their parents with a story about their victory 'o'er sensual folly and intemperance'.

Later Milton's father made possible another victory, over his own life-denying son's melancholy. He agreed to finance a trip through France, Italy and Switzerland (with a servant in attendance) from May 1638 to August 1639. John's mother had died in 1637 and his father had decided to close down his own household and to live with the family of his younger son Christopher, who was earning a good income. John could now be sent to talk with his intellectual equals, who could be trusted to appreciate his Latin verse and his mastery of their own languages. The tourist enjoyed himself, admiring antiquities and landscapes but concentrating on the scholarly conversations. Towards the Catholicism of the Counter-Reformation he felt nothing but a hostility which he could not always keep silent, yet towards the 'academies' or private groups of friendly intellectuals taking shelter from the clergy's censorship he felt nothing but admiring envy. Many memories of those fifteen months of travel and talk were to influence his future. In Paris he met Grotius, the advocate of reason and liberty in religion; near Florence he met Galileo, condemned by the Church for having observed before his blindness that the earth moved round the sun; in Rome he heard Baroque music and wrote Latin poems assuring a famous singer that in her 'God speaks'; in Venice he saw an old republic still flourishing; in Geneva he talked with theologians and was reminded that Cambridge was second-rate.

When abroad he heard of the outbreak of resistance to the attempt of King Charles to impose Anglican-style bishops and prayers on Scotland. Two 'Bishops' Wars' began on March 1639 and ended in the occupation of the North of England by the Scots at the expense of Charles, who to raise money had to summon Parliament after eleven years (1629–40) without it. But Milton did not hurry home, perhaps sensing that once back he would never leave England. And a sadness had clouded his holiday, for he had learned of the death of Charles Diodati, still in his twenties. In recent years they had not been close geographically; after studying theology under his uncle in Geneva Diodati had begun to practise as a physician like his father. But they certainly had been close emotionally, at school and later, and a long Latin poem of mourning resounded with echoes of the literature they had studied.

On his return to London he began to use much of his time as tutor to his two nephews, Edward and John Phillips. When freed from his uncle's strict regime John was to react by publishing a collection of naughty poems including some which mocked the Puritans, and in 1656 Milton would have to intervene as his protector from official wrath. Edward was also no Puritan but his biography after Milton's death is the most intimate picture we have of his life and it is full of admiration. Other pupils arrived. Tutoring was, however, not the main source of income: right up to his death in 1647, when he left him a considerable legacy, his father supported Milton financially; for example, he assigned to him the interest on a loan made to an Oxfordshire gentleman named Richard Powell. Schoolmastering was not the greatness of past dreams but it seemed preferable to becoming a lawyer like his brother; in his poem to his father he had called the law 'noisy stupidity'. And some employment was necessary now that he had made the decision not to be a priest.

As late as 1632 he had been willing to sign his assent to the Articles of Religion and thus to the doctrines and discipline of the Church of England, for he had needed to do so in order to become MA. So his change of course must have been a hostile reaction to the policies enforced by William Laud, made Bishop of London in 1628 and Archbishop of Canterbury in 1633, the year of George Herbert's death. It is impossible to be sure how Herbert would have reacted to Laudianism, a mixture of ideas not all of which he is known to have had himself.

Working closely with his king but always under him, Laud was a hyperactive administrator driven by a determination to revive both the dignity and the discipline of the clergy. Their often grinding poverty and their often cringing subservience to the gentry must be ended, which meant reversing the whole tendency of the last hundred years. Their sacred functions in worship must be performed with a sense of awe within churches cleaned, restored and beautified. To inspire devotion, crucifixes and images of saints should be brought back and prayers must be offered in the humility of kneeling. The communion table must be treated as sacred and railed off from the rest of the church; preferably it should be returned to the medieval position of the altar at the church's east end. Communicants must kneel to receive the sacrament from the priest, for sitting round a casually treated table might suggest that Holy Communion was essentially a meal where well-fed people simply remembered an absent Christ. The clergy must be bold to rebuke misbehaviour by the laity, in suitable cases punishing it more severely through strengthened ecclesiastical courts.

But the raising of the clergy's spiritual and social status must be accompanied by an insistence on their duties as officers in an army. They must dress, and always act, as men of God different from other men, and they must teach what the Church teaches. The Book of Common Prayer must be used without variation; the Articles of Religion must be accepted without controversy; the authorised catechism with its respectful questions and assured answers must be used in the instruction of children and of childlike adults. The Church's canon law of 1604 must be revised (and it was in 1640) so as to make the regulations firmer and more extensive, and the bishops must enforce them, being the successors to Christ's apostles. Sermons on Sunday morning must expound to the whole parish what is laid down in the Prayer Book and in the afternoon communal sports are to be enjoyed, having also been authorised by a royal decree read out in church despite Puritan objections to Sabbath-breaking. Probably most parishioners had no objections to sports but could be worried by changes which might be signs that the Laudian bishops planned to restore Popery.

Laud could also be accused of supporting tyranny, for the personal rule of Charles I, without an argumentative Parliament but with a Bishop of London as Lord Treasurer, could be interpreted as a sign that there was a plot to make England a Catholic kingdom with an all-powerful, semi-divine king as in Spain or France. The Laudian doctrine was that just as bishops governed 'by divine law', so did the king – only more so, being consecrated at his coronation to establish justice like the kings in the Old Testament. So the king and his law courts must counteract the tendency of local magistrates to further the interests of their own class: the 'enclosure' of common fields by landlords, already a process Shakespeare's day, must be halted or reversed, and manufacturing and commerce must be encouraged but also regulated in some detail. Such policies were already putting the clock back and men who had profited from the changes made in the previous century could be alarmed. Would lands and incomes (tithes) which had belonged to the clergy in the Middle Ages be restored to them? Would capitalism as practised by (for example) Milton's father be curbed drastically? Would the gentry-controlled Parliament never meet again? But pamphleteers who protested had their ears cut off.

Without putting his own ears at risk, Milton was one of those who wanted the Protestant Reformation and the rise of the middle classes to be speeded, not stopped, and he indicated this in *Lycidas.* It was a poem after the death of Edward King, another graduate of Christ's College in Cambridge, who had been drowned in a storm in the Irish Sea before he could proceed to ordination. Milton does not seem to have known him well and may not have known that he admired Laud, but he contributed to a memorial volume published soon after his departure for his European tour. The poem is in English but there are again many allusions to the Latin classics.

And again the deepest emotions are about himself. Despite the horror of his death King 'is not dead': his soul has been rescued by the 'dear might' of the Christ 'that walk'd the waves'. 'Weep no more!' Milton is more disturbed by the thought that he, too, may be claimed by death before his life's work has even started. The opening lines include the words harsh, crude and rude, shatter and bitter, and the shattered memories of the Cambridge years are now indeed bitter, for

> Comes the blind Fury with th' abhorred shears,
> And slits the thin-spun life.

Why had God, who could be trusted to take care of King in heaven, not taken care of him on earth? The 'all-judging Jove' who 'pronounces lastly on each deed' is asked why he permits the death of a man who has scarcely any deeds to be judged – and no answer is heard. Milton has begun the spiritual journey which will end in *Paradise Lost* with its need to justify to human scepticism the mysterious ways of the Christians' God. And as an independently minded Christian who is not afraid to question or criticise, he has no intention of taking King's (or Herbert's) place in the Church of William Laud. Instead he ends with an outburst which is almost hysterical.

The 'pilot of the Galilean lake', St Peter, declares that had other clergymen died he would have been less sorry. He does not supply names or details because the poet (identified only as J.M.) keeps the official censor in mind. But the generalised condemnation is very severe. These clergy work only for pay, for 'their bellies' sake'; they do not notice that the hungry sheep are not fed as they could have been by the preaching of the Gospel, being themselves 'blind mouths'; they ignore the danger to the flock from the 'grim wolf' from Rome; they deserve to be executed by the 'two-handed engine' which is already 'at the door'. This is the sword of justice to be wielded by Protestant Englishmen if not by Christ returning to be the Judge. Eight years later Laud is to be beheaded after three years in prison.

Lycidas ended with words inappropriate for a mourner: 'Tomorrow to fresh woods, and pastures new'. The poem was published soon after the start of Milton's grand tour and presumably he had that in mind – but after Italy, what? Back in England with a new vigour, it might seem inevitable that he should have a strong connection with the battlefields of the civil war – if not as a soldier, then as a writer able to stir up support for Parliament. But he did not throw himself into the good new cause. Instead, he put his energy into pamphlets about church government, divorce, censorship and education, in the process displeasing Parliament.

One factor seems to have been that like many Englishmen he was not confident that the war begun in August 1642 would have a good outcome. Until the battles of 1644–45 it could seem likely that the royalists would defeat the rebellion and that the reaction against Parliament would be severe; yet a victory by Parliament would be without precedent in English history and full of dangers to the whole structure of English society, in which the Milton family had been comfortable enough. He had himself been immensely privileged by being free to devote himself to literature at his father's expense, with open contempt for the lower classes in society. So during most of the 1640s he wanted the king to remain on the throne with a new set of ministers excluding the bishops, and he said so clearly in one of his attacks on the bishops. His brother was a committed royalist and he himself was not deterred by politics from marrying a girl from a stoutly royalist family. His ardent identification with the fully republican cause was therefore delayed for ten years after his return to England. During that time he got on with his own work and confined his public role to the passionate advocacy of causes dear to him because of his own experiences.

He said that his pamphlets were written with his left hand so that his full power could be reserved for poetry which would 'leave something written to after times as they would not willingly let die' and the possibility of an epic about King Arthur was among the projects in his hopes. But with that left hand he managed to wave goodbye to a number of institutions which, although they survived or revived in his own century, eventually did die. His prose was that of a poet, full of images and epigrams, but it had a strength in argument which his poetry had seldom displayed: full of a passionate earnestness, and of hatred and contempt for the other side, it marshalled his learning not as decoration but as artillery.

The whole atmosphere which he now breathed in England was as intoxicating as Italy had been, although in a radically different way. The war unleashed verbal as well as physical violence as the forces of conservatism were challenged by the enthusiasts for an new age, idealists with whom Milton could have sympathy so long as the class system was not too disturbed. In particular he had a fellow feeling with fellow Protestants who read their Bibles with a new excitement now that the end of history could be imminent: was Christ about to return and reign with his saints for a thousand years? One of the fellows of Christ's College during Milton's years in Cambridge had been Joseph Mead, an expert in the interpretation of the Book of Daniel and the Revelation of John, and in 1643 Parliament ordered the translation of his Latin treatise about such prophecies. It predicted that Christ's second coming would occur in 1653. At the very least, Milton hoped that in England a new stage of the Protestant Reformation was being inaugurated and was sure that his eloquence in this crisis did not result from 'the heat of youth or the vapours of wine'.

His first target was the Laudian bishops who had given evil advice to the king and who had 'church-outed' him and good Protestants like him in the 1630s. He called them 'prelatical', by which he meant pompous and dictatorial. In five fierce pamphlets he did not merely accuse them of conspiring to admit the 'grim woolf' from Rome into the Anglican sheepfold. He mocked their 'swan-eating' at table, their indulgence in drink and their fraudulence as scholars. With his own learning he demonstrated that bishops (*episkopoi*) ranking above elders (*presbuteroi*) were not clearly on view in the New Testament, and claimed (wrongly) that letters of St Ignatius of Antioch showing that they had emerged within a hundred years of the Church's birth were all forgeries. These Anglican bishops were depicted as gross impostors whose claim to govern their church was laughable – and such was his confidence that he did battle with two bishops who were known to spend more time on their knees or at their desks than at their dinner tables. John Hall of Norwich had himself been a witty satirist in earlier days but his *Art of Divine Meditation* was the work of a man of prayer and his defence of the 'divine right' of bishops since the apostles' time echoed a claim which had already been normal in the Church of England before Laud's leadership. James Ussher, Archbishop of Armagh, made a similar claim but wanted bishops to work in collaboration with the clergy and not to trouble the consciences of the Puritans. An immensely learned scholar, able to work out the Bible's date for the creation of the universe (in October 4004 BC), he was to be given a state funeral by Cromwell. Yet these men were among the prelates who, Milton wrote, were so lukewarm in religion as to make God 'vomit'. Even Cranmer and other bishops martyred as Protestants during the English Reformation were treated as time-servers, not servants of God, and the corruption of the Church under bishops was traced right back to the arrival of wealth and power in the fourth century.

The target became even wider, to include the clergy who had served or idled under such bishops. He asked 'where was there a more insolent, profane and vicious clergy, learned in nothing but the antiquity of their pride, their covetousness and superstition?' And while history has largely vindicated his attack on William Laud and his closest associates, Milton's positive ideal for the shape of church life has seldom been adopted in its entirety, based as it was on the individual's right to interpret Scripture and on the congregation's right to worship exactly as it considers helpful. It was only in the twentieth century that Milton's do-it-yourself religion became more popular, for then many people could identify themselves as Christians without feeling any obligation to defer to any authority or to belong to any congregation.

While denouncing the bishops in the 1640s Milton took care to distance himself from the theologians commonly then regarded as the arch-heretics: Arius who denied the full divinity of Christ and died *c.*336, Socinus who denied the traditional doctrine of the Trinity and died in 1562, and Arminius who affirmed freedom to accept or reject salvation and died in 1609. But he soon moved very close to their positions and in the late 1650s he wrote a frank and long exposition of his own theology in Latin, *De Doctrina Christiana*, revising it subsequently and calling it 'my best and most precious possession'. No censor would allow its publication during his lifetime – not even in Latin – but after his death a former student got hold of the manuscript and sent it to a Dutch publisher who refused the risk. It was returned to the ex-student's father who passed it on to the government. Buried obscurely in the national archives, it was discovered by accident in 1823 and initially greeted with excitement: Parliament discussed it, the king ordered a rapid translation by a favourite clergyman (a future bishop), and this was published by the Cambridge University Press in 1825. But when looked into, it was seen to be so different from the standard interpretation of Milton's poetry as an exposition of mainstream Christianity that little notice was taken of it for another hundred years. Only in the twentieth century was its radicalism widely seen to be what Milton really thought in his maturity.

Postponing theology, we may observe that his vision of the Church in *De Doctrina* was of a community without many paid clergy, for all incomes derived from tithes are to be ended. Congregations are to be at liberty to pay their own minister if they so wish but their meetings (which need not be on Sunday) may be held in people's homes, or in barns since 'he who disdained not to be laid in a manger disdains not to be preached in a barn'. Compulsory church attendance, or any form of jurisdiction by the congregation over other people, is of course out of the question. No set form of worship is to be obligatory and anyone is to be encouraged to expound his (but not her) faith as the Spirit guides his use of the Bible. Baptism is to for be converted adults, not children: by itself it cannot bring salvation or regeneration. Holy Communion is to be available when the believer feels that a time and a place for it are 'convenient' but it requires 'holiness of life' to take effect. The eucharistic bread is not 'Christ's actual flesh' as 'papists' are said to maintain: if it were, it might be eaten by a mouse and then mice would 'attain eternal life'. And so far from Holy Communion being a sacrifice to God offered by a priest ordained by a bishop, 'there is nothing in the Bible about how the Lord's Supper should be administered. So I do not know why ministers should forbid anyone except themselves to celebrate it.' Other 'sacraments' in the Catholic system are prayers for blessing or forgiveness, which all Christians may equally well offer for, and by, themselves.

That, however, was not how most of the English wished to worship in his own lifetime or for some two hundred years later. The intensely spiritual and radical movement nicknamed the Quakers, or the later and more intellectual Unitarians who openly rejected the doctrine of the Trinity, never became numerous. In *The Caroline Captivity of the Church* (1992) Julian Davies demonstrated that in the 1630s 'for the majority of the political nation the breaking of the ecclesiastical yoke was essential', meaning by 'the political nation' men with property who elected the House of Commons, but in *The Personal Rule of Charles I* (also 1992) Kevin Sharpe produced other evidence to show that in the same period the majority of the population routinely conformed to the Established Church as a part of the familiar landscape: 'most of the parishes remained devoted to *their* Church of England – to its fabric, customs and rituals.' In 1660–62 this Church was to be released from its brief spell as an underground movement and its restoration to most (not to all) of its privileges seems to have been generally acceptable. Between 1640 and 1660 there had been limited explosions of hostility including riots and vandalism – against bishops with political power, against cathedrals which seemed to be idolatrous, idle and rich, against ecclesiastical courts which controlled marriages and punished sexual activities outside marriage – but when things had settled down most people were, it seems, willing to return to Church as well as to King, mainly perhaps because the restored Church would interfere with their lives less actively than the kill-joy Puritans. And the 'Dissenters' from that Church endured penalties imposed by the Anglican state because they wanted to be pilgrims in closely knit groups which accepted the authority of Scripture. Whenever possible they built their own chapels with pulpits.

Milton's own vision of the Church did not lead him to much, if any, churchgoing. Although the absence of evidence about regular membership of a congregation in the 1640s and 1650s proves nothing, there are clear reports that after 1660 he seldom, if ever, left home to worship. His Anglican parish church would have seemed an idolatrous temple and he did not take the risk which he would have run, had he identified himself with a Dissenting congregation such as the one to which John Bunyan preached when not in prison. One does not get the impression that he thought he was missing much.

The removal of the bishops and other objectionable features of the Church in the 1640s depended on the will of the House of Commons, which after the exit of the royalists consisted largely of Presbyterians. These insisted that all ministers (no longer called priests) should be equal in status, but they did want them to have a considerable status – to be orthodox Calvinists, paid out of the customary tithes, and if possible learned, with authority in their parishes. Yet Milton did not follow up his literary demolition of the bishops by writing in support of the Commons in the civil war; instead, he embarked on a series of pamphlets bound to scandalise Presbyterians.

Indeed, he became almost completely isolated. In those turbulent times other sects arose and seemed scandalous to the respectable gentry on both sides of the civil war: the Levellers and the Diggers who were idealistic Socialists, the Socinians who believed in One God exclusively, the Quakers who believed in the Christ and the Spirit at work in everyone, the Seekers who could not believe that any God had been revealed, the Ranters who could not believe that any God existed, the Muggletonians who believed in Lodowick Muggleton as a prophet of the coming End, the Fifth Monarchy Men who believed in themselves as qualified to help the End to come, the Family of Love who did not believe in marriage. But Milton – a gentleman and a scholar whose only connection with such radicalism was his belief that it should be answered, not silenced by the law – was regarded as the founder of a sect which almost everyone condemned: he was a Divorcer.

He felt himself obliged to write on this very sensitive subject for two reasons. One was that marriage mattered intensely to most people, yet the Church's jurisdiction in this field had been abolished and he believed that now the only 'preeminent and supreme authority' left for Christians in any field was Scripture interpreted by the Spirit within the individual. So as an inspired individual, he must say something. But the other reason was painfully personal. In May 1642, now at 34 almost halfway through his life, he visited Richard Powell in Oxford, probably in order to rebuke that small-scale landowner for failure to pay him interest on the loan arranged by his father. As poets know, May can be an unsettling month and (to the astonishment of his pupils) before the end of June Milton was back in London with a wife. Much later he was to write about Adam's first sight of Eve:

> here passion first I felt,
> Commotion strange, in all enjoyments else
> Superior and unmov'd, here only weak
> Against the charm of beauty's powerful glance . . .
> yet when I approach

Her loveliness, so absolute she seems
And in herself complete, so well to know
Her own, that what she wills to do or say
Seems wisest, virtuousest, discreetest, best;
All higher knowledge in her presence falls
Degraded.

She was Mary Powell, then aged seventeen. But a month or so after her marriage she wanted to return to her lively family, near Oxford to which the royal court had moved. Her husband agreed to a short absence which grew longer and longer. What had gone wrong may be guessed from what he wrote about the failure of a marriage, although without naming her or discussing desertion. He wrote about sex without love as being so disappointing as to be disgusting, about happy conversation as being the heart of a marriage, and about 'constant contrariness' as being its destruction. He wrote, too, that although the courts of the State must decide the financial arrangements if these are in dispute, the decision to dissolve the marriage must rest with the man. Marriage was a covenant, not an indissoluble sacrament, and God had explained in Genesis 2:18 why he had founded this institution: 'It is not good that the man should be alone.' Another convenient text was Deuteronomy 24:1–4, where a wife may be dismissed if 'unclean'.

But the chief objector to any divorce was well known: Christ. Taking Matthew 19:3–9 as the most authentic record of Christ's teaching, Milton was faced with the problem that divorce had been forbidden except after adultery, which could not be proved in this case. So he advanced two interpretations, one that 'adultery' really meant incompatibility and the other that in all Bible-based decisions charity is the best guide; as he was to write elsewhere, 'no ordinance, human or from heaven, can bind against the good of Man'. His task would have been easier had he anticipated what was to be agreed by most modern biblical scholars – that Mark's is the earliest gospel which Matthew uses and edits; that Mark records the original teaching of Jesus; that marriage is intended by God to be lifelong; and that Matthew reflects the decision by the church behind him to allow divorce after the specific offence of adultery, adjusting the ideal for a pastoral reason after a human tragedy. As it was, Milton had to argue that the passage in Matthew made everything depend on the husband's feelings, whether or not adultery had been committed. This was precisely opposite to the way in which almost all the teachers of the churches have understood the passage, although he was able to quote one or two who agreed with him. Into a sequel he slipped a brief admission that a wife, too, ought to be able to initiate a divorce.

But he did not actually seek a divorce and about two years after her exit an older Mary was on her knees before him, begging for forgiveness. His heart melted and the resumed marriage produced three daughters before Mary's death in 1652. For a year it also resulted in the invasion of Milton's house by the entire Powell family, refugees from their own home as Parliament's army began to control the whole country. Milton's father, now a widower in his eighties, was a more welcome lodger.

In the long run many parliaments around the world, and many churches, were to make the emotional breakdown of a marriage the sufficient reason for a divorce, just as Milton had advocated, but for the time being he caused a scandal. Further outcries came when it was noticed that he defended polygamy. He based this unprovoked but highly provocative position on Scripture, which he could use when and as he wished (there are more than three thousand biblical quotations in *De Doctrina*). In the Old Testament the patriarchs and King Solomon make good use of this arrangement and in the New it is not explicitly forbidden. In the future this was to be a real issue for churches in other times and places (in Africa for example), but it was not in Milton's England, and his raising of the question did not make Parliament's sympathetic attention any more likely in his next controversy.

He protested against the Act of Parliament which in 1643 reimposed censorship on all printed matter and was not to be repealed before 1694. His pamphlets about divorce had not been submitted to any censor and now he addressed *Areopagitica* to Parliament in a 'speech' giving his own full name but not the name of the printer or bookseller. He got away with it: he had to appear before the House of Lords but was dismissed. No one took the trouble to answer him at length.

He protected himself against the full force of a storm by advocating only a limited freedom. Although he protested against licences being needed for books, pamphlets or newspapers before publication, he agreed that once in the public arena those responsible could be justly punished if they fell into one or other of a wide variety of categories – if they were blasphemous, if they defended 'popery and open superstition', if they spread treason or libels, or even if they offended against 'manners'. And he left the more precise definition of all these crimes to the authorities. Under Cromwell he was to be for a time willing to act as the chief censor under a regime which prohibited royalist publications (in vain) on the ground that they were treasonable, and he was the editor-in-chief of the official weekly newspaper in order to make sure that its contents were politically correct. In the circumstances such employment was perhaps excusable, and when he had licensed the translation and publication of a Polish pamphlet which was not orthodox about the Trinity, he withdrew from this unwelcome duty during the ensuing minor storm, reminding his critics that he had written *Areopagitica.*

More serious was the intellectual argument to be found amid the rhetoric of the 'speech', for that argument is: virtue is strengthened by being challenged, truths have never harmed virtue but are only fragments of Truth, Truth is discovered by being debated. And that argument justifies the whole modern struggle for a free press. On that splendid basis, he ought to have wanted a toleration wider than he felt able to advocate in 1644.

However, there is unlikely to be disagreement about the power and value of much of the rhetoric, which accords with his description of 'true eloquence': it is 'possessed with a fervent desire to know good things and with the dearest charity to infuse the knowledge of them into others'. He knew one good thing: a good book is 'the precious life-blood of a master spirit, embalmed and treasured up on purpose to a life beyond life'. And another: 'Who ever knew truth to be put to the worse in free and open encounter?' and 'yet it is not impossible that she may have more shapes than one', since 'truth lies scattered in pieces' and 'we have not yet found them all . . . nor ever shall do, till her Master's second coming'. And another: 'I cannot praise a fugitive and cloistered virtue, unexercised and unbreathed, that never sallies out and seeks her adversary.' And another: 'When God is decreeing to begin some new and great period in his Church, even to the reforming of Reformation itself, what does he then but to reveal himself to his servants and, as his manner is, first to his Englishmen?'

The scope of a pamphlet on education was similarly limited: it advocated free grammar schools for the 'able' sons of the gentry, to be established in every town. Such boys could grow up to write the kind of books which Milton thought should be allowed, however controversial they might be. He had imagined them as adults in *Areopagitica*, 'sitting with their studious lamps, musing, searching, revolving new notions and ideas', and writing for readers who would assent to 'the force of reason'. But they should grow up as Christians, since 'the end of learning is . . . to know God aright', and as competent 'to perform justly, skilfully and magnanimously' any task, 'public or private, needed in peace or war'. Modern language, recent history and some science were to be included in the curriculum, as was physical exercise for some hours every day and relaxation after supper (reading the Bible).

He worked on two history books which would educate the young – a small one on Russia and a big *History of Britain.* He reached 1066 before he was summoned to be closer to British history in the making and the book was not published before 1670. He wanted to show how the disorganised, indeed spineless, British lost their liberty first to the Romans, then to the Anglo-Saxons, then to Danes and then to the Normans: so the confusion of the present must be ended. Slightly more in keeping with a modern idea of history is some effort to discriminate between the sources then available, which were largely a collection of legends such as the foundation of London by refugees from Troy. To present-day readers the only interest may lie in connections with Shakespeare which, however, do not reproduce the plots of the plays. Lear, 'more and more drooping in years', flees from his wicked daughters but is cherished by order of Cordelia in 'some good sea port' in France, before she takes him back to Britain where he is buried (in Leicester) and where she reigns for five years before her suicide, having been overthrown and imprisoned by her wicked sisters' sons.

Poems reflect Milton's experiences during the civil war – experiences which were certainly not those of a combatant. The first sonnet in this series is detached from the conflict; when a royalist army seems to be about to capture London in the autumn of 1642, he begs whatever 'knight in arms' may be at his door to remember that it is the house of a poet. The second encourages a young woman to remain as she is, virtuous and devout: it has been suggested that she was Mary, and Edward Phillips was to recall that 'she took much delight in his company' at first. The third offers proper compliments to a neighbour's wife who has been kind to him after Mary's desertion: he praises her father, an earl who had struggled to keep Crown and Parliament together. Others pour scorn on critics and would-be censors of his pamphlets about divorce, mocking them for being put off by titles in Greek. He also attacks 'shallow Edwards', a Presbyterian who in *Gangraena* had listed all the current heretics and demanded the application of a surgeon's knife to the whole lot. Milton objects to the condemnation of men of 'learning, faith, and pure intent' such as himself. 'New Presbyter is but old priest writ large' – and to him that is a clinching insult.

Another sonnet is addressed to the widow of a bookseller who had collected, and saved for posterity, some twenty-two thousand publications issued during recent controversies, but he rises above controversy when he praises music composed by Henry Lawes, who had remained a royalist. And in August 1648 he praises the Earl of Halifax, assuring that general of 'unshak'n virtue' that after leading Parliament's army to victory a 'nobler task' awaits him – winning the peace, a peace with an aristocrat in command.

A few months later Halifax is going to retire to his estate rather than agree to the execution of the king, and nothing in these poems makes it seem likely that in March 1649 Milton will be offered, and will accept, appointment as a senior civil servant under Cromwell. He never gave a full and public explanation of this new commitment, but his attitude was clear and explicable. The king's behaviour in defeat, escaping from imprisonment when possible and intriguing endlessly in order to regain some power (he even told the Scots that he would abandon the bishops), showed that if he lived to make trouble, the England which Milton wanted had little chance of birth and survival. But who could replace the king? Cromwell, now in full control of the army, was the only man who could control the country, take the enormous risk of the king's execution in January 1649, and defeat the Scots and the Irish. It is significant that the 59 signatures on the order for the king's death included George Herbert's stepfather: Milton was far from alone in thinking that the utterly discredited Charles needed to be removed. Some previous kings had been removed by being deposed and quietly murdered but now it was possible to take some pride in a formal trial and a public execution as dramas of justice.

Milton became 'Secretary for Foreign Tongues' to the revolutionary Council of State, listening to its varied views and after its decisions composing letters in Latin to be sent to other governments – which was no easy task, for almost everyone on the council knew nothing of foreign affairs and all other nations were hostile to the revolutionary regime. Scholars have studied the state papers which he drafted without being able to report that his influence was often decisive. Cromwell went to war against Catholic Spain but made a treaty with Catholic France. He protested against a massacre of Protestants in Italy (the subject of a powerfully angry sonnet by Milton) but got involved in a war against the Protestant Dutch inspired by commercial rivalry. Once again dreams of greatness as poet and prophet had been disappointed, but duty called. With the job went a salary and a house near Whitehall Palace, still the centre of power although under new management, but it would be excessively cynical to say that these were the main reasons why Milton accepted the invitation, for he could have lived off his recent legacy from his father and his income as a tutor to devote himself with fading eyesight to the fulfilment of his long plan to write great poetry.

A part of the arrangement was that he should support the government by his own writing. One pamphlet was a prelude to Cromwell's triumphantly brutal campaign against 'barbarians' in Ireland. More philosophically, a short book maintained that 'kings and magistrates' should have only limited 'tenure' of their positions, which rightly depended on the will of the people. He wrote during his own king's trial, but implied clearly enough that a tyrant had forfeited the throne which the people had leased to him. His main task was to argue against the denunciations of the unprecedented trial which were pouring from many Presbyterian ministers at the time; Anglicans were less of a problem because they had to use illegal print, not public speech. And a treatise in Latin defending the republican regime was commissioned and distributed abroad, in reply to an attack by a French scholar which voiced the outrage of Europe.

The most influential of his semi-official publications was, however, *Eikonoklastes* which appeared nine months after the king's execution. It was a reply to *Eikon Basilike*, a best-seller claimed to be the prayers and sacred thoughts of the royal martyr. Actually that book had been compiled by a clergyman, John Gauden, under the king's supervision, but Milton ignored rumours already circulating that it was no more than a forgery. This was a decision taken so that his fire might be concentrated on Charles himself. All the 'sanctified bitterness' with which he had attacked the living bishops was now directed at their dead master, with passion in making the point that the people were being lured into forgetting that the king had been a tyrant. His life had been disastrous for the nation, his prayers in prison had been stolen from the Bible or Philip Sidney's *Arcadia*, and his brave death had been a piece of play-acting – a masque like those performed in the Banqueting House, the background of the execution. It had been intended to deceive the 'image-doting rabble'.

Delighted that this poet and civil servant had fully recovered his energy in personal abuse directed at its enemies, the Council of State asked him to reply to a second critic of the king-killing regime. This was another French scholar, Pierre du Moulin, but Milton was wrongly informed that the true author was Alexander More, an Englishman who in fact only wrote the preface and supervised the printing. The immorality of More's life was not totally exaggerated in the onslaught now delivered.

Milton was proud of all this journalism, claiming in a poem that 'all Europe talks from side to side'. But the work had been done over most of a year, at an hour a time and at a terrible cost: his left eye was already useless and in the winter of 1651–52 his right one also failed. As spring came, unseen by him, his wife Mary died after giving birth to their third daughter and six weeks later their only son, John, also died. His immediate despair was expressed in a dictated sonnet published 21 years later:

> When I consider how my light is spent,
> Ere half my days, in this dark world and wide,
> And that one talent which is death to hide

Lodged in me useless, though my soul more bent
To serve therewith my Maker . . .

He fears that he will never write the poem of his dreams. But the angels of *Paradise Lost* are already beginning to fill his imagination, for he reflects that angels can obey God merely by standing to await his command:

His state
Is kingly: thousands at his bidding speed,
And post o'er land and ocean without rest;
They also serve who only stand and wait.

This does not suggest that he accepts inactivity for the rest of his life: it means that he waits for the divine command, which he is to hear as the order to begin *Paradise Lost.*

Inevitably his moods changed. For a time he could remain busy with public affairs since assistance was provided, and a light-hearted poem has survived in which he invites a former pupil to a 'cheerful hour' when they may 'drench' their cares. But inevitably also, he lost influence now that he could no longer see what was going on in minds behind faces. In May 1652 he wanted to urge Cromwell to veto the new republic's interference in the national Church being established; he could now denounce even non-Anglican ministers as 'wolves' if they depended financially on tithes collected from parishioners with the authority of the State. He could address Cromwell as 'our chief of men . . . guided by faith and matchless fortitude' but he argued not by face-to-face discussion but in a sonnet – and he argued in vain. Three years later he had to semi-retire from his secretaryship.

Blindness added to his sense that he was lost with a young family but without a wife. After four years of loneliness a wife was brought to him, Katherine Woodcock, for whom respect and love were increased by dependent gratitude. They had a daughter but she lived for scarcely more than a month longer than her mother, who was buried in February 1658. He saw the dead Kate only in a mourner's dream, and then not her face:

Methought I saw my late espoused saint
Brought to me . . .
Came vested all in white, pure as her mind.
Her face was veiled, yet to my fancied sight
Love, sweetness, goodness in her person shined
So clear as in no face with more delight.
But O as to embrace me she inclined,
I waked, she fled, and day brought back my night.

A public tragedy followed. He had supported Cromwell against successive Parliaments, and had even accepted the semi-royal status assumed as Lord Protector at the end of 1653, and had not protested against the intolerance needed to counteract the continuing loyalty to the exiled Charles II, but after May 1654 he produced no more public defences. When Oliver died in September 1658 he paid no public tribute, and he did not admire the son and heir (Richard) although he did some work for him until May 1659.

The regime collapsed by stages. The Long Parliament elected in 1640, or what was left of it, was reassembled but power lay in the army, whose leading general, George Monk, had a dukedom in mind. The restoration of Charles II to the throne of his ancestors in May 1660 became inevitable. Yet in March 1660 'J.M.' took the opportunity to follow up a series of pamphlets with a manifesto entitled *The Ready and Easy Way to Establish a Free Commonwealth*, with an enlarged edition in April. He urged that the army should be subordinated to a senate, a 'Grand Council', elected for life by men both propertied and virtuous. In each county the gentry should be responsible for law and order and should control the voluntary militia. There should be no political interference in church life and of course no king would be needed. The proposal was wildly unrealistic at the time (for example, the separation of Church and State seemed inconceivable until the first amendment to the constitution of the USA) and in his heart Milton, who was no fool, may well have known this – but he still wanted to state the ideal called by him the 'good old cause'. And he was prophetic in a sense, for within thirty years the Stuart monarchy was to be replaced by one which Parliament chose. And what he wrote proved that he was a very brave man.

Had he kept silent, or signalled a willingness to accept the king's return, or emigrated to New England, history would probably have forgiven him, for he had attacked the memory of the king's 'martyred' father more publicly than anyone else and he knew how horrific was the punishment traditionally inflicted on traitors. But he was not a traitor to his own ideals despite some compromises thought necessary. It seems to have been in 1659–60 that he wrote a tribute to an imaginary angel, Abdiel, which we may apply to the poet himself, blind, bereaved and probably doomed:

> Among the faithless, faithful only he;
> Among the innumerable false, unmoved;
> Unshaken, unseduced, unterrified,
> His loyalty he kept, his love, his zeal;
> Nor number nor example with him wrought
> To swerve from truth, or change his constant mind,
> Though single.

The defeat of the republic by what he regarded as the forces of evil, and the hope that the defeat could be reversed if the good could be heroic, suggested a subject to which he could dedicate his whole heart and mind; as we have seen, previously his poetry had been largely about himself. And as he turned to this task his blindness saved him. He had thought that it would make him useless but it was what enabled him to be a great poet, who was to be placed next to Chaucer and Shakespeare in English literature's gold-and-marble House of Fame. In the late 1650s it meant that he was not exhausted by writing propaganda for Cromwell's doomed commonwealth: instead, he spent most of his time at home and it seems that most of *Paradise Lost* was dictated during this period, around his fiftieth birthday. In the 1660s it meant that he was not subjected to the usual fate of traitors (being hanged but soon cut down so that he might see the beginning of the butchering of his body). Friends could argue that God had already punished him by blinding him and the men now in power could see that the public hanging of a blind scholar might not be popular, but we know that many people were astonished that he survived.

He did not entirely escape. He feared that he would be lynched by the mob that celebrated the king's return, or assassinated if he left the house. He was imprisoned for two months, which must have been terrifying for a man physically dependent on others. He lost most of his savings. He knew that if he fell foul of the censor the deadly case against him could be revived. But it is striking that he was spared when many of those who had sentenced the royal martyr were executed in their turn or, if dead, brought out of their graves for conspicuous humiliation. And Milton was not finally silenced.

Paradise Lost is an extraordinary poem. Undertaken when its author had lost almost everything which most authors think essential, it is not only a demonstration of the power to rise above tragedy and make out of it whatever is still available for a life of great courage, dignity and usefulness. It is a flight of the imagination, taken not merely to escape from the censorship which would have grounded any explicit republicanism: it is fuelled by Milton's own brand of theology, which would also have been censored had it been stated plainly. It is staggeringly ambitious: it imagines conditions before the creation of the world, it journeys without faltering through space (a 'vast infinitude'), it alludes to much of history, it invites readers to be intimate with God. Its height and breadth are very much larger than anything achieved by the Elizabethan poets whom he admired. Philip Sidney had envisaged a glorious future for English 'poesy' in a tradition looking back to Chaucer, and had written about an unsuccessful courtship in the language of high romance, but had died a soldier's death at the age of 31 before any of his work had been printed. When he had been at leisure during a long stay with his sister in Wilton House in 1580, he had used the time to write a novel, *Arcadia*, with a plot as complicated as any of Shakespeare's comedies and with no more than a scattering of poems in the prose. Edmund Spenser had lived to edit *Arcadia* by adding more morality, and to write *The Faerie Queene* as his massive answer to Sidney's plea for poetic magnificence which would delight and instruct. For him that meant more than mere flattery of his queen, although there was plenty of that. It meant taking seriously the ideals both of chivalry and of Protestantism, and combining them in a narrative so full of allegories that no one has ever been able to decode them all.

Now Milton was determined to praise God and not a mortal, and to use the Bible not the conventions of romance, comedy or chivalry, and to write in the blank verse of Shakespeare's plays instead of in the convention that poetry must rhyme. Both Sidney and Spenser had escaped from the often sordid realities of Elizabethan politics – in Sidney's case from the queen's half-hearted and half-financed involvement in the Protestants' resistance to Spain in mainland Europe (the half-crusade which cost him his life), in Spenser's case from his employment as a civil servant working for the colonial regime in rebellious Catholic Ireland. They had escaped into richly fanciful dreams of a golden past. Now Milton, too, would escape from public and private griefs, but his escape would be into the Bible. The Scriptures meant far more to him that did all the literature on which Sidney and Spenser drew, and they were in this period familiar territory for the English whom he wished to address. He would interpret the biblical story in a way which was not orthodox but would do no more than hint at his heresies. This strategy would leave the censor and most of his readers undisturbed, but the discerning – 'fit though few' he expected – would hear what he wanted to say and would take it to heart. Making them think about God was a good alternative to the epic about King Arthur, previously envisaged as the fulfilment of his long hope and work in the ambition to become a great poet.

So that *Paradise Lost* may get close to being music, he often concentrates on the sound rather than the sense. He arranges the words in an order which, although somewhat like Latin, is in English harder to grasp than the subject-verb-object pattern which Francis Bacon had recommended as a part of no-nonsense modernity. And so that the poem may be sublime without being artificial, he avoids that rhyming which can sometimes make even George Herbert sound like a literary workman: he took a special pride in this, claiming that it was 'ancient liberty recovered' from 'the modern bondage of rhyming'. In the 1920s T. S. Eliot led a fashion which preferred Donne to Milton, claiming that when Donne handled someone or something it was as if he was smelling a rose. But *Milton's Grand Style* was the title of a defence by Christopher Ricks in 1963 and readers agreeing that this style did what this poet wanted it to do have included a more reflective Eliot. Here is the only poet of a stature near Shakespeare's, and he is not to be matched until, almost a hundred years after his death, William Wordsworth is born.

Essentially he writes about ideas, but these are always personified and dramatised. There is a great deal of activity in eternity, God himself takes part in the conversations, and angels have much in common with Adam and Eve. And frequently the story is unexpected. The title suggests that Paradise will be eternal and perfect peace until it is lost through some sin which is obviously appalling, and that the punishment which follows will be hellish. But none of these expectations will be fulfilled. In eternity there is a colossal war. The human activity which is related at length takes place in the Paradise on earth. Although Adam and Eve do fall their sin is of a kind which many readers will not think wrong, and the poet's attention is given as much to the relationship between them as to to their relationship with God. Although they are punished, they are also rescued and encouraged: it seems that after all God loves them. And the description of the life of devils in hell at the beginning of the poem arouses both amusement and the question whether Satan is not more admirable than God. Satan is at first said to be chained in torments, but we soon see him seated on a throne and lifting the spirits of other devils. Then we see him on a voyage through space to Earth, and in *Paradise Regained* we shall meet him as the ruler of the world who gives unwanted advice to Jesus. So *Paradise Lost* is surprisingly original and complex – yet its purpose could be stated with a simplicity not always matched in Miltonian scholarship:

> I may assert Eternal Providence,
> And justify the ways of God to men.

In a paraphrase of Psalm 136 'done by the author at fifteen years old' (as he had boasted in 1646), he had seen no such need to defend God:

> Let us with a gladsome mind
> Praise the Lord, for he is kind;
> For his mercies aye endure,
> Ever faithful, ever sure . . .
>
> Who by his all-commanding might
> Did fill the new-made world with light . . .

And it seems that Milton never seriously doubted God's existence. In *De*

Doctrina he writes that 'in every nation it is believed that either God or some supreme evil power . . . presides over the affairs of men', and despite all the tragedies which he knows about he cannot believe in that alternative to God. Instead he believes that God is One, infinite, eternal, never changing, never corrupted, present everywhere, omnipotent, completely free, all-knowing, supremely pure, holy, just, faithful and 'kind'. All these adjectives traditionally applied to God are echoed here.

But his experience of human failure and suffering had made him think, more deeply than Edward Herbert ever did, that the 'ways of God' needed to be defended, and his most important move was to say that God's 'omnipotence' does not mean that he is 'all-commanding' in the sense of exercising a direct control over every event. One reason for this departure from what was then orthodoxy had been given to him by the experience of blindness. He could not believe that this had been inflicted by God as a punishment for sin: on the contrary, it had been caused by his zeal as a writer in what he was convinced was God's cause. God had allowed him to go blind, but that was all. He tells us so in a sonnet ('Cyriack') written at the turn of 1653–54:

> I argue not
> Against Heav'n's hand or will, nor bate a jot
> Of heart or hope, but still bear up and steer
> Right onward. What supports me, dost thou ask?
> The conscience, friend, to have lost them overplied
> In liberty's defence, my noble task.

At about this time he begins *Paradise Lost*, knowing that ahead of him lie 'things unattempted yet in prose or rhyme', about the origin of 'all our woe' in humankind's general refusal to live as God wills – to live in 'Paradise' which represents what God wants for humanity. The need which he does admit is for more spiritual sight while physically he cannot see anything at all. He is sorry for himself as a blind man but as a poet he knows at last the gift of vision:

> Hail, holy Light . . .
> Thee I revisit safe,
> And feel thy sovran vital lamp; but thou
> Revist'st not these eyes, that roll in vain
> To find thy piercing ray, and find no dawn . . .
> Seasons return; but not to me returns
> Day, or the sweet approach of ev'n or morn,
> Or sight of vernal bloom, or summer's rose,
> Or flocks, or herds, or human face divine;
> But cloud instead . . .

After 1660 he wrote another, even sadder prayer:

> On evil days though fall'n, and evil tongues;
> In darkness, and with dangers compassed round,
> And solitude; yet not alone, while thou
> Visit'st my slumbers nightly, or when morn
> Purples the east. Still govern thou my song,
> Urania, and fit audience find, though few.

But his grief is also for his country. He makes a coded reference to Charles I when he says that the 'game' of Nimrod (Genesis 10:9) is 'hunting men' although God never intended any lordship of 'man over men'. And he has the ultimate failure of the rebellion against that king in his bitter memory when he says that allowing 'tyranny' to prosper is God's just judgement on rebels who do not know what 'rational liberty' is. So Charles II is brought back and

> All now is turned to jollity and game,
> To luxury and riot, feast and dance,
> Marrying or prostituting, as befell,
> Rape or adultery . . .

From early days *Paradise Lost* has been interpreted as a lament for the loss of the English Paradise which in the 1640s had seemed within the grasp of idealists and the classic exposition of this theme is now Christopher Hill's *Milton and the English Revolution* (1977). But it has proved possible to move from this generally correct interpretation to the mistaken suggestion that because Satan led the rebellion of the fallen angels against 'the throne and monarchy of God' readers are entitled, even intended, to be on his side. Some highly distinguished readers have taken that side. Among the great poets Blake concluded that Milton himself was 'of the Devil's party without knowing it', while Shelley thought that morally his Satan was 'far superior' to his God. Long after Blake and Shelley, modern or postmodern critics have welcomed Milton the rebel, with his rebellion as his most attractive feature. So it seems necessary to remind ourselves that Milton is convinced that he is on God's side, a position which involves treating Satan as 'the Enemy', which is the meaning of *satan* in Hebrew. His whole life shows that his instinct was to defend the authorities which he believed could be defended rationally – he was no Shelley – and *De Doctrina*, with which Blake did not reckon, presents the God he thought defensible.

Some confusion is understandable because Milton had his own views about God and was associated with a rebellion against a king; so why not guess that he was at heart a rebel against a God who could be pictured as the King of Kings? But when it is taken as a whole, *Paradise Lost* refutes the idea that its author admires Satan: that is as far-fetched as would be any suggestion that he is a fan of King Charles. If his account of the war in heaven is influenced by memories of the English civil war – as it is – there is much in it to connect the devils of his soaring imagination with the royalists of his recent experience. The good angels who triumphantly defend the rights of God are not unlike the good Englishmen who fight, also triumphantly, to defend the rights of the people as represented (more or less) in Parliament, and King Charles is the real rebel, presented in Milton's journalistic prose as a satanic figure.

Certainly Milton can state the arguments which are used on Satan's side to encourage the rebels against God. 'Awake, arise, or be for ever fall'n!' After such eloquence, 'out flew millions of flaming swords, drawn from the thighs of mighty cherubim'. They manage to invade heaven and a titanic struggle is needed before they are defeated. Satan weeps in sympathy but he asks

What though the field be lost?
All is not lost; the unconquerable will,
And study of revenge, immortal hate,
And courage never to submit or yield

will, he promises, finally prevail, even though he is now speaking in a lake of fire amid 'torture without end'.

Milton also shows some sympathy with Adam as he protests in a rebellious prayer after his own disaster. He makes him say

Did I request thee, Maker, from my clay
To mould me man, did I solicit thee
From darkness to promote me . . .?

Like Hamlet Adam wants to die:

How gladly would I meet
Mortality, my sentence, and be earth
Insensible, how glad would lay me down
As in my mother's lap!

But like Hamlet he fears that his hostile Maker will be 'satisfied never', 'both death and I am found eternal', and he will be sentenced to 'endless misery'. And like Satan he weeps over those who will be condemned with him, asking

Why should all mankind
For one man's fault thus guiltless be condemned?

So Adam is utterly confused about whether or not 'the ways of God' are either loving or just:

> O Conscience, into what abyss of fears
> And horrors hast thou driv'n me; out of which
> I find no way, from deep to deeper plunged!

Such questioning of God's goodness is as powerful as any protest in William Blake's attack on the 'Not Human' in Milton's theology, or in William Empson's modern classic of morally indignant atheism, *Milton's God* (1961).

Plainly there is a bit of Satan, and a lot of Adam, in Milton, who rejects much 'orthodox' teaching about God. But before we ask whether his defence of God is sound, it is important to find out from the text what his intention was. His literary strategy was first seen clearly by Stanley Fish in *Surprised by Sin* (1967), a book which has been criticised as not doing justice to the eloquence of Milton's sympathy with Satan and with Adam and Eve. But Fish has been defended by pointing out that the Miltonic strategy is to make his characters, good or bad, intelligible by making them seem to be like us. Thus God can sound both boastful and defensive, Satan can sound like a democratic politician, Adam can look like a rather weak husband who will do anything for his wife and Eve like a loving wife who wants some time to be on her own and to take care of herself. But all the time, to Milton God is God, Satan is evil and Adam and Eve are potential or actual sinners. As he presents them to us, his belief is what he advocates in *Areopagitica*: Truth is to be reached through debate, but there is such a thing as Truth.

Thus Satan is allowed to argue against God and to think aloud in five speeches to himself, and Adam and Eve are positively encouraged to say what is in their hearts and minds, but God also holds forth. This is because Milton wants God to be vindicated after all the arguments that can be thrown at him. He tells us that when he makes his great speech of defiance against God Satan is not being honest with his audience, for he is really in 'deep despair'. He also tells us that Satan's despair is about the defeat of evil, for

> To do aught good will never be our task,
> But ever to do ill our sole delight.

And he tells us that Adam, so far from being on the right side in his argument with God, is a very insecure man. After confessing that he is in a miserable muddle, he immediately proceeds to pick a quarrel with his wife whom in fact he adores. In contrast, when we are allowed to overhear God's private conversation with his Son we find that both are being both calm and good. God explains his intentions about humankind: in them 'mercy first and last shall shine'. It is clear that Milton believes that the Son is then correct in assuring the Father that all his judgements are 'only right'.

Any readers who feel that Milton's heart is with 'the Devil's party' should inspect the second tier of that party's leadership. The devils who are the first to join the 'great emperor's call' to be positive in defeat are headed by Moloch, 'horrid king besmeared by blood'. Mammon has a more comical character: in heaven he was always stooping to admire the pavements made of gold, and when exiled to hell he teaches the other fallen angels to dig for gold. In the palace called Pandemonium 'the great Seraphic Lords and Cherubim' sit like the House of Lords in Westminster and as a 'conclave' like the cardinals in Rome. For Milton those are two insults and his report of the devils' debate suggests that he has laughed silently during the meetings of the Council of State under Cromwell. First Satan announces that 'none sure will claim in hell precedence', so he will preside. Then Moloch urges 'open war' against 'the Torturer': the going ought to be easy, but if they die that will end their present problems. Then Belial smoothly urges caution, for the present situation is not so bad as Moloch has claimed and it may improve if they remain inactive. Mammon wants their greatness to be 'conspicuous' but the economy is what matters and 'magnificence' can be achieved by developing more goldmines in hell. Then Beelzebub advises them to invade Earth: that would be easier than the conquest of heaven and more profitable than staying in hell. Everyone votes for the brilliant idea and Satan, who has no doubt put Beelzebub up to it, announces that it suits the dignity of his throne for him to volunteer in a one-devil expedition without asking anyone to share his mission's profits.

The other devils are left to wait for his return. Some play theological games about

providence, foreknowledge, will and fate,
Fixed fate, free will, foreknowledge absolute . . .

– time-wasting debates which have 'no end'. Others become tourists around hell, discovering only that it is 'a universe of death'. And at the start of his voyage to Earth, Satan meets hell's gatekeepers, Sin and Death. Sin was born out of his head but Satan raped her and she became the mother of Death. This is not a party which Milton hopes his readers will join.

On the contrary, we have been invited to take sides in a three-day war in which Satan's army is defeated. God/Parliament claims that Satan/Charles has provoked the war. A righteous cause is defended by the discipline of the good angels in heaven – and in England by an army of soldiers who fight for liberty but not for equality, and who in their own ordered ranks are

> Equally free, for orders and degrees
> Jar not with liberty, but well consist.

The devils win the first fights under 'their king', but God/Parliament keeps its nerve and musters 'armed saints' against 'that godless crew'. The devils fight on but the divine/Parliamentary army develops a new discipline under new generals; at his Father's command the Son of God grasps 'ten thousand thunders' in his 'fierce chariot' and drives his enemies into hell. But it must be admitted that Milton could not resist attributing to the devils the dramatic first large-scale use of artillery to destroy castles, when to be accurate any blame should rest on the Parliamentary troops, who believed that their guns fired thunder and lightning from God.

Satan's flight from hell takes him to the Paradise of Fools. In this connection Milton makes crude fun of the theological speculation that souls neither baptised nor guilty (infants for example) end up in 'limbo': he suggests that it is a suitable receptacle in eternity for friars and hermits among other 'fools' whose minds are feeble. More interesting nowadays is Satan's earlier visit to Chaos, a region where 'chance governs all', because Milton's report comes quite close to modern science – unintentionally of course: in *De Doctrina* he writes that the universe was 'created in six days for a few thousand years'. Science now teaches that the universe emerged out of particles which behave unpredictably when smaller than atoms.

When he accounts for the strength of human evil in human history he sees that the freedom which produces chaos in that mysterious region of the universe also produces sin on Earth. His explanation is that the first man is essentially good but is free to choose to be bad. About this God is firm:

> I made him just and right,
> Sufficient to have stood, though free to fall.

God explicitly disagrees with strict Calvinism, for he denies that people have sinned because 'divine predestination overruled their will'. Because he expected them to sin, that does not mean that he commanded them to do so. On the contrary,

> If I foreknew,
> Foreknowledge had no influence on their fault.

And the widespread collapse of strict Calvinism, even among Christians who honour Calvin as a great reformer, has supported the wisdom of

Milton's God. For it to be possible to believe that God is good, it seems essential to believe first that he does *not* foresee the future exactly, for the future will include much which almost everyone will judge to be evil. The evil must result not from what he can predict with certainty but from what he has decided to allow but not to control – which seems to be a lot. In nature and in history many things appear to happen by chance or coincidence and in our own experience decisions are made by humans with free will. Milton's God stresses that his 'high decree unchangeable, eternal' has commanded not people's fates but 'their freedom'. And when they use their freedom wrongly, that is not the end of the story.

To some sinners will be offered 'peculiar grace' but (as Arminius argued against Calvin) all without exception will be invited to 'pray, repent and bring obedience due'. The invitation will be offered by God through 'my umpire, Conscience', planted in everyone. And this response to the misuse of freedom is, in Milton's view, what makes the Son right to say that God's intentions are indeed merciful. Against William Empson's charge that Milton's God is 'wicked', Daniel Danielson's defence of *Milton's Good God* (1982) could argue that sentence should not be passed until all the evidence in the poem has been examined. And *De Doctrina* is also important, for there Milton was less orthodox than he was in his censored poem. The poem may be open to the charge that God's way of showing mercy is itself 'wicked', but we can now know what Milton really thought.

An objection can of course remain even when God has explained that the misuse of human freedom will always be met by the offer of 'grace', for God goes on to say to his Son that justice as well as mercy must be in his character if what Conscience tells humans is to be true about the creator of Conscience. Therefore if Adam 'disobeys' and thus rejects the life which God wills for him, 'die he or justice must' – which have been quoted as monstrously evil words. But even then, the Son of God is very quick to offer to die as the substitute for all who deserve to die eternally: 'on me let thy anger fall'. And God is very quick to tell the Son that this one death will satisfy his justice, provided only that sinners humbly repent:

> thy merit
> Imparted shall absolve men who renounce
> Their own both righteous and unrighteous deeds.

In Milton's time (as in our own) many millions of Christians would have placed that interpretation of the cross at or very near the centre of their faith (as George Herbert did) although many would have wished to add that Christ's merits are not only 'imputed': they are also 'imparted', transforming sinners. But *De Doctrina* makes it clear that Milton did not really believe that Christ had to satisfy the Father's wrath. The centre of his faith was Christ's heroism in his life: God's justice is satisfied, he believed, whenever anyone imitates that example. And he was not dogmatic about the nature of hell as a consequence of any rejection of God. In *De Doctrina* he lists the biblical texts but sees that they should not all be understood literally and his own understanding does not solve the mystery. The guilty must be punished somehow if they do not repent, yet human lives which come out of God cannot be finally extinguished. Logically it is possible that they will be punished for ever, yet God always wants what comes out of him to have a good end, and therefore it seems more likely that anyone who finally wants to be saved will be. Milton never wrote a serious poem either about the cross or about hell, but his clear belief in *De Doctrina* is that 'God hates nothing he has made and has omitted nothing which might provide salvation for everyone.'

His poem also says something about what he thinks the Son of God is although he still keeps an eye on the censor. The Son is 'throned in the highest bliss, equal to God' and the announcement to that effect causes Satan's rebellion, for that bad angel hates being inferior to God, let alone to God's Son. Milton is willing to use the traditional words about the Son being 'only begotten'. The Son alone is, says God, 'my Word, my wisdom'; he alone is commissioned both to create and to judge everything and everyone on Earth; and in addition he is called Son of God 'by merit more than birthright' because he is willing to quit all this dignity in order 'to save a world from utter loss'. No touch which can be called heretical comes until the angels sing in praise of the Son. They are traditionally orthodox when they affirm that in the Son's face the glory of 'th' Almighty shines', for that is a quotation from 2 Corinthians 4:6. But they drop a brick when they go on to sing that he is 'of all creation first', for when Christology was defined more precisely by the Church in the fourth century it was eventually agreed that the Son was 'begotten' not 'created'. Thus the meaning of 2 Corinthians 1:5 was not that the Son was created first but that he has the primacy over all creation.

In *De Doctrina* 'God imparted to the Son as much of the divine nature as he wished.' Although 'the Son existed in the beginning' and 'all other things, both in heaven and earth, were made through him', yet he himself was 'the first of the created things'. This is said to be necessary in logic. A God who does not exist necessarily, who did not beget but is begotten, who is not the first cause of everything but is the effect of that cause, is therefore not the supreme God. But it is also stated that like the rest of creation the Son was created 'out of God'. Even what is material can come 'out of God': 'there must be some bodily power in God's substance, for no one can give what he does not have'. So the creation of a spiritual being such as the Son 'out of God' does not face any difficulty at all. Nor is there any difficulty which Milton can see in God's decision to give his created Son a unique honour, which makes it right for angels and Christians to worship him.

Milton has been criticised for obscurity when writing about such matters for the public but the denial of the traditional doctrine of the Trinity was a crime throughout his lifetime: it was to be excluded from the Toleration Act of 1689 and threatened with hanging in the Blasphemy Act of 1698. And in the seventh book of *Paradise Lost* the angel Raphael attempts to explain these mysteries in terms which the censor will pass. The Almighty is represented as saying about 'the deep' which exists before the creation of heaven and the universe:

> Boundless the deep, because I am who fill
> Infinitude, nor vacuous the space.
> Though I uncircumscribed myself retire
> And put not forth my goodness, which is free
> To act or not, necessity and chance
> Approach not me, and what I will is fate.

These difficult words – we may pity the censor – may be simplified as saying that God is infinite but has a capacity to 'put forth' his goodness by deciding to create. In the poem, however, it is not made absolutely clear that God created first the Son and then through the Son's workmanship the rest of creation. God never clearly tells the angels that the Son created them and only in the fifth book does Raphael tell Adam that Abdiel told Satan that it was by his Word that 'the mighty Father created all things, e'en thee'. Hostile critics of *Paradise Lost* have therefore been able to claim that, had it been fully explained to the bad angels who the Son has been from the beginning, they would not have rebelled when told that he is to be their king.

It must be left to readers to decide whether Milton's thoughts are acceptable. Only a few other thoughts may be submitted here, briefly.

One is that Milton never seems to have experienced in his depths the sense of being distressed and 'saved' which we find in George Herbert's poetry. There seems to have been no great emotional crisis in his life apart from his blindness, to which he soon rose heroically: like Herbert he came from a devout home but his own decision not to be a priest was comparatively calm because always his highest vocation was to be a poet. As a result, he had no profound understanding of the experiences which have made so many Christians in so many centuries want to affirm the full divinity of the action which has come to their rescue in a time of great weakness and confusion.

Nor does he seem to have had deeply the experience which accounts for the Holy Spirit being called a 'person' in the Trinity – the distinctively Christian experience of the power given by the Spirit within the fellowship which can be called the Body of Christ. In *Paradise Lost* the Spirit is far from prominence. In *De Doctrina* the Spirit means God at work in the world. When Milton says that the Spirit is a person, he stresses inferiority both to the Father and to the Son: if the Son is a servant, the Spirit is a messenger. He can never say that the Spirit at work in the Church is a vital part of what 'saves'. Inspiration is given to the individual.

From boyhood he has had a strong sense of the presence and power of God as benevolent Creator and demanding 'Task-Master'. This 'natural' religion is voiced in the evening prayer raised by Adam and Eve before they enjoy the 'crown of all our bliss', the 'rites mysterious of connubial love' – and it is made even more eloquent in the morning prayer which they offer after Eve's disturbing dream that night. Needing to recover 'firm peace', the two think about the angels praising 'him first, him last, him midst, and without end'. They seem to hear the whole creation praising 'the world's great Author':

> Hail, universal Lord, be bounteous still
> To give us only good.

But it is less clear how Christ comes into this picture. Milton tells us that the Son created the universe as God's agent, but not that the arrival of God embodied in the Son is needed to make the universe seem God's good gift despite what is utterly daunting in it and what seems pointless or positively cruel. When God's ways are 'justified', the argument is that originally things were perfect, that humans spoiled things, and that God sent his Son to the rescue. But in the prologue to John's gospel 'the Word' is nothing less than God, the ultimate Reality, and all things in the universe, without exception, came into being through the Word. The Word, also and more often called the Son, is God's self-expression, and Jesus is that fully divine word made flesh, made understandable. This alone enables believers to see the Creator's 'grace' which is the 'truth' about the creation – and if they see this, they have the one light which is not overcome by the world's darkness.

There remain modern objections to Milton's stories about angels and about Adam and Eve. It may be granted that the characters of God and of the Son of God in *Paradise Lost* are not so objectionable as they may seem to be at first sight – but it can still be asked: need a modern reader take these tales seriously?

When Raphael is sent to warn Adam and Eve about the interest which

Satan is taking in them, Eve lays on a vegetarian feast with non-alcoholic wine and is assured that this guest loves good food. He does not appear to notice that his hostess is naked ('undecked, save with herself') but when she has withdrawn after the meal he talks at leisure with Adam and what he says takes up most of four books of the poem, so that his hostess is not to be blamed. One of his teachings agrees with modern science, since he explains that there is no gap between the delicious food and the rest of creation:

> one first matter all,
> Endued with various forms, various degrees
> Of substance, and in things that live, of life;
> But more refined, more spiritous, and pure . . .

But he adds a promise that by eating the right food Adam and Eve may themselves become more spiritous:

> Time may come when men
> With angels may participate, and find
> No inconvenient diet, nor too light fare;
> And from these corporal nutriments perhaps
> Your bodies may at last turn all to spirit . . .

He also adds that if they do 'ascend to God' by such steps, humans will not find that they have lost their free wills, for (despite what orthodox theologians teach) angels too perform only 'voluntary service': 'freely we serve, because we freely love.' What is true about angels can be true about humans. Nor will people be timeless in heaven: 'we have also our ev'ning and our morn.' Nor will they be sexless, since 'without love no happiness' and 'whatever pure thou in the body enjoy'st . . . we enjoy in eminence'. In *De Doctrina* there is of course no equivalent to that promise about eternal sex although the rewards in heaven will include 'all those creatures which may be useful or delightful'.

Raphael's parting advice is sensible and highly congenial: 'Be strong, live happy and love.' Although 'first of all' they must love God, 'whom to love is to obey', that too will be a delight. Yet when Raphael's back is turned, a modern reader is likely to ask: 'what in all this can I believe?'

The modern answer is that the whole conversation has taken place in Milton's imagination, which is also true about the war and the debate in eternity, and about the talk between God and his Son. And in much of *De Doctrina* Milton seems prepared to agree with that deflating answer, for the theological book is in a severely plain style with little mention of, for example, angels. But in Greek *angeloi* means 'messengers' and all the flights of the human imagination take off from a simple faith: the Eternal needs powerful messengers because evil may also be in the air around vulnerable humans. It may be most helpful to think of devils as personifications of whatever causes evil while good angels are personifications whatever spreads goodness. At least that would give us permission to enjoy the fertility of Milton's seventeenth-century imagination, telling us about eternity 'as earthly notion can conceive'.

He allowed his imagination to work on the Bible very freely. He imagined Satan after reading the first two chapters of the Book of Job; the war in heaven after reading that 'Michael and his angels fought against the dragon' (Revelation 12:7); the devil's fall from heaven after reading a prophecy about the fall of Babylon (Isaiah 14:12). But in the Bible none of these passages refers to the beginning of history.

In the best texts of the Old Testament Adam appears only near the beginning of Genesis and is mentioned as a name at the beginning of Chronicles. He is not mentioned in the teaching of Jesus. Paul refers to him as the first man, who brought death into the world, and 1 Timothy adds that he was not 'deceived': Eve was. There is also a glance in the Letter of Jude. But that scanty material needs a lot of imagination before *Paradise Lost* can be written.

The Hebrew creation myth preserved in Genesis 1:26 merely says that God created human images of himself, male and female but with no name. Here plants have flourished since the third day of creation, although Genesis 2 pictures the making of Adam out of dust since the ground is dry: there has never been rain and therefore no plant has grown. So Genesis itself does not tell one story, for here too human imaginations have been at work although neither story imagines any angelic activity until a guard is needed to prevent a return to Paradise. The Bible is a good precedent for the vigorous use of the imagination in religion, to adorn what is believed to be Truth.

Milton's own imagination gives us, in its own style, his mature reflections after a lifetime of preparation, activity and defeat. He has experienced events which can be symbolised in Satan's arrival in Paradise saying 'myself am hell'. But he has also found that people need not be destroyed by evil, for they are well equipped to 'be strong, live happy and love'. When Adam and Eve are first seen by Satan (and this is our own first sight of them), they are 'God-like erect' in 'their naked majesty' and Satan so admires then that he 'could love' them if he could love anyone. Moreover, Milton does not hesitate to disagree with the great St Augustine by saying that their feelings for each other are sexual. Eve remembers when she first awoke, first falling in love with her own reflection in water, but then seeing the far more exciting Adam.

Her husband has his own memory of how he called when she nervously ran away. So we are told that despite his sorrows Milton has learned what for many years he did not know: that marriage is 'heav'n's last best gift' which God 'declares pure, and commands to some, leaves free to all'.

But when Satan stays, spying on them, he overhears Adam reminding Eve that among all their happiness they must respect a single prohibition: they must never eat the fruit grown on the Tree of Knowledge which stands next to the Tree of Life. If they do eat that, 'God hath pronounced it death.' When he has learned of this, Satan silently asks a question which many will wish to repeat: what is wrong with knowledge? Later he will ask Eve what can be wrong with eating the fruit which has made him, now a lowly snake, able to speak – and Eve will answer by eating. Many readers have had great sympathy with her, for they dislike, despise and even hate authoritarian religion – in particular religion which oppresses women – as the enemy of knowledge. And Milton himself seems uneasy as he tells this tale, for he has been an enthusiastic spreader of knowledge. As a poet he likes flights of imagination but for about half a century he has worked to acquire knowledge. When Eve has a nightmare that she will eat the forbidden fruit, during the night before she does he makes Adam tell her to trust in 'reason' and not to worry about 'imaginations, airy shapes'. Milton seems to sense that the whole story about the trees is unreasonable, for in *De Doctrina*, a prosaic plea for reasonableness, he feels compelled to offer a rational explanation of the myth. But this makes matters worse, for he interprets God's command about the Tree as the prohibition of something 'which was in itself neither good nor bad'; it was simply a test of obedience. That makes his God behave like a tyrant who cannot give a reason as he demands blind obedience.

Modern biblical scholarship has, however, provided an explanation which may seem reasonable. The myth about the Tree of Knowledge seems to have originated in a not uncommon folk tale about the gods not wanting humans to know too much – as the myth about the Tree of Life may have been derived from a tale about the gods not wanting humans to live too long. But such myths are now best placed in the context of the whole Bible, which often celebrates both knowledge and life. (Adam, Eve and their descendants knew how to use their hands and brains to good effect, and the man said to have brought death into the world is also said to have lived for 930 years.) And when taken as a whole, the Bible suggests an explanation of the myths which a reader who is repelled or baffled by this feature in *Paradise Lost* may find more convincing. The message is that humans court disaster if they 'know', in the sense of deciding without reference to anyone else, the difference between right and wrong. The disaster comes not because of an arbitrary edict by a tyrant but because what is called 'wrong' is in the end found to be truly evil because anti-life.

It is of course understandable that many modern readers of Milton should think that he is anti-life because anti-women, so in preparation for the great drama of the Fall, for which Eve bears the chief responsibility, we may take a quick look at the evidence.

When Raphael arrives with a warning about Satan's diabolical plan, Eve retires after the meal, to tend her fruits and flowers rather than doze during the lengthy and 'studious thoughts' of angel and husband. In her absence Adam wants to satisfy his curiosity by asking questions about the universe but Raphael advises him to 'think only what concerns thyself and thy being'. This encourages a down-to-earth discussion about 'that which lies before us in daily life' and in particular about Adam's relationship with Eve, on which much will soon turn. Raphael reports God's views on marriage which coincide with Milton's and are not crudely masculinist. The angel urges the husband never to forget Eve's sensitivity since 'oftentimes nothing profits more than self-esteem' and she needs and deserves to be affirmed. Adam agrees and declares that what delights him most is not her body but

> Those thousand decencies that daily flow
> From all her words and actions . . .

That can refer to Milton's second wife, as his heartbroken sonnet after her death suggests. But it is also a tribute to Elizabeth Minshull, a woman half Milton's age as his first wife had been. He married her in 1663 on the recommendation of his doctor. John Aubrey knew her as someone who was gentle, peaceful and agreeable and she seems to have coped with a blind old man who suffered acutely from gout and was not always heroic. The only problem which is known about their marriage of eleven years arose from the fact that Milton already had three daughters not much younger than her and motherless since 1652. They found it impossible to accept her authority as she reorganised the household and they felt distanced even further from their father, who must often have been sad, remote or demanding although he was genial enough when visitors called. So these daughters must be at the centre of any discussion of Milton's attitude to women in daily life.

Immediately it must be admitted that he did not handle them as well as he handled the boys who were his pupils, and that when his brother Christopher came to see him shortly before his death he grumbled about them. He told Christopher, who was a lawyer, that what he intended to leave to them in his will was nothing more than the money promised by their grandfather as a dowry for their mother and never paid. Fortunately his plan was overturned when taken to court in the absence of a written will. Milton can perhaps be defended up to a point. He had little money to leave to his widow, who had many years ahead of her; he had been paid only ten pounds for the two editions of *Paradise Lost.* He may have had a serious hope that those children of the Mary Phillips he had married would be able to extract a thousand pounds as a fulfilment of that contract on marriage, because currently the senior Phillips was much better off than he was. But other evidence points to a sad lack of understanding between Milton and his daughters.

According to his brother he complained that they had been 'unkind', but one hopes that this was never said to the oldest, Anne, who was handicapped physically and, it seems, mentally as well. She could not write and may have been unable to read. When no one else was available Mary and Deborah had to read to their father books in a variety of languages which they could not understand but had to pronounce properly. They also had to be his hands when he could not see to write and his eyes when he could not see to revise. They resented this work and the family's poverty, and sold some of the books without their father's knowledge. A maid reported to Milton that when told of his new marriage Mary's reply had been that she would rather have heard of his death. But when they left home against his wishes, probably in 1670, they had been trained to earn a living as embroiderers, and he had paid for this. Deborah, who married, spoke kindly of him after his death.

Milton's retelling of the story of the Fall says more than Genesis does about the man–woman relationship. He imagines how Eve came to be alone with Satan after his return to Paradise. As advised by the angel Adam has encouraged her 'self-esteem' (a word Milton invented) and this has had an effect, for she dares to suggest that in future each should work alone in their massive garden. Every day they need to 'lop overgrown, or prune, or prop, or bind', before 'one night or two' derides all their labour with further 'wanton growth'. Yet when they work together they are distracted by 'looks' at each other, by 'smiles' and 'casual discourse', so that 'th' hour of supper comes unearned'. Adam does not want them to be separated at all and warns her of dangers, but Eve insists that she is a strong woman and he yields after her promise to be back by noon.

Once again Satan seems about to fall in love with Eve when he sees her beauty, but 'the hot hell that always in him burns' makes his flattery of her as 'Empress' or 'Goddess humane' sinister:

> Fairest resemblance of thy Maker fair,
> Thee all things living gaze on . . .

And he flatters her goodness also. When she quotes God's prohibition, Satan remembers it more fully as forbidding 'knowledge of good and evil' and points out that evil, if it is 'real', must be 'known' before it is 'shunned'. He also knows what Raphael has promised, so his own promise is that Eve will not only survive but will also become divine if she eats this fruit, for

> . . . what are gods that Man may not become
> As they, participating godlike food?

Meanwhile Eve is getting hungry at noontime. So the climax comes in one line:

> Forth reaching to the fruit, she plucked, she eat.

She then tells the tree of her hope to 'grow mature in knowledge, as the gods who all things know' – and to be 'more equal' with Adam and perhaps ('a thing not undesirable') sometimes 'superior'. But what if 'the great Forbidder' knows and will kill her as threatened? She cannot bear to think of 'Adam wedded to another Eve'. So she hastens to join her husband who eagerly awaits her (and lunch) with a bouquet of flowers but who, when he hears her news, immediately says that he will join her in death. Even if God were to 'create another Eve', he could not bear to live without her: 'to lose thee were to lose myself'. So he, too, eats and this is one of the rare occasions on which Milton abandons his disguise as the poet and tells us plainly what he thinks:

> He scrupled not to eat
> Against his better knowledge, not deceived,
> But fondly overcome by female charm.

When the modern feminist movement has commented on such words, they have rightly been condemned as a man's attempt to escape responsibility for many evils in the world by blaming it all on a woman. And even worse is his description of Adam and Eve as this man sees them even before Eve has exercised her charm with allegedly fatal consequences:

> For contemplation he and valour formed,
> For softness she and sweet attractive grace,
> He for God only, she for God in him.

In the considerable modern literature on Milton's Eve two defences have been offered (more than once by scholars who happen to be women).

One is that he had been taught this nonsense, at home as well as in church, from childhood, like everyone else in that period. The other is that despite his conformity to his culture, he is known to have treated women as his companions. His complaint about Mary had been that at first she was not a companion, but he took her back. His loneliness when Katherine had died, and his happiness with Elizabeth ('Betty'), need no comment. Indeed, the second quotation just given as evidence for the prosecution describes what Milton imagined Satan first feeling when he saw 'the loveliest pair that ever since in love's embraces met', a couple which seemed to him 'lords of all' (not lord and lady). In contrast, Adam's attitude to his wife after their shared Fall shows that one of its results is damage to their love. He grabs her in order to 'enjoy' her and the pair have 'their fill of love' – but it is not love. Their sleep is not contented and in the morning they have their first quarrel. Paradise has been lost even before their expulsion from the Garden of Love.

Astonishingly, Milton puts more emphasis on the couple having problems with each other than on their new exposure as sinners in the hands of an angry God. The divine 'Forbidder' of whom Eve had been frightened turns out to be relaxed. He tells the assembled angels not to be troubled and he does intend to trouble himself by a direct intervention. He appoints his Son to represent him in a mission to Earth, with the vague instruction to combine mercy with justice.

In his turn the Son shows that the heart of his own divinity is not now full of wrath: humans are to be treated differently from the rebellious angels. What George Herbert had celebrated as the love of the King of Glory, overwhelming guilt by the offer of a new life, is now indicated by Milton in his own less ecstatic style.

Adam is rebuked not for disobeying God but for obeying Eve: 'Was she thy God?' The question is accompanied by the complaint that 'thou didst resign they manhood' but implies more than an accusation about a failure to uphold male supremacy. For Milton and therefore for the Son, being a man ought to mean being rational; before the Fall Adam had told Eve that she ought to obey (not him but) Reason, for 'Reason is our law'. Always in their relationship there had been a danger of unreasonable idolatry: she had almost worshipped her own reflection in the water, she had got nearer to idolatry in what she said about him, and he had got nearer still in what he said about her. So both had been in danger of slavery to Passion, abandoning 'rational liberty'. Such liberty can be properly combined with obedience to the God who alone deserves worship, who has given them freedom and who always means the best for his creation. Indeed, such liberty results from that obedience.

However, the Son's verdict on Adam is less annihilating than was to be expected, and that is true about the other sentences. Although the snake is condemned to crawl in the dust, Satan has made his escape – admittedly to hell. Although Eve is condemned to pain in childbirth, her descendants will 'bruise' the serpent: in other words, they will fight against Satan. And although Adam is sentenced to death after a term of hard labour, he is spared the immediate capital punishment which has been threatened, and the Son becomes a tailor: 'he clothed their nakedness with skins of beasts'. This is before their full repentance, but he knows that they have begun to feel shame about the human body. Then comes another light-hearted touch in the story: when Satan has boasted about his exploits to the other devils, the response is not applause but 'a dismal universal hiss': they are all turning into snakes.

The humiliated Adam is now full of self-pity, fearing that the long life which is promised will prove to be 'a long day's dying'. But he cheers up when Eve takes all the blame and begs for the renewal of his love, even offering to join him in suicide if that is what he wants. In response he encourages her: having children will make her the 'mother of all mankind' and she need not worry about his own life of labour, for that will be better than unemployment.

God himself adds to the good cheer. Although a little earlier he has furiously cursed Sin and Death, now he shows that he is one of the 'mortalists' who in Milton's time are condemned as heretics. He predicts that when death comes to Adam and Eve, they will die completely but he declares that this will be better for them than immortality, for it will be the 'final remedy' for the 'sharp tribulation' of life on Earth after the Fall. But their deaths are not to be unending. They are to be followed by resurrection, by the glorious 'renovation of the just' as well as by the sending of the unrepentant to hell.

The angel Michael is, however, now sent to Earth with the sadder news that Adam and Eve must leave Paradise: they can't have everything. Her first reaction is to cry because she will miss her flowers (which she has named) and her home with all its good memories, but she is reminded that she will still have her husband. Adam submits more calmly and is assured that God will not be 'far off' wherever he goes, for the Creator's presence can fill 'land, sea, and air, and every kind that lives', through days 'good or bad'. Michael is realistic about the suffering which must now be endured by individuals and societies: individuals will suffer in old age, societies will suffer in wars. The angel knows this but he still holds out the prospect of a 'Paradise within'. People who obey and trust God will find that it is possible neither to love nor to hate one's life, but to 'live well'. After such a life, death will be 'like a sleep', followed by a 'gentle uplifting to eternal life'. The loss of Paradise is very far from being complete.

Milton allows himself one more attack on clergy who make their living out of a religion more formal and superstitious than the one recommended, but the finale of his masterpiece is Adam's prayer of thanksgiving to God's 'goodness infinite', with a declaration of his intentions for his life. He will walk in dependence on his Creator all the way to the 'abyss' of eternity; he will trust in 'good still overcoming evil, and by small accomplishing great things'; he will suffer for truth's sake in fortitude until he finds 'death the gate of life'. Milton also allows himself one more bow to orthodoxy (to please the censor?). Adam acknowledges 'my Redeemer ever blest', for the angel has given him a preview of the history of Christianity and thus he is able to be a Christian before Christ. But the belief that faith is a heroic patience that will eventually be rewarded by God, rather than trust in the Redeemer, is what Milton most wants his great poem to teach. It was licensed for publication in 1667, with a second edition shortly before his death.

The exercise of heroic patience by Jesus is the theme of the sequel, *Paradise Regained*. A poem with that title could be expected to be about the crucifixion, but Milton had failed to write about the cross as a young man and had no intention of attempting the task again. Instead he chose to write about the temptations inflicted on Jesus by Satan, in the order given in Luke's gospel and with a result stated in the Letter to Hebrews: the Son of God is made 'perfect through sufferings', he is 'tested in every way, only without sin', and he learns 'obedience in the school of suffering'. For Milton, Jesus does perfectly what Adam has resolved to do after the Fall, and his responses to the temptations are deeds 'above heroic'.

The unique honour which the Father had bestowed on the Son is concealed when the Son becomes human: among men this 'man of men' is no more than 'th' exalted man' and his temptations test 'one man's firm obedience'. A secret agent, he has entered a world ruled by Satan ever since 'Adam and his facile consort Eve lost Paradise'. The 'Most High' plans to drive his enemy 'back to hell' through the work of 'this perfect man, by merit called my Son', but first he will 'exercise him in the wilderness'.

Before we see Jesus entering that battleground, we hear him musing. A 'multitude of thoughts' swarms in his mind, with memories of a childhood like Milton's:

When I was yet a child, no childish play
To me was pleasing; all my mind was set
Serious to learn and know, and thence to do
What might be public good . . .

But this young man's ambition in Nazareth had been more than the writing of poetry: it had been the conquest of 'all the earth', by 'heroic acts' as well as 'winning words'. Then, taught by his mother about the miraculous circumstances of his birth, he had come to understand that before his promised kingdom he must

. . . work redemption for mankind, whose sins'
Full weight must be transferred upon my head.

That task, however, is not in the foreground and one may wonder how important Milton really thinks it is. The action begins when in the wilderness Jesus meets Satan disguised as 'an aged man in rural weeds'. Despite the Devil's other suggestions, Jesus is calmly sure that he is (as Milton does believe) the 'living Oracle' sent by God into the world – sent to teach God's 'final will' which will be interpreted by the 'Spirit of Truth' dwelling in 'pious hearts'. His silence about the Church is not good enough for Satan, who in Miltonic style wonders why God allows hypocritical priests to 'tread his sacred courts'. Nor is the prospect of the all-too-human history of the Church enough to satisfy the disciples of Jesus, or his mother: in his absence they complain that he has not immediately set about the conquest of the world.

Satan intends to conquer Jesus but already knows enough about him to reject Belial's advice to tempt him with a woman. Instead, as Jesus grows more hungry Satan appears before him, now disguised 'as one in city or court or palace bred', and offers him not fruits from a tree but a whole lavish banquet. When this is spurned, Satan reminds him that he is 'unknown, unfriended, low of birth', and needs money to gain friends and realms – to be answered:

Yet he who reigns within himself, and rules
Passions, desires and fears, is more a king.

Then Satan tempts him with the prospect of fame, only to be told that 'the blaze of fame' is despicable because it depends on public opinion and the public is 'a miscellaneous rabble' in which the intelligent and the wise 'are few'. Satan can scarcely believe his ears when Jesus rejects even a comprehensive vision of the cultural glories of Rome and Athens, for Jesus shows that he is both knowledgeable and scornful in an equally comprehensive rejection. This renunciation may be connected with the fact that about this time Milton sold many of his books. As an old man he needed the money and as a blind man he had learned to live without reading:

> many books,
> Wise men have said, are wearisome; who reads
> Incessantly, and to his reading brings not
> A spirit and a judgement equal or superior . . .
> Uncertain and unsettled still remains,
> Deep versed in books and shallow in himself.

Satan becomes exasperated. If Jesus wants neither to be active and gain fame, nor to be studious and gain wisdom, 'what dost thou in this world?' So he falls back on the final temptation. Jesus believes that at his baptism he was called to his mission as 'Son of God' – but what does that mean? The title 'bears no single sense', Satan comments correctly, adding that he is himself in one sense a son of God. So he takes Jesus through the air to Jerusalem, where the temple is 'topped with golden spires'. He invites Jesus first to stand on the highest pinnacle, which 'will ask thee skill', and then to throw himself down to be held in the arms of angels. But what Jesus now does is not related in the gospels:

> To whom thus Jesus: 'Also it is written,
> "Tempt not the Lord thy God".' He said, and stood.
> But Satan smitten with amazement fell.

In those three lines, more precisely in *and stood*, Paradise is regained. There is no need to wait for the crucifixion or resurrection. Christ did not need to undergo self-sacrificing agony and the Father did not need to raise him from a totally humiliating death. The heart of traditional Christianity is missing.

This is a clever scene in the drama because it implies what Milton believes while not alarming the orthodox censor. It quotes 'Tempt not the Lord thy God' from the Bible and that can sound as if the fully divine Son is resisting temptation but for Milton, as for the Bible, it means that the Almighty must not be tested about his ability to save Jesus from falling to his death. Then it changes the Bible: the temple's parapet from which Jesus is invited to fall becomes a spire on which he manages to stand. And it adds to the Bible: Satan now falls, reversing the fall of Adam and Eve. So the acrobatic feat of Jesus is the hour of salvation but the censor's attention is not drawn to this marginalisation of the cross. And Milton's cunning continues when Jesus the semi-divine hero is honoured by the angels who provide a banquet in heaven. They acclaim him as 'Son of the Most High' which is theologically diplomatic. Then Milton's heresy is further concealed because he does not give the Most High an after-dinner speech which might have been too revealing about the status of the Son. Instead Jesus becomes a human hero who goes home 'to his mother's house' in Galilee for a rest and the remainder of his life is not recounted.

If Milton had been more explicit about his own theology, the censor would not have been so indulgent as he had been when licensing *Paradise Lost.* But in 1671, the year after the Conventicle Act which was the high point of the Anglican persecution of the Dissenters, *Paradise Regained* was licensed.

Another long poem, *Samson Agonistes*, was licensed along with it. It can be treated as an alternative parable about the conquest of evil by Christ and in the orthodox Christian tradition Samson the hero of Israel has often been regarded as a forerunner of the Saviour because of the self-sacrifice of his own death. But in the poem Christ is never mentioned and it seems more likely that the self who is uppermost in Milton's mind is himself. Like Samson he is blind but like Samson he feels able to destroy a temple, in his own case the one in which Anglicans, like Roman Catholics, worship idols and support tyrants. Like Samson, Milton will achieve his victory through dying: his poems will not be rapidly influential but victory will come – as Milton certainly believes, thanks to the inspiration given by God and the supreme example of heroism set by the Son of God.

It is presented as a 'dramatic poem' but with an emphasis that it was never intended for the stage, and as a tragedy but with an assurance that it avoids Shakespeare's habit of 'intermixing comic stuff with tragic sadness and decorum'. Milton submits to the judgement not of the public but of those who are 'not unacquainted' with the work of Greek tragedians. He is proud that his poem imitates the Greeks' decorum, their use of a chorus as commentator, their confinement of the action to one place, and their restriction of the time to 24 hours. And certainly this drama is not comic. It opens with the blind Samson sitting 'before the prison in Gaza', troubled by hornet-like thoughts about 'what once I was, and am now':

> Why was my breeding ordered and prescribed
> As of a person separate to God,
> Designed for great exploits, if I must die
> Betrayed, captived, and both my eyes put out,
> Made of my enemies the scorn and gaze . . . ?
> O dark, dark, dark, amid the blaze of noon,
> Irrevocably dark, total eclipse
> Without all hope of day!

His worst memory is about the women he has married on an 'impulse', first one who was 'the daughter of an infidel' and then Dalila who was a 'monster'. (But the second was not Samson's wife according to the Bible.) They had made him 'sung and proverbed in every street' as a fool. Dalila had cut off his magic hair while he was asleep and so had made him impotent to lead the Israelites' rebellion against her fellow Philistines. When his father appears in a feeble attempt to console him, Samson can only repeat that 'vile hath been my folly'. When his father tells of his hope that money may be used to ransom him during the current festival of his captors, Samson is not interested and continues in deep depression. When Dalila appears, dressed in the finery made possible by the reward paid to her, her gushing apologies and excuses are rejected bitterly even before she shows what kind of a woman she really is:

> I leave him to his lot, and like my own.

How many of Milton's memories are hinted at here – the silent years after the elaborate education, the disloyalty of his young bride, the failure of what he wrote about divorce and censorship, having to write diplomacy or propaganda when he wanted to write a great epic, the blindness which destroyed any political influence, the suicide of the good old cause, an afterlife patronised and censored by enemies!

But Samson is aroused out of self-pity by the arrival of the Philistine giant Harapha (not in the Bible), whose taunts arouse his self-esteem at last. He challenges him to a fight and when this offer is dismissed still assures him defiantly that he was raised

> With strength sufficient and command from Heav'n
> To free my country; if their servile minds
> Me their deliverer sent would not receive . . .
> The unworthier they.

Here Milton deviates from the Bible, where Samson becomes impotent not because the Israelites are ungrateful to him but because Delila has cut his hair off. But the deviation is made in order to refer to the poet's own disappointments and the Bible is rejoined as Samson recovers his heroic manhood. At first he refuses, then he accepts, an order to perform his tricks as a strong man within the pagan temple where 'lords are lordliest in their wine' and the 'well-feasted priest' looks forward to the entertainment after dinner. And one of his tricks is to bring the whole temple crashing down on the lot of them, at the sacrifice of his own life.

We do not see this happening but we hear his father's tribute:

> Nothing is here for tears, nothing to wail
> Or knock the breast, no weakness, no contempt,

> Dispraise or blame; nothing but well and fair,
> And what may quiet us in a death so noble.

And the chorus tells us how to conclude our reflections:

> All is best, though oft we doubt,
> What th' unsearchable dispose
> Of Highest Wisdom brings about,
> And ever best found in the close.

In the history of ancient Israel, which his early readers knew well, Samson's self-sacrifice had no quick impact on events, for the Philistines remained in power. That was also true about Milton's influence on his own time. But *Samson Agonistes* recaptures the sublimity of *Paradise Lost* with those words about a noble death being used by 'Highest Wisdom' to bring about what is best 'in the close'. That sounds like Shakespeare's belief in 'Providence', although that is defined by both poets less sharply than in any doctrine about

> providence, foreknowledge, will and fate,
> Fixed fate, free will, foreknowledge absolute.

And the implication seems to be that despite his failures and his blindness, Milton believes that what he has written will eventually help to destroy the power of those whom he regards as the enemies of God. He was right.

He died in 1674. Within fifteen years the last of the Stuart kings was to be in exile and Protestant Dissenters were to be assured of toleration, and within a century his plea for republican liberty was to be an inspiration for American independence. Dryden who had once been his assistant in Cromwell's civil service was to make his poetry rhyme; Handel was to set him to music; Addison was to rank him with Homer and Virgil because of the 'sublimity of his thoughts'; in most of the eighteenth century he was to be considered more important than Shakespeare; Wordsworth was to revere him; Coleridge was to ponder why he was so great; Blake was to be obsessed by him; Matthew Arnold was to applaud his poetry but not his 'Hebraic' religion; Denis Saurat was to call his theology 'rubbish'; F. R. Leavis was to reckon him incapable of precise thought; Douglas Bush was to write that 'the question is not how far the poem is worthy of our attention but how far we can make ourselves worthy of it'; C. S. Lewis and C. A. Patrides were to commend him highly for making Christian orthodoxy sound new; more recent critics have illuminated his work from positions Christian-orthodox or Christian-radical, rationalist or Marxist, psychological or sociological, feminist or deconstructive; and almost every year during the second half of the twentieth century a good study of his poetry appeared, usually from an American university. Shorter recent criticism has been reprinted in five volumes. His life has been recounted in many laborious modern studies. But to honour his grave in London six words were cut into stone: JOHN MILTON AUTHOR OF PARADISE LOST.

FIVE

WORDSWORTH

In contrast with the high hopes and deep defeats of Milton, William Wordsworth (1770–1850) lived during the slow birth of a new society. The population doubled and millions of people now lived in large towns, worked as hands applied to machines, were restless under control by capitalists, and asserted their independence at least by making up their own minds about religion. In his young manhood he briefly found it 'bliss to be alive' as a new age dawned in the French Revolution. Later, he was dismayed by developments in France and reacted to an actually changing England in a more conservative spirit, to the dismay of many then and now. Always his spirituality was strong, first as a worshipper of nature and then as his own kind of Christian. Until his late fifties he was often ridiculed but he was taken more seriously when old or dead. His poetry became influential on both sides of the Atlantic, with a considerable effect on thoughts and lives from 1830 to 1930. Since then other influences have been larger but the continuing interest in his personality and work produced well over a hundred full-length academic studies during the twentieth century and his most famous poems have continued their impact in schools. In many eyes he still resembles one of the mountains which inspired him, whether or not one has so far become aware that this mountain repays a decision to climb.

Geoffrey's Hartman's close reading of *Wordsworth's Poetry 1787–1814* (1964) is regarded as a landmark because the approach was psychoanalytical rather than awestruck. In *The Revolutionary I* (1998) Ashton Nicholas provided a convenient summary of the subsequent discussion between scholars and advanced students. He argued that the emphasis on the poet's selfhood in 'Romantic' poetry was revolutionary but that suspicion about a poet's self-presentation is right, especially in Wordsworth's case. He wrote: 'The past three decades have called into question the stability of all texts, arguing first – deconstructively – that all language uses are potentially equivocal, and more recently – new historically – that no text is less complicated than the cultural circumstances which give rise to its production.' In cruder terms, the recent discussion has taught us not to rely exclusively on what he chose to tell the public about himself and his changing beliefs. However, it still seems possible to take the evidence as now known and to find in it a real man – and one who was not unusually complicated.

From an early age he felt called to be a poet responding to things and people. He was barely fourteen when he contemplated a tree's bare branches against the evening sky and wanted to be the first poet to celebrate the beauty. He walked home after an all-night dance and as dawn broke

> I made no vows, but vows
> Were then made for me: bond unknown to me
> Was given, that I should be – else sinning greatly –
> A dedicated spirit.

The key points in his interpretation of nature were such moments, which he called 'spots of time'. These were experiences, familiar in the history of spirituality around the world, when perception is suddenly intensified, 'time stands still', and one feels briefly united with an oceanic reality, infinity in a small space, the 'eternal now'. For Wordsworth the message was that nature is unified and sacred, overwhelming but on the whole benevolent: 'I saw one life, and felt that it was joy.' And he could have revealing moments when he met people and admired their ability to endure and rise above suffering – a detachment possible, he thought, because the human mind can rise above the adversities of life as well as above the more puzzling parts of nature. It took time for him to believe that the Creator was even higher than nature and human nature, in the one

> Surpassing life, which out of space and time,
> Nor touched by weltering passion, is
> And hath the name of God.

When he did so believe, however, his faith made him feel all the more that he had a duty to combine true religion and sound philosophy in a poem about 'Nature, Man and Society' which would answer the spiritual questions of the modern age with a grandeur comparable with *Paradise Lost*. When he had been persuaded to undertake this project, in 1798, he had told a friend that 'I know not anything which will not come within the scope of my plan'. But when he wrote that he did not know his limitations. He experienced these 'spots of time' as a kind of mystic, but his visions only supplied hints about any reality beyond what he actually saw. Unlike Milton, he had no ability or wish to reach theology.

Since he did believe that he had a mission to teach his fellow countrymen how to live, it may be thought that he could have thrown himself into politics, but in practice he had no alternative to being an onlooker. Like Chaucer he needed money and eventually had to earn it as a tax-collector. Even as an onlooker he was limited because by temperament he needed rural quiet and a small domestic circle: thus his pamphlet criticising the conduct of the war in Portugal and Spain in 1809 could not be written effectively in the English countryside. It would be more realistic to ask whether he could not have been a parish priest like George Herbert (and other poets) or his own son John, or a leading clergyman like his brother who became Master of Trinity College, Cambridge, or his nephew, a bishop who wrote his biography and other hymns of praise.

When he went to Cambridge in 1797 it was assumed that he would be ordained and would be helped in his family's expectations of promotion by an uncle who had been tutor to a prime minister (Pitt) and to the sons of a king (George III) and whose own rise ended in the chapel of Windsor Castle. As a middle aged layman he celebrated the history, buildings and ceremonies of the Church of England in 102 *Ecclesiastical Sonnets*, and in 1839 he was given an honorary degree by Oxford University, then heavily clerical, with praise from the poet of Anglo-Catholicism, John Keble, as a defender of 'high and sacred truth'. But an ecclesiastical career would have had to begin in the 1790s by 'vegetating on a paltry curacy' at first, and we can see why he rejected the possibility if we look at his relationship with Richard Watson, the most intelligent among the bishops. In May 1792 he wrote about his intention to be ordained 'in the approaching winter or spring' and in February 1793 his sister Dorothy was still excited by the prospect of sharing a parsonage with him. But during that spring he wrote an open letter to Watson which would have taken him to prison had it been printed, for although anonymous it was to be announced as coming from 'a Republican' and the government had a security service.

Both he and the bishop had been born and educated in the Lake District before studies in Cambridge. As a Fellow of Trinity College Watson became a priest more or less automatically and volunteered as the university's professor of chemistry although, as he confessed, he 'had never read a syllable on the subject, nor seen a single experiment'. One of his experiments demolished the laboratory but others led to discoveries noted by less amateurish scientists. After seven years a better-paid professorship fell vacant and he procured the required doctorate. After appointment he began to study the subject, which was theology, but without troubling to become familiar with dead theologians. A liberally minded Protestant, he bestowed his attention on the

Scriptures alone and the pamphlet which he wrote was *An Apology for the Bible*, defending it against the sneers of Tom Paine and Edward Gibbon. (But William Blake was to write on his copy: 'To defend the Bible in this year 1798 would cost a man his life.') He was also interested in the collection of incomes from parishes where he did not reside, and of fees from an archdeaconry in the diocese of Ely. In 1782 he transferred these limited labours as a professor to a deputy, for the government made him Bishop of Llandaff: the appointments of priests to most of the parishes were in the hands of lay patrons but the government kept the best jobs for its own nominees.

He felt it his duty to inspect the clergy of his diocese every three years, encouraging their ministry although he never learned to speak Welsh. A legacy enabled him to acquire an estate and to build a mansion worthy of his new dignity outside Wales, returning to the Lake District where he consoled himself for his failures to secure a richer bishopric and became enthusiastic about the improvement of his property. He wrote some pamphlets or speeches advocating full civil rights for the Protestant Dissenters, who were now tolerated, and welcoming the French Revolution in its early stages since the foreigners seemed to be catching up with the British decision to limit the powers of their own monarchy, a step taken a hundred years previously.

The touches of radicalism now enabled Wordsworth to pay a compliment: 'While, with a servility which has prejudiced many people against religion itself, the ministers of the Church of England have appeared as writers upon public measures only to be the advocates of slavery civil or religious, your Lordship stood almost alone as the defender of truth and political charity.' But he could not stomach the bishop's new pamphlet, which denounced the recent execution of Louis XIV and defended God for arranging British society in classes, so that the poor should be encouraged to be industrious and the comfortable to be happy and perhaps useful in their own chosen ways. No revolution was needed in Britain, and not much improvement.

Wordsworth, in contrast, argued that the French king's execution had been the natural 'overflow of spirits' in admirable zeal for necessary reforms, and he added that in Britain the hereditary aristocracy should be deprived of power along with the monarchy. A government must govern but the interests of the governors must always be subordinated to the interests of the governed, who must be allowed to change the government. Privately he confessed that he was a 'democrat', however 'odious' that word might be, and therefore would never 'bow down my mind' to the church established, privileged and corrupted by the state.

At this stage he did not express himself so freely on matters outside politics but it is clear that in religion too he was not conservative. When he had moved back to the Lake District in 1799 it was his habit not to attend the parish church. Until 1806 its resident priest was a curate deputising for the rector, who had been insane for some sixty years. Although this curate was 'often intoxicated it was never, I believe, at his own expense'. Nevertheless Wordsworth had his eldest son baptised by him in 1803. He began regular churchgoing in 1806–07 while staying in a cottage on the estate of a devout friend and patron, Sir George Beaumont, but years later told a friend that when at home he went for the prayers, never for the sermon.

During his lifetime standards were raised all over the Church of England and Wordsworth became content to give in public a general assent to its teachings. In middle age he opposed any alteration to the Book of Common Prayer or the Articles of Religion because, he said, he could not imagine a better alternative. But in private he could sometimes be less discreet about what he did not believe. As a poet he could see that the Bible is not an infallible record of accurate facts and permanent laws, and as a humane man he 'could not explain to my satisfaction how an infinitely pure Being can receive satisfaction from the sufferings of Jesus Christ'. Nor could he explain to himself how such a Being could send to hell all those who before their deaths had not put their trust in Christ's self-sacrifice as usually interpreted in theology. The classic definition of Christ in terms of two natures and wills, divine and human, seemed to him 'needless and mischievous attempts at explanation'. He came to believe in the theoretical possibility of miracles ('I consider as superstitious the imagined knowledge and certainty which men suppose that they have as to the laws of nature') but in practice he still did not write about, or rely on, any supernatural interference in the course of events. While admiring much in the characters of many Evangelicals, and while seeing that their 'self-examination' could nevertheless make them believe that they needed a Redeemer, he felt no such need himself. Or so he told a friend in 1812: later, he seems to have become more normally Christian, even in private.

He appreciated history and beauty in the Catholic tradition but as a layman who in 1814 called Milton 'the holiest of men' he could not share the Anglo-Catholics' insistence on bishops and priests, Baptism as spiritual regeneration through a sacrament and the Eucharist as the only really important act of worship. Least of all could he share the fascination with Rome which was so strong in Newman and in some other leaders of the Oxford Movement whose aim was to renew Anglicanism. In the early 1840s an ardent Anglican High Churchman, Frederick Faber, expressed enthusiasm for his poetry in visits and letters and persuaded the poet to hang a crucifix in his bedroom, but when he was received into the Roman Catholic Church the discipleship was terminated. Later a Roman Catholic faith was not the least of the objections to Edward Quillinan's relationship with this firm Protestant's daughter Dora and he delayed their marriage for three years.

Many visitors or correspondents tried to persuade him to say more clearly what he did believe but they had to be content with imprecise assurances: he accepted the 'truths of Christianity' although he had been 'averse to frequent mention of the mysteries of Christian faith' because they were too sacred to be spoken about freely. Back in 1798 Coleridge had told a friend that 'he loves and venerates Christ and Christianity – I wish he did more' and a 'great philosophical poem' was suggested in the hope that he would do more. Two years later Wordsworth, still under Coleridge's influence, ended with a quotation from Milton when he wrote a prologue to the great poem:

Of Truth, of Grandeur, Beauty, Love and Hope,
And melancholy Fear subdued by Faith;
Of blessed consolations in distress;
Of moral strength, and intellectual Power;
Of joy in widest commonalty spread;
Of the individual mind that keeps her own
Inviolate retirement, subject there
To Conscience only, and the law supreme
Of that Intelligence which governs all –
I sing: – 'fit audience let me find though few'!

But he grandly dismissed Miton's use of myths which to him were 'mere fiction of what never was':

Jehovah – with his thunder, and the choir
Of shouting Angels, and the empyreal thrones –
I pass them unalarmed.

Even when he took a more favourable view of the myths to be found in the Bible, he never took the trouble to work out how the public might be told about their revelation of 'Truth and Beauty'. He was content to rely chiefly on truths and beauties he had experienced for himself in the nature around him,

For the discerning intellect of Man,
When wedded to this goodly universe
In love and holy passion, shall find these
A simple produce of the common day.

However, in his latter years he took great pleasure in his religious or spiritual influence which he saw beginning. In earlier years he had said that he wanted 'to be a teacher or nothing'. And while avoiding theology he wanted to teach religion: he told a friend that 'piety and religion will be best understood by him who takes the most comprehensive view of the human mind' and 'for the most part' an understanding of religion 'will strengthen with the general strength of the mind'. In particular he was pleased that his reticence about his own beliefs had enabled him to reach and help many who shared his interest in religion and were outside the ranks of the firm believers. After his death this appreciative public grew. A considerable amount of his life's work was anthologised in Francis Palgrave's *Golden Treasury* (1861) and in 1879 Matthew Arnold edited a selection with a widely noticed commentary. He scorned the poet's public references to religion as 'illusion', but claimed that the best poetry had an emotionally convincing force. Wordsworth, he wrote, had directed attention to nature as 'the truest and most unfailing source of joy'. The 'simple, primary affections', with the sense of duty to people in general, could be inspired by that universally accessible joy. Here was a poet with the 'high seriousness' which, Arnold maintained, was lacking in Chaucer – and he had the merit of being really serious not about religious doctrines which had become incredible but about spiritual realities which had survived the Victorian stage of modernisation. There could still be contact with what was left of unchanging nature, love within a family, compassion for the unfortunate and a willingness to work.

The next year in England saw the formation of the Wordsworth Society, a fan club from which emerged the National Trust dedicated to the preservation of natural beauty. That led in time to the designation of National Parks and to planning restrictions on all new building. By now Wordsworth's influence was also considerable in the United States, through the writings of Emerson and Thoreau, through a new concern to conserve the wilderness and through the whole Transcendentalist movement which spread idealism in colleges and schools. Later he might sound like a preacher, so that the impatient could live their lives without needing to listen to him or to any other eminent Victorian. Yet those who were willing to listen would love the music of his words and want that music to be one of their most valued possessions. In their own styles people to whom English literature as a whole was boring or totally unknown could, without being aware of it, live according to Wordsworth's gospel as interpreted by Arnold. They could still gain joy from beauty outdoors, from people dear to them, from work which took them out of themselves, and usually also from a belief that human life, being supported by some mysteriously higher power, is not ultimately meaningless. They could still care about the unfortunate. And in that strange way a prophecy come true which Wordsworth had made in

1805, and which he was to place at the end of *The Prelude* of 1850. Addressing Coleridge, he had predicted that

> Prophets of Nature, we to them will speak
> A lasting inspiration, sanctified
> By reason and by truth; what we have loved
> Others will love, and we may teach them how:
> Instruct them how the mind of man becomes
> A thousand times more beautiful than the earth
> On which he dwells, above this frame of things
> In beauty exalted, as it is itself
> Of substance, and of fabric, more divine.

That influence has flowed from what he wrote about his intense experiences. Keats could poke fun at 'the Wordsworthian or egotistical sublime' but in fact the emphasis on the ego was right at the centre of the vast cultural revolution which has been called Romanticism and at the centre, too, of the modern mind. (Where would modern poetry be without the acutely sensitive ego?) He was the first English poet to write so explicitly, and at such length, about himself. This was a poem begun in the late 1790s in a draft made public in 1970. It was expanded in the early 1800s in a draft made public in 1926. After further revision ended only by his death, it was published in 1850 as *The Prelude: Growth of a Poet's Mind.*

Its story begins with his birth in the small town of Cockermouth. He imagines himself as a 'five years' child' bathing on a summer's day in the adjacent river. This passage had been written while he was homesick in Germany during the most severe winter for many years and it avoids foregrounding some cold facts about his parents. His mother died at the age of 31 when he was only eight. At the time he had been sent out of the way, to the house of his mother's brother, who ran a successful shop in distant Penrith. There he was to spend many miserable months while the home of his years with his mother was full of visitors on business. Five years later his father died and he never forgot waiting for the horse to take him home for the Christmas holiday in which this happened. Now he had no home at all for ten years. He was separated from his beloved sister Dorothy for almost the whole of this period and was (he admitted years later) 'stiff, moody and violent', especially when thrust into the resentful Cookson family above their draper's shop.

A lasting grievance was the refusal of his father's employer to honour a very large debt which if repaid would have supported the five orphans: he preferred to influence the court, which obediently took his side. The father had sacrificed his own honour in the service of Sir James Lowther, later the first Earl of Lonsdale. This man was a totally ruthless bully who had acquired wealth and influence from the mining of coal and slate and the acquisition of land and property. He bought up most of Cockermouth and Wordsworth senior occupied its best house without rent because he was Lowther's agent, as his brother and father also were. He may have used methods of which his master would approve, but Lowther's response had been to encourage him to spend his own money on the work.

William, the most sensitive of the cheated orphans and the most in need of a good education, might have been marginalised and traumatised beyond repair had he not enjoyed three pieces of very good fortune. He was sent to an excellent grammar school where the reading and writing of poetry was encouraged. He lodged near that school house in a cottage in the remote village of Hawkshead with Ann Tyson, a working-class woman who became his second mother. And he was left free to roam alone and to play as a member of a 'noisy crew' in an 'excess of happiness'. That freedom lies behind the passages in *The Prelude* which declare that the mountains and the lakes also became motherlike, as when the hills looked down on his delighted skating. Nature 'fostered alike by beauty and by fear' and there were times when it seemed to be exercising parental discipline. One night the boy felt guilty because he had stolen 'the captive of another's toil', a snared woodcock, and on another night a boat was taken without permission for a row over the lake before the hills became frightening. There was a 'spot of time' when he stumbled across a place where a wife-murderer had been executed and buried, and near it saw a girl struggling against the wind as she carried a pitcher. Such moments gave him 'an obscure sense of possible sublimity' in life and death but as he 'served in Nature's temple' his predominant feeling was not one of fear or awe: it was gratitude for 'blessings spread around me like a sea'. When he hooted like an owl, the birds hooted back, and when that merry noise ceased he could listen to the voices of the mountain streams and look at the changing reflections of the clouds in the 'steady' lake.

It is no wonder that while a student in Cambridge he had

> A feeling that I was not for that hour,
> Nor for that place.

At first he was excited by the reminders of the past (in particular of Chaucer and Milton), and by the pleasures of friendship in idleness as he ran up bills with a 'gladsome' thoughtlessness; and at first he performed well academically, playing that game. But 'the world about me' was 'my own' only when he could walk around the green Backs behind the colleges in the evening. He soon developed a contempt for his 'grotesque' elders who taught a curriculum irrelevant to his emotional needs, although he read widely in private, learned Italian and Spanish and composed or translated poetry. He had almost as little respect for his contemporaries who competed for prizes within the system with 'passions unworthy of youth's generous heart'. Cambridge could give him nothing which he had not already received from Hawkshead and its environment – received not only from his teachers and friends, and not only from 'the speaking earth and heaven', but also from ordinary adults including the poor with whom he had talked naturally. In particular he was to remember a discharged soldier whom he met tramping along a road by night. According to *The Prelude* he had said very little except

'My trust is in the God of Heaven
And in the eye of him who passes me!'

In July 1790 it seemed more important to walk with a friend through France, the Italian lakes and Switzerland, than to prepare for his final examinations. The twin results were an undistinguished degree and an informal education which prepared for 'some monument behind me which pure hearts should reverence'. By that he did not mean the poetry he was able to write before 1795: that was conventional. His monument would be what he later wrote, reflecting on momentous experiences in France.

He had not gone to observe the French Revolution; he did not visit Paris. Nor was he deeply interested in historic sites; his elaborate passage about the Grande Chartreuse, a monastery now doomed, was written years later. He walked almost all the way, mainly to save money but also because it was democratic not to use a carriage, and being sociable he learned from temporary companions about

France standing on the top of golden hours
And human nature seeming born again.

But 'Nature then was sovereign in my mind' and his main motive in going was to see mountains. Mont Blanc did not live up to expectations, and he did not realise that he had actually crossed the Alps, but the gorge through which he now descended into Italy was remembered as teaching that

Our destiny, our being's heart and home,
Is with infinitude, and only there;
With hope it is, hope that can never die,
Effort, and expectation, and desire,
And something ever more about to be.

The woods, the waterfalls, the winds, the rocks, the darkness and the light were (and once again he remembers Milton)

The types and symbols of Eternity,
Of first, and last, and midst, and without end.

After that long holiday and a consequently undistinguished graduation he spent some time in London. In *The Prelude* of 1850 he presents himself as an eager tourist who admired most the oratory of Burke, the leading spokesman of conservatism, and who noticed most a father nursing a sick baby with 'unutterable love' and a blind beggar carrying a placard to say 'who he was'. Visiting a fair was, he wrote, a sight of a 'Parliament of Monsters' and he preferred the city's empty streets at night. But research has found that he read and listened very carefully as he met the London equivalents of the revolutionaries in Paris and sensed what might be 'about to be' in British politics. That experience explains why in 1792 he did not listen to a suggestion that he should return to Cambridge and immerse himself in Hebrew and other oriental languages in preparation for life as a scholarly clergyman. Instead, he announced that he needed to improve his French and in November returned to France.

After a brief visit to Paris he moved to quieter Orléans and found that the local bishop was a leading supporter of the revolution. Moving to Blois he made friends with some army officers of aristocratic birth who shared the bishop's views. He never forgot how one of them, Michel Beaupuy, exclaimed when during a walk they met 'a hunger-bitten girl' leading an emaciated cow: ''Tis against this we are fighting'. Later that officer fought gallantly and fatally against an invasion of republican France, and his main motive throughout was one to appeal to the Milton in Wordsworth: a man must fight injustice but always with love for his country. However, that position was much harder to maintain as the revolution killed off both any survivors from the *ancien régime* and its own moderates, the Girondins. In dismay about its development into terror, in *The Prelude* Wordsworth claimed that he had affected 'more emotion than he felt' about the revolution in general, but the fact was that before long he identified himself with the Girondins as wholeheartedly and as actively as was possible for an English visitor.

That became a problem when he fell in love with Annette Vallon, a woman older than him who after her own early sympathy with the revolution joined her family in support for the royalist reaction, even when foreign monarchs sent troops into France and royalists could be executed as traitors. In *The Prelude* of 1805 this whole experience was concealed in a sentimental story about Julia and Vaudracour: the pregnant Julia is sent to a convent and her lover is left with the baby who dies, so that he never smiles before his own early death. It is a tale totally out of keeping with the rest of *The Prelude* and its insertion indicated the author's embarrassment about the real events. Not long after Annette's news of her pregnancy he left her, explaining that he needed to return to England in order to raise money to support mother and child, with a promise to be back soon. It seems right to think that at least half of him was sincere but he must have known that his uncles, who still controlled the supply of money, were very unlikely to respond and that his own poetry could produce a few pounds at the most. Moreover, he now spent six weeks amid the excitements of revolutionary Paris.

When Anne-Caroline was born in December 1792 her father was absent but her mother gave his name when the baby was baptised and subsequently called herself a widow with the surname of Williams: she never married. Although she wrote impassioned letters and Dorothy replied affectionately, communication stopped when war between their two countries broke out in February 1793. It is just possible that he made a very risky return to France that autumn, for he told Thomas Carlyle that he had witnessed the execution of the Girondin journalist Gorsas in Paris, but so far as we know he never described any such adventure in detail and it seems that in any case the war made it impossible for him to see Annette. He did not forget her: many deserted women were to stumble through his poems and presumably also his self-accusing dreams.

A few people knew about this during his lifetime, but any references to the scandal were so guarded that they did not wreck his reputation as a wise man who could perhaps be avoided as a moralising bore. More than a century passed before some of Annette's letters, confiscated by the censor during the war of the 1790s, became known in 1916–22 and then they caused no great shock because Victorian standards were being rejected widely during and after another war. And it has never been sensible to suggest that William should have joined Annette permanently in France. Had he done so, he would have been treated as a spy; had he survived physically, probably the marriage would have died; and in any case it must be very doubtful whether he could have survived as a poet.

On his return to England he did what he could to deal with his guilt and to share any remaining hopes of a revolution in Britain, but he was homeless in body and mind. He published two poems: the conventional *An Evening Walk* written largely in Cambridge to express his love for the Lake District, and the picturesque *Descriptive Sketches* about his expedition further afield in 1790, written largely during his return to France; he had not yet escaped from the prison of poetry in rhyming couplets. But he did not settle down to new work in any real sense. Having rejected the Church he was not interested in any other paying profession and he stayed in so many houses owned by other people, with such disturbance in his mind, that he wrote little poetry.

The Prelude indicates that he soon fell under the influence of a very radical (and atheistic) philosopher although William Godwin is not named. This sage taught that if the 'circumstances' which mould characters are changed through better education, the minds of the young can be washed by such a tide of rationalism and idealism that, with patience rather than violence, 'political justice' can be established anywhere, even in Britain. In London's intellectual circles, divided between would-be revolutionaries and the reactionaries who were now more powerful and more popular, this project was bound to seem intellectually stimulating but also unrealistic – and this was what Wordsworth eventually concluded. When he read the second edition of Godwin's *Political Justice* he saw through it. The plan to 'set all things right' involved (as he judged in *The Prelude*) 'resolute mastery shaking off infirmities of nature, time and place'. He had seen enough of the real world to know that it was imperfect and would never be made perfect by Godwinian reasoning any more than Utopia could be reached by a bloody revolution or defended by a blind reaction. And he preferred to think about what is the world

> Of all of us – the very place where, in the end,
> We find our happiness or not at all!

In this world he saw two countries which he loved at war, to his intense surprise. He expected it to be a long war although he did not know it would continue almost without interruption until 1815. He never forgot standing on the coast of the Isle of Wight and seeing the British fleet assembling; he was horrified. Nor did he forget being in church when prayers were offered for a British victory – and hoping for a British defeat. He gradually recovered his patriotism as he saw France moving away from the sponsorship of an international liberation of the peoples towards militant nationalism and even imperialism, but a decisive change in his loyalties was not to come until Napoleon invaded an old and neutral democracy, Switzerland, in 1798, and began his dictatorship in France next year. But even then, the Britain which he now supported in heart and soul was not worshipped by his mind. In *The Prelude* he cannot accept as the alternative to war the ideal of peaceful and free trade which would increase the wealth of nations – in particular of Britain, the world's first industrial nation – for that too was the worship of a materialistic idol. And the idol would not even bring material gain to 'the man whom we behold with our own eyes', for this wealth would end up, and grow, in only a few hands. Britain was no democracy.

So the ideologies clashed in his mind like the armies and navies in the war and he found himself 'now believing, now disbelieving'. The result seems to have been a mental breakdown during which he lost

> All feeling of conviction, and, in fine,
> Sick, wearied out with contraries,
> I yielded up moral questions in despair.

And there is some evidence that he contemplated suicide.

In *The Prelude* of 1805 the impression is given that he recovered quite rapidly from this collapse. He mentions his long walk in the summer of 1793 when he 'found hope' by talking with people whose poverty, endured courageously, had not destroyed

> Grandeur upon the very humblest face
> Of human life

– although such people were to be met in 'Nature's presence', not in overcrowded cities

> where the human heart is sick
> And the eye feeds it not, and cannot feed.

But poetry which he wrote at the time, condensed into *Guilt and Sorrow* and first published in 1843, stressed the horror of what he saw on Salisbury Plain as men and women told him stories of the effect of war or of dehumanising poverty. In this period he often dreamed that he was defending the innocent before a tribunal which would not listen, whether in France or in Britain, and at Stonehenge near Salisbury he imagined the human sacrifices then believed to have been performed by the Druids, in the early years of British religion.

A reference to the Druids' more edifying knowledge of stars prepares us for the climax of *The Prelude* in 1805. 'In one of those excursions' he climbs to the peak of Snowdon and is overwhelmed by one of the most important of all the 'spots of time'. We can be forgiven if we suppose from the poem that this occurred in 1793, as he walked into Wales from Salisbury trying to recover from great distress, but there is no evidence that he had such an experience then. If he did, and if it was clearly decisive for his whole outlook on the world, it is very strange that in the summer of 1794 he was still so much under the influence of Godwin's philosophy that he discussed the project of a monthly journal in order to spread arguments which were far from mystical. The truth seems to be that the ascent took place soon after his graduation in 1791, when he was with the Welsh friend who had accompanied him to the Alps in 1790. No doubt he would have been deeply impressed then, when his emotions were already confused, but only later did he think that his life had been changed.

It seems that this event, not described at the time in any surviving evidence, was remembered and thought about until in *The Prelude* of 1805 it could be interpreted as a disclosure of 'transcendent power' given to the human mind which itself is on top of nature, 'truly from the Deity'. What he had seen undeniably was a magnificent landscape by moonlight, with a mist covering the lesser hills in mystery, but with the sound of streams audible and the calm sea visible in the distance. The rest was an interpretation more or less in keeping with his religious tradition and his own psychology, as is probably the case in most or all accounts of mystical experiences. What he wrote in 1805 celebrated a 'spot' of 'highest bliss' in 'reason's most exalted mood' – and he wrote after undergoing much further suffering since the 1790s. But not before the 1850 version was there an explicit reference to 'Holy Writ' as an influence on the interpretation; in 1805 it was enough to feel

> The sense of God, or whatsoe'r is dim
> Or vast in its own being.

From this sense could flow 'the fountains of his future life', already in 1805. These were 'cheerfulness for acts of daily life' and readiness for love towards humanity as well as nature, for 'by love subsists all lasting grandeur' and 'that gone, we are as dust'. Even 'faith in life endless' could flow from this brief encounter with 'Infinity'. At the same time he must be 'Power to thyself' since 'no Helper last thou here'. The Deity resembles the moon, distantly and serenely shedding a cold light which at present seems enough. But when he revised that 1805 version it did not seem enough and he introduced more explicit references to the Christians' God and to 'Eternity'.

However, *The Prelude* of 1850 kept silent about experiences which he still found too disturbing to be put into poetry intended ultimately for the public. That final version does not fully express the outrage he felt about his family's treatment by his father's employer, which was typical of Lowther's treatment of people in general and must have been a large factor in the poet's radicalism in the 1790s. Nor does it stress the permanent damage done to him by being orphaned, which must have been connected with his compensating love of nature. Nor does it show the extent of his sympathy with the revolution or the depth of his guilt about his relationship with Annette. And the greatest silence of all was that he did not wish *The Prelude* to be printed before he was safely dead. Publication would have answered the contempt, or aroused the indifference, which he had to endure until the late 1820s, and later on, when he was revered and even became a tourist attraction, it would have been the clinching evidence that he deserved a place alongside Chaucer, Shakespeare and Milton. But it appears that the ridicule which had greeted his earlier poetry had hurt him very deeply. He dreaded what might be the response to this self-exposure without any precedent in English literature. So even after his death the public was not to learn from him the whole truth about the growth of his mind.

Only in October 1795 did Wordsworth begin to write poetry at the level now associated with his name, because it was only then that he had the stability of an income, a house and a view of life which he could call his own. Even then his finances were to some extent under his control only because he was left a legacy by a friend whom he had nursed during three months, and he remained acutely worried about money. In 1795–98 he lived in large houses, first in Devon and then in Somerset, but the first was rent-free thanks to a benefactor and the second was let only for a year at an extraordinarily low rent. And even then he took some time to find the voice we know.

He was still full of anger as he worked on his memories of the destitute folk on 'desolate' Salisbury Plain and denounced the rich in satires modelled on the savagery of the Roman poet Juvenal. *A Somersetshire Tragedy* was so unlike his later restraint that he later destroyed it. His best work was on the angry first draft of 'The Ruined Cottage' which was eventually to appear at the beginning of *The Excursion*. There, Robert does not intend to cause the despair of his wife Margaret when he leaves the cottage because he needs the money which the army pays. But he never returns; presumably he is a casualty of war like the maimed, brutalised or famished people who were now still haunting the poet's imagination. No one helps her to survive; one child has to be sent away as a 'servant boy'; another dies, as she does. However, all this material was too gloomy to be published at the time and when he had spent many months of 1796–97 on an equally tragic play, it was not accepted for the stage and not printed before 1842.

The Borderers was written in blank verse imitating Shakespeare without being a sufficiently impressive drama of action. (Duncan Wu wrote that 'Wordsworth's art lies in encapsulating the drama in a mere glance'.) Set on the lawless frontier between England and Scotland in 1265, it explored themes vitally important to its sad author. The villain, Rivers, applies his 'independent intellect' in the manner of William Godwin, but it is to a cruel world where mastery depends on being ruthless in the exercise of strength, in the manner of Robespierre and the other terrorists who gained power during the French Revolution. He is a reincarnation of Iago, while the captain of the little private army (almost a police force), Mortimer, reproduces the gullibility of Othello. This is an honourable man but his mind is poisoned by the lies of Rivers about a blind, and now landless, old baron, Herbert.

He is morally indignant and after much hesitation agrees to execute the alleged villain – as many in France had at first accepted the revolution which became a bloodbath, and as many in England had accepted a social system which condemned the poor to destitution and death. But Mortimer does not offend his conscience by striking a blow; instead he leaves Herbert alone on the moor without a guide or food. It is *Macbeth* without blood. Then Rivers, himself already a murderer, tells him that he has lied in order to make him guilty and to teach him that the proud should feel no compassion or regret. Being proud himself, he hates Mortimer who in the past had saved his life. He wants to be released from the humiliation of being grateful, much as Sir James Lowther refused to be in debt to his agent. Mortimer has not been a murderer by clear intention any more than Wordsworth had always intended to desert Annette, but the deed was done. Mortimer admits to himself that he would not have done it had he not been in love with Herbert's innocent daughter, said by Rivers to be no daughter but a sex-slave about to be handed over to the evil Lord Clifford. Now she would not touch her father's murderer – and would any decent woman look at Wordsworth? So Mortimer condemns himself to a life of wandering in flight from the past, as had been Wordsworth's fate, while Rivers is killed as an act of justice. Action is short, the poem says, but suffering 'hath the nature of infinity'.

How, then did Wordsworth see any hope of escape from guilt and sorrow? He learned how to cope in the real world where happiness is not easy to find but where brave lives are possible. In that spirit he wrote a long tale called 'Peter Bell', in the style of a popular ballad. Contemporary magazines were full of such poems but he did not publish this one before 1819 because it had seemed to need revision if it was to be fit to 'fill *permanently* a station, however humble, in the literature of our country'. Its purpose was to show that the transformation of a life does not require 'the intervention of supernatural agency' and the prologue, about a journey on a magic boat among the stars ending in a garden on 'mother earth', clearly implied the message that nature itself can lead a sinner to virtue.

Peter Bell is the villain who has deceived 'a dozen wedded wives' and been guilty of many other crimes. As he stumbles thoughtlessly through a wood (does this represent Godwin's philosophy which does not recognise guilt?) he comes across an ass (nature incarnate) which he proposes to steal, but the ass will not budge although beaten brutally. This is because his owner lies dead in the lake and Peter feels compelled by conscience to drag the body out of the water. The ass now licks his hands but, when he mounts, forces him to go where he does not wish to go – to the late owner's family. On the way he is taken past an inn which reminds him of years of debauchery including the seduction of a girl who died of a broken heart (Annette?). Then he is made to ride by a Methodist chapel and to hear the preacher's 'repent! repent!' but his own repentance takes the form of making it possible for the drowned man to be buried, as any human being deserves.

> And now is Peter taught to feel
> That man's heart is a holy thing
> And Nature, through a world of death,
> Breathes into him a second breath,
> More searching than the breath of spring.

But what is this 'nature' which can heal? One day in June 1797 a friend he had met with fascination two years before came bounding across the field into Wordsworth's garden; this was Coleridge, whom we shall meet for ourselves in the next chapter. He brought with him an enthusiasm about Wordsworth's existing work which was much needed, for he was at least a published poet and a great talker with intoxicating ideas. A very unusual depth of love and collaboration developed at a very unusual speed. In the family-like group Wordsworth was the most serious thinker and his sister the most attentive observer of the world, but Coleridge's brilliance was what they needed to convince them that their combined imaginations could produce poetry with a new power and a new gospel. This poetry would tell the world that nature is One, that the life which runs through it all is One, and that all life comes, or may come, from God. Wordsworth was not yet clear about God and Coleridge thought him 'at least a semi-atheist' as well as a republican, but it could be agreed that if God exists beyond as well as within nature he, too, must be One. Wordsworth, who at this stage found it difficult to believe that anything could be more grand or more redemptive than nature, had no wish to believe in more than that one god and Coleridge, who had a decided faith, was at this stage a Unitarian, rejecting the orthodox doctrine of the Trinity because it was thought to teach nonsense or idolatry about three gods. But for the time being, it was agreed not to argue about religion.

Coleridge had rented a cottage some distance away for his wife and child. That did not keep him from spending many days in talk with the Wordsworths but they decided to move to be nearer him in Somerset, and again they were lucky, in their housing as well as in the great beauty of the neighbourhood. They were also lucky to escape from the government's campaign against radicals who might be revolutionaries and, in wartime, traitors. A senior intelligence officer was sent down from London to investigate when bewildered neighbours believed that the strange intruders into their tranquil society might be French spies. The

Home Office was reassured but the Wordsworths were told that, by what may not have been a coincidence, an aunt of the landlady needed the house.

Had people been able to read 'The Old Cumberland Beggar', that local alarm might have been soothed, but that poem was not published before 1800. There Wordsworth showed how far he had moved from revolutionary dreams. He felt for the poor – *for* them rather than *with* them, Coleridge could say – but he saw merit in the practice of letting the poor beg. Not only would that fate be better than confinement to a 'house of industry' where the conditions were degrading and labour was expected in return for minimum rations. He pictured an old and destitute man who moves from village to village and improves the community spirit of the residents by giving them opportunities for charity. The lesson drawn is that 'we have all of us one human heart', but his poem did not probe the heart of the beggar, or the heart of the growing cancer of mass poverty.

So the three friends walked, talked and wrote during and between the summers of 1797 and 1798. For them it was a time of excitement and astonishing creativity and out of it came two suggestions, both made by Coleridge. They needed wider knowledge if they were to be as great as they intended to be, so despite the war they must go to Germany, then the centre of Europe's intellectual life. They needed cash for this purpose, so that they must be paid for a collection of their poems. It would have to be anonymous; Coleridge explained to the potential publisher that his own name 'stinks' as a well known radical while Wordsworth's is 'unknown'. But it could have a title to make it saleable by promising both beauty and popularity, *Lyrical Ballads.*

At first Coleridge was to write the preface and contribute a substantial number of poems, but he backed out of both assignments. Probably he found to too difficult to see what unity could be claimed for the little book and there seemed to be only three poems which were ripe for their first publication, a tall tale in a pseudo-medieval style and two short extracts from a play not yet performed. So Wordsworth wrote the 'Advertisement' which was a substitute for a carefully reasoned preface. With an acceptable modesty it excused the poems as 'experiments' made 'chiefly with a view to ascertain how far the language of conversation in the middle and lower classes of society is adapted to the purpose of poetic pleasure' – an explanation of his own style but not of Coleridge's. But he then snubbed readers who 'may disapprove of the style': 'if poetry be a subject on which much time has not been bestowed, the judgement may be erroneous.'

It was a mistake to pick a fight, particularly since pride of place in this book which might be by a single anonymous author was given to

Coleridge's baffling 'Rime of the Ancyent Marinere'. The other poems were also not in the normal 'language of conversation'. They were strict about grammar, they used metre or rhyme, they avoided indelicacy, dialect and slang. When larger prefaces were added to the editions of 1800 and 1802, it was admitted that people using the language of such poems would have to be 'in a state of vivid sensation' and would only use a 'selection' from their everyday speech. Moreover, few of these poems shared any obvious pleasure. Since the 1740s many poets had practised 'sensibility' by being sentimental about human distress, which was usually given a picturesque background, but here the distress was usually thrown at the reader without any 'lyrical' softening and the 'ballads' were far more disturbing than the poems popular in that period. No extraordinary malice would be needed if reviewers and readers suspected that the poems had been published in the hope of making money – which was the truth.

The arrangement of the poems was another mistake which made it hard even for sympathetic readers to see what message was intended. The arrangement avoided any logic before it was changed in the next edition, but even amid the original disorder a pattern could be glimpsed.

The first of Wordsworth's poems to be included rejects the mood of a disillusioned priest who had brooded and wept in a seat which he had carved in the trunk of a tree near a lake. When young and 'by genius nurs'd' he had been 'big with lofty views', but had found the world neglectful and therefore he now fed his mind with the food of wounded pride. He was depressed both by the barren landscape around him and by the thought that any 'loveliness' glimpsed in the distance might be imagined by a human 'benevolence' which he did not share. Such pride, Wordsworth now comments, 'is littleness'. 'True dignity' is shown by the man who in 'lowliness of heart' can both 'suspect' and 'revere' himself, presumably because with all his weakness he is still able to hear what nature really says, to arise from self-pity, and to do some work. And near the end of the little collection the poet is moved when he meets an 'Old Man Travelling' – a man in whose 'settled quiet' there seems to be no need either of 'effort' or of 'patience'. Certainly he has no need of encouragement from people who see him. His mind is set on his one purpose: to walk to the distant hospital where his son is dying from wounds after a battle at sea.

The flowers and the birdsong of spring cannot stop Wordsworth's thoughts about 'what man has made of man'. Yet he wants to persuade any readers, who by definition must be educated and privileged, that even the destitute can retain some dignity because they, too, are human – and to honour them individually by sympathy and charity is more important than helping them systematically. From the agonised writing of his Salisbury Plain period he prints the story of the Female Vagrant. Her idyllic childhood was ended when a wicked landlord drove her and her father from their cottage to an ugly town and to dire poverty, and her survival there was ended when her unemployed husband had to enlist in the army sent to fight the rebels in America. She went with him but in that war he and her children died after great suffering and now she is penniless and hungry as she tramps an English road with no equipment except her tongue.

That is a story said to be true, and there are others about women. A book about Canada is the source for a ballad about a sick Indian woman left to starve and freeze to death because her nomadic tribe including her child must move on. A book by Erasmus Darwin is the source for a ballad about a Warwickshire farmer who rebukes an old woman for gathering sticks from his hedge in midwinter – only to be cursed by her and to die of cold in the belief that she had the power of a witch. A report from a 'lady in Bristol' about a mother who is 'mad' after her husband's desertion is turned into another ballad: she clings to the baby at her breast. Another ballad tells of another mother, also deserted, who sits and moans near the grave of the baby she may have killed.

In this sympathy with women in distress Wordsworth curbs his own self-pity. He does this also in his ballads about men. The shepherd who has to sell the last of his flock in order to feed his children is not treated as a victim of any particular oppressor: he has had to be responsible for ten children of his own, in happier days he took pride in his success at work, and in the thought of this period it is impossible for the state to solve his unavoidable problems. The old huntsman who is too feeble to wield an axe, or even a spade, was once exuberant in his love of life and only his imminent death can be the solution now: his gratitude for a little help is polite but ultimately irrelevant. Two poems are about convicts in chains: they are guilty and the chains are deserved. But that does not mean that the four men do not suffer like the women: to be human is to suffer.

By now Wordsworth derives his humanitarianism not from a belief in the French Revolution, nor from any British form of radical politics, nor from the shallow sentimentality of some other poets, but from a deep emotion about nature: to love that beauty is to love the spiritual beauty which can rise to the top in humans. Life tends to be tragic but the response has to be the courage to endure because that is the only realistic hope. What is needed is a 'wise passiveness' with the beauty of nature as a consolation and the defiance of fate as the spiritually victorious response. If we attempt to chop up nature into little bits (as scientists do) we shall not be wise, but wisdom can come from the courage to accept reality in a single vision:

> Sweet is the lore which nature brings;
> Our meddling intellect
> Mishapes the beauteous forms of things;
> – We murder to dissect.

Insights are put into the mouths of children who cannot well express what they feel. 'The Idiot Boy' was written with unusual speed because a friend had told him of a boy who had said about the moon 'the sun did shine so cold'. Wordsworth could expand this into a long story about Johnny's delighted ride when he decides to take a horse through a moonlit wood. (Nowadays the boy's handicap would be diagnosed as Down's syndrome.) A shorter poem was about a simple-minded girl who insisted that 'we are seven' although most of her family had died: her love of her family mattered more than the sad facts.

Three poems are entitled 'Lines Written . . .' and they are about the consolation which can be received from nature. One is an invitation to Dorothy to come outdoors 'on the first mild day of March': 'bring no book' because 'silent laws' about love can come 'from earth to man'. Another is inspired by the Thames at evening: the peace of the calm river should go with the poet 'to the tomb'. And the third poem was added to the collection when the printer thought it complete. This was entitled 'Lines Written a Few Miles above Tintern Abbey' although years later he said that 'I began it upon leaving Tintern . . . and concluded it just as I was entering Bristol that evening . . . Not a line of it was altered, and not any part of it written down till I reached Bristol.' The important point is that it was 'published almost immediately', unlike the account of his similar experience on Snowdon seven years before.

He rejoices once again in the 'wild secluded' beauty which he has remembered 'in lonely rooms' since his first visit in 1793. New Historicist critics have recently pointed out that the abbey was then a camp for the destitute while the valley was a Mecca for tourists although busy with the production of guns for the war, with forges smelting the iron mined locally. But it is no discredit to Wordsworth that he ignores such snags in order to recapture 'that serene and blessed mood' and 'the deep power of joy'. In 1798 the poet still needs healing: that is what matters to him. When 'we see into the life of things', is it 'a vain belief' that things ultimately mean well? He is full of 'sad perplexity'. He remembers that when he first came here in 1793, he had been

> more like a man
> Flying from something that he dreads, than one

Who sought the thing he loved. For nature then . . .
To me was all in all.

Then he had found in nature 'aching joys' – but 'that time is past' and he has been compensated because he has heard more of 'the still, sad music of humanity' – including his own heartbroken humanity – and in that music a whisper has reached him that human suffering is a part of a mystery greater than he had known either in 'the hour of thoughtless youth' or in 1793 when events in France had made him think deeply. He added '13 July 1798' to the poem's title, it seems mainly because that was the eve of Bastille Day which marked the start of the French Revolution. It was also the anniversary of an execution which marked the beginning of the Terror. Nine men had been condemned for counter-revolutionary activities, the chief witness being Léonard Bourdon who alleged that he had been nearly killed in a brawl in Orléans. Bourdon had been admired as an idealist by republicans in London and Annette's brother Paul had been involved in the little riot, only escaping death by disappearing.

Such memories of 'what man has made of man' made Wordsworth concentrate on reviving

That blessed mood . . .
In which the heavy and the weary weight
Of all this unintelligible world
Is lightened.

And the mood came. He felt

A presence that disturbs me with the joy
Of elevated thoughts; a sense sublime
Of something far more deeply interfused,
Whose dwelling is the light of setting suns,
And the round ocean, and the living air,
And the blue sky, and in the mind of man,
A motion and a spirit, that impels
All thinking things, all objects of all thought,
And rolls through all things.

Many critics have pointed out that it is not clear what is this 'something' present 'in all things' but it seems that Wordsworth wishes to escape from well-defined philosophy or theology, as he wishes to escape from the unromantic realities to be seen in the valley. The retention of the word 'god' without a capital letter in what he was to write next year seems to point to this wish not to close down any of his religious options. He sounds like a pantheist:

All things live with god, themselves
Are god existing in one mighty whole
As indistinguishable as the cloudless East
At noon is from the cloudless west . . .

However, he turns to his sister with 'this prayer', that 'through all the years' nature will lead them both, whether 'from joy to joy' or through 'solitude, or fear, or pain, or grief'. At present he is 'a worshipper of Nature' – of Spinoza's 'God or Nature' – but when 'these wild ecstasies shall be matured' they will learn what nature will still be willing to teach. 'Nature never did betray the heart that loved her': so he said and so he hoped in July 1798. But quite soon he was to think that not even nature could teach him what he most wanted to hear: that death, which is everywhere in nature, and often cruel, is not always the final reality.

It seems that the Wordsworths went to Germany in September 1799 because the lease on their house in Somerset had not been renewed and William had been persuaded that he needed to learn the German language and the rudiments of science. But the idea of such an expedition during a war had come from Coleridge, who now threw himself into doing what he wanted, while William and Dorothy had bigger problems about money and, as it turned out, no great interest either in the language or in the science. They landed up in Goslar because lodgings there were cheaper than in Coleridge's university city, they made very few friends and shivered through the severe winter. Dorothy was miserable and William would have been had he not retreated into drafting the poem about his childhood which eventually began *The Prelude.* He also wrote poems about loss and grief, the 'Lucy' and 'Matthew' poems. These sound like long sighs after 'strange fits of passion' and although large parts of those being mourned must be imaginary, there may be connections with real people. The innocent Lucy may be linked with Annette or Dorothy and Matthew with himself, for like that serious-minded village teacher he feels that he is 'unprofitably travelling towards the grave'. His draft for *The Prelude* started with a contrast between childhood's glory and an adult's waste of nature's gifts: 'Was it for this . . .?' And although he could use the word 'God' (then on almost everyone's lips) he did not believe that the personality can survive death:

No motion has she now, no force;
    She neither hears nor sees;
Rolled around in earth's diurnal course
    With roots, and stones, and trees.

All this made him glad to be back in England and happier still when he decided to make his home in the Lake District of his youth. He would live cheaply with Dorothy, but at first without Coleridge who strenuously objected to the district's dampness and then rented a house not far away. As a further prelude to the great philosophical poem of his continuing hopes he began *At Home in Grasmere*, intended as a long poem but never completed; what he wrote was not printed before 1888. At first he pictured himself as a delighted explorer of 'blissful Eden':

The unappropriated bliss hath found
An owner, and that owner I am he.
The Lord of this enjoyment is on Earth
And in my breast.

Soon, however, he found that the inhabitants were not all as innocent or as happy as Adam and Eve. He and Dorothy identified themselves with two swans recently brought to the little lake, only to find that some neighbour had thought that the strange and noisy birds would be more useful when eaten. A poem inspired by a memorial seen in Yorkshire showed his feelings about animals as well as birds. A deer being chased by hounds made a long leap ending in death and to commemorate the event the rich hunter had built a 'pleasure-house', now a ruin. But Wordsworth heard a different message from 'the Being that is in the clouds' and 'in the green leaves':

Never to blend our pleasure or our pride
With sorrow of the meanest thing that feels.

And his withdrawal to the Lake District did not mean that he had no further contacts with human sorrows. On these rural roads he still met the victims of war and people without work or home, and in this neighbourhood he found many signs that fewer families could survive on work done in cottages or in a few inherited fields. In 1800 he sent a copy of *Lyrical Ballads* to the great Whig politician Charles James Fox with a letter reporting his experience, but Fox replied by discussing the poetry.

On the whole he remained glad to be home again. He loved to have Dorothy at his side in their many walks and used her detailed diary as some of his inspiration for many future poems. When daffodils were to be symbols of the renewal of nature and of human hopes, they were to spring out of what Dorothy wrote, and when a leech-gatherer was to teach the poet 'resolution and independence' by his stoicism he too had been met first on Dorothy's paper. He loved having his brother John to stay for eight months in 1800. But they had to separate again because he had to earn his living as an officer in the merchant navy and 'The Brothers' came out of the poet's fears about such separations. A sailor returns to his native village and in the churchyard meets the vicar who speaks about the parishioners buried there. Eventually he tells the unrecognised sailor about his brother. The two were orphans devoted to each other and when the one went to sea the other grew depressed, took to sleepwalking and died in an accident. His body lies in an unmarked grave.

The fact that many families were being broken up by economic pressures (including overpopulation at that stage of history) was the reality which he begged Fox to consider. During a walk round the local lake he and his companions (Coleridge has joined them) enjoy the beauty and the sounds of the harvest being gathered in. Then they see a tall man in the distance, fishing, and tell themselves that he ought to be doing an honest day's work on the harvest. When they get to him, however, they find that he is too weak and emaciated to be able to hope for anything except a fish to feed his family; he may not be able to do even this much longer, and they are ashamed. And the greatest of the poems of this period is about Michael, a 'statesman' who is proud to own his own small territory for his sheep and who has lived and worked in order to be able to hand this heritage to his son Luke. Now Luke has had to earn his living in a far town, has fallen into debt, and has had to flee overseas. Yet Michael, now old and alone, still comes to the sheepfold which father and son had begun to build.

That recognition of the quiet suffering to be observed even in this 'blissful Eden' was written as the climax to a new edition of *Lyrical Ballads* which included a new preface about the proper character of poetry. It is now defined as 'the spontaneous overflow of powerful feelings' in a poet who is able to think 'long and deeply' and able also to remember 'in tranquillity that overflowing emotion with such power that by a species of reaction the tranquillity disappears' and he creates something very different from the conventional artificiality.

After that outburst of creativity Wordsworth relaxed during much of 1801. Then in December he resumed work on *The Prelude*, recalling his years in Cambridge. The revival of memories of young enthusiasm and ambition seems to have made him feel that he would never recover his full powers as a poet. In March 1802 he therefore began the 'ode' which became *Intimations of Immortality from Recollections of Early Childhood*, at first lamenting that nature no longer seemed to be robed 'in celestial light' but then removing his depression by celebrating spring with all the old power. He showed a draft of this ode to Coleridge and was dismayed to receive from his friend the passionate 'Letter to Sara Hutchinson' which was a long cry of despair: despite the joys of spring, nature reveals nothing about our destiny. In reply he tried to talk Coleridge out of this mood, saw the significance of the patient leech-gatherer whom Dorothy had met, and wrote his own despair-defying poems which culminated in his 'Ode to Duty'. A man must do what he knows he ought to do, whatever the difficulty and whatever his mood; a man must be manly. And then he completed his ode about immortality: we do not depend entirely on what nature may teach, the glory of childhood is a revelation of the origin and destiny of Man, the soul lived before birth and will live after death, duties must be done in that context of eternity.

His own household dared to tease him about the praise of duty, knowing that he kept on postponing the great philosophical poem which was meant to be his life's work, and Christians rebuked him for seeming to accept the heresy of the pre-existence of the soul. The educated knew that in ancient Greece Plato had thought that souls already alive in eternity were inserted into bodies at birth, but the orthodox insisted that the one Creator made a new soul for each new person. Yet Wordsworth, who was now beginning to move back into Christianity, declared that

> Our birth is but a sleep and a forgetting:
> The Soul that rises with us, our life's star,
> Hath had elsewhere its setting,
> And cometh from afar . . .
> . . . trailing clouds of glory, do we come
> From God, who is our home.

Thus the child is the 'best philosopher' because when everything seems new the world seems to resemble an 'imperial palace' in this 'vision splendid' before adulthood locks the 'prison house'. When challenged, he claimed that he had not been meaning to teach Platonism but had used such poetic language in order to speak of the soul's immortality as a gift from the eternal God.

He had not spoken more clearly because he was still not sure about what he believed. He gave thanks

> for those obstinate questionings
> Of sense and outward things,
> Fallings from us, vanishings;
> Blank misgivings of a creature
> Moving about in worlds not realised . . .

and he hoped for a fuller revelation through his experience of 'spots of time' which make him 'tremble' but

> be they what they may
> Are yet the fountain-light of all our day,

Are yet a master-light of all our seeing;
Uphold us, cherish, and have power to make
Our noisy years seem moments in the being
Of the eternal Silence . . .

Those moments when we listen to 'the eternal Silence' can make us feel like children who play on the beach with 'the mighty waters' of the 'immortal sea' near them. But nature gives us more than joy:

To me the meanest flower that blows can give
Thoughts that do often lie too deep for tears.

Indeed, when there are deep thoughts about the 'mighty waters' there can be 'the faith that looks through death'. William Blake was so excited by this poem that his stomach was upset when he thought about what he would have said himself. But Coleridge was unimpressed, in particular by the marks given to a child for being the 'best philosopher'. And it seems that Wordsworth himself was not impressed deeply enough. He had not yet experienced the agony of bereavement as an adult. When that came, a faith which had to be expressed by a poetic use of Plato, flowers and the seaside did not offer sufficient strength. When he had to listen to the silence of death, would 'the eternal Silence' speak up, so that an adult could hear?

In May 1802 a death gave him ill-concealed pleasure, however: the life of James Lowther ('Wicked Jimmy') ended. His successor as Earl of Lonsdale, his cousin William, soon promised to pay the outstanding debts with interest. Since expenses and legal fees had eaten up so much of what had been due to the orphans almost twenty years ago, Wordsworth still had to exercise a strict economy but the improvement in his finances meant that he could support a wife, and hopefully children, as well as Dorothy. He still had Annette on his conscience, but in March a peace or truce had been patched up between Britain and Napoleon. It was likely to be temporary but it made contact with the deserted mother and child possible. Annette responded without hysterics and in August William and Dorothy travelled to Calais in order to reach an arrangement without going further into France or into the emotions of the past.

Dorothy's diary was for once not vivid, but it seems that agreement was reached without great difficulty. Annette had now accepted that she would never be married and was worried mainly about Anne-Caroline, to whom her father could now promise an annual income until her own marriage. As they walked on the beach the relieved father communed with nature:

The holy time is as quiet as a nun
Breathless with adoration, the broad sun
Is sinking down in its tranquillity;
The gentleness of heaven broods o'er the sea:
Listen! the mighty Being is awake
And doth with his eternal motion make
A sound like thunder – everlastingly.
Dear child! Dear girl! That walkest with me here,
If thou appear untouched by solemn thought,
Thy nature is not therefore less divine.

The child may have been thinking about this strange Englishman, her father whom she had never seen before and was never to see again.

But Wordsworth's thoughts were also intense about the politics of 1802, and his month's absence from England made him more patriotic than ever before. He looked across the Channel and felt that the evening star was the 'Star of my Country!' He looked south to the Adriatic and lamented Napoleon's extinction of the Venetian republic. He looked across the Atlantic and hailed Toussaint L'Ouverture who faced death after resistance to Napoleon's reimposition of slavery. And when he returned to England, he immediately composed a celebration of the white cliffs and the white shirts of the cricketers. When he had left London, the city seen from Westminster Bridge in the early morning had seemed almost as lovely as the Lake District. But he grew anxious for his country as the peace disintegrated and England lacked leadership worthy of it. So

Milton! thou shouldst be living at this hour:
England hath need of thee . . .
Thou hadst a voice whose sound was like the sea,
Pure as the naked heavens, majestic, free . . .

The association of Milton with the sea was odd but significant, for only the Royal Navy now stood between Napoleon and England. In April 1803 the *Morning Post* published another patriotic sonnet, speaking of the proud 'flood of British freedom' which must not be 'lost for ever'.

We must be free or die, who speak the tongue
That Shakespeare spake; the faith and morals hold
Which Milton held.

An extra reason for being patriotic (he even drilled with the Volunteers who would have defended the Lake District against the French had they ever reached it) was that he was now married, from October 1802, to Mary Hutchinson. He had known and loved her since 1787 although people thought her plain, and she had got used to his habits. She was, indeed, ready to accept patiently whatever life might produce, helped by a quiet faith which was to curb her husband's heresies (in an influence exercised by many Victorian wives). It says much for her that John, the shyest of the Wordsworth brothers, had also hoped to marry her. She needed this peace of heart and mind on her wedding day. Dorothy had slept with the ring on her own finger and in the morning she said that she was not up to being present at the ceremony. When the married couple appeared she embraced William with more exhibitionism than the bride. But the two women had been friends for many years and continued to remain friends in their new relationship. This was partly because Dorothy recognised that Mary was as devoted to William as she was: both were willing to copy and recopy versions of poems. Mary knew that Keats was a fellow poet but still rebuked him: 'Mr Wordsworth is never interrupted.' His poem of 1804 about this 'perfect woman', and letters published in 1997, are evidence that husband and wife were passionately and permanently in love.

They were also to be unfailingly tender to Dorothy during the years (from 1829) when she was to suffer from Alzheimer's disease, then called senile dementia, while remaining in their joint home until her death in 1847. She was often expressively affectionate towards William and in a book of 1954 it was suggested that their relationship was so intense as to be at least on the border of incest, but this idea probably owes more to the twentieth century than to the nineteenth, when love between siblings (as between friends of the same gender) could be ardent without involving any action which would be condemned by moralists, who were then plentiful. So far as is known, at the time only Coleridge dropped even a hint about anything wrong – and then his hint was about Annette, not Dorothy.

He dropped it when very bitter about William's growing alienation from him and about his own failure as a husband and as a poet. His ode to *Dejection* cut out some of the references to himself but the date of its appearance in the *Morning Post* was pointed: it was the day of Wordsworth's wedding, which he did not attend. And a week later a shorter and more clearly malicious poem appeared in the same newspaper:

> My Father Confessor is strict and holy . . .
> But yet how oft I find the pious man
> At Annette's door, the lovely courtesan
> Her soul's deformity the good man wins
> And not her charms: he comes to hear her sins.

William welcomed his first son, born eight months after the wedding, and named him John after his father and his brother, who was to be the central figure in the next spiritual crisis. First he took Dorothy on a tour of Scotland (he also took Coleridge but this forgiven friend walked off on his own). The best poem resulting was about a river he did not see, the Yarrow. It showed his enthusiasm for Scottish history, including some located by that river, and he brooded over the grave of Burns before making friends with a living poet, Walter Scott. All this might hint that his inspiration was beginning to be literary rather than natural, but when 1804 began he had almost completed *The Prelude.* He was at the height of his powers and of such contentment as was possible for him while he was still close to the years of misery.

Then work was interrupted. In February he received the news that his brother John had died at the start of a voyage intended to make him rich enough to settle into a retired life in the Lake District. William had invested most of his own capital in the cargo on board, hoping that the profits would solve his financial problems permanently while with John's encouragement he dedicated himself to the composition of the great philosophical poem as the new Milton.

It was some consolation that the cargo had been well insured but the loss of John broke William's heart. The ship had sunk in the bay between Weymouth and Portland in Dorset, driven by the strong tide onto a notorious shoal of rock and shingle. The only man who could be blamed for the disaster was the pilot, who arrived late and then in his hurry chose the wrong route past the danger. As captain John had sent passengers off in the ship's few boats and had calmed the sailors but like most of the crew was frozen during the night and dropped helpless into the shallow water while the other ships were too nervous to attempt a rescue. His last reported words were 'God's will be done' and William's agony was now shared with Sir George Beaumont in a letter which modern biographers have rightly seen as crucial:

> Why have we a choice and a will, and a notion of justice and injustice, enabling us to be moral agents? Why have we sympathies that make the best of us so afraid of inflicting pain and sorrow, which we see dealt about so lavishly by the supreme governor? Why should our notions of right towards each other, and to all sentient beings within our influence, differ so widely from what appears to be his notion and rule, if everything were to end here? Would it be blasphemy to say that, upon the supposition of the thinking principle being destroyed by death, however inferior we may be to the great Cause and ruler of things, we have *more of love* in our nature than he has? The thought is monstrous; and yet how to get rid of it except upon the supposition of *another and a better world* I do not know.

Here was something which nature could not teach. Milton's belief that God is perfect had been strengthened by the idea that originally the world had been very good, and he had imagined the lost Paradise. Now Wordsworth's more vulnerable belief that 'the great cause and ruler of things' is good had been rescued by the idea of a better world after death, although he could not imagine heaven. The future had replaced the past at the centre of faith, and he could believe and trust in such a future not because it was the obvious fulfilment of the beauty to be seen before death but because 'pain and sorrow' meant that a life terminated by death could have no ultimate meaning or significance, just as Macbeth had said before going to his death.

His poetry was now a cry from grief. One poem was about a daisy growing on his brother's grave; it had been John's favourite flower. Another, in 1806, was about a picture Beaumont had painted of a ship struggling in a storm near a castle. It ended 'Not without hope we suffer and we mourn.' Another was added to a book of his poems in manuscript, intended to go with John to the East, and it was more clearly a petition to God than was any of the book's earlier contents. And around Easter 1806 he could write to his brother Richard with a pointer to his full acceptance of the 'supposition' about the 'better world' of eternity: 'he went a brave and innocent spirit to the God from whom I trust he will receive his reward.' The life and death of John had made William a Christian believer.

As a major poet Wordsworth died not long after his brother but the man had 45 more years to live. Instead of being almost suicidally distressed or ecstatically elated and joyful, he was now either happy or worried, and neither mood made for great poetry. Instead of dreaming about an ideal republic he had to observe from a distance, or to experience to a small extent, the realities of a society moving into modernity in ways which he found worrying or deplorable. But there were consolations for middle and old age. Instead of a small domestic circle and brief encounters with poor folk met on the road, he now received visitors on pilgrimage and enjoyed social contacts with people in other parts of the country, even in London. These new friends had the education and money needed to support their cultural interests and they could welcome his advice about landscaping their gardens. He could earn enough from a job which was steady although not glamorous. He had a happy marriage, children he loved and worried about when ill or idle, pleasure in beauty found not only in nature but also in buildings which echoed with impressive history. He had come from, and had always written for, the middle class; now he happily belonged to it. To regard him as the 'lost leader' of

English radicalism is to forget how immature he had been in early manhood.

Easily understood poems written in middle age, quite often for magazines which paid, could be popular. For example, 24 sonnets out of the 525 which he wrote at one time or another were prompted by his tour of Scotland in the autumn of 1831 and collected as *Yarrow Revisited.* They came very near to the conventional and artificial style about picturesque scenes which he had denounced in the time of *Lyrical Ballads*, and they had less energy than, for example, the smaller series of poems linked by the river Duddon which he had published in 1820 as musings on the stages through which life flows to the sea. The question which he had already heard had now caught up with him:

> Whither is fled the visionary gleam,
> Where is it now, the glory and the dream?

The earlier confession that he was a democrat also seemed distant while he agitated against the Reform Act of 1832 which gave votes to property owners in the new industrial towns and abolished old constituencies which had now very few and very bribable electors. But this was not entirely the blind reaction which readers are nowadays likely to condemn. Some of his worries were not despicable. The enlarged electorate still fell far short of a representation of the people; the new electorate had its own vested interests; and if eventually all men (and even all women?) were to be included in the political system, first there must be a national system of education. This constructive cause, which prevailed twenty years after his death, now aroused real passion in him. Meanwhile he did advocate some changes which were not inconsistent with the passion of his republican immaturity. In 1835 he praised the Britain which was now beginning to be Victorian: it was the 'happiest and worthiest' of all the countries 'of which there is any record since the foundation of civil society'. That should, he thought, be remembered by any workman who 'runs the risk of becoming an agitator', or of becoming a slave 'without a will of his own' by 'being enrolled in a union'. Yet he did argue that 'all persons who cannot find employment, or procure wages sufficient to support the body in health and strength, are entitled to maintenance by the law'. And he did support legislation to take children out of factories and to limit the hours worked by adults.

What has sometimes made him ridiculous in the eyes of readers who have lived through changes in the world far larger than those which he experienced is his hostility to the impact of relatively minor changes in his own backyard. He opposed the building of a railway from Kendal to Windermere although some of the tourists who would use it had been attracted by reading his own poetry. They had countryside already near them, he argued: let them be less exhausted and better paid so that they might regularly enjoy it and not be a nuisance in the district to which he wrote a guide book for the benefit of discerning walkers. He denounced the building of brick houses and the whitewashing of cottages, for the cottages of his boyhood (or was it an earlier period?), inhabited by proudly independent 'statesmen', had seemed to be neat piles of stone at home on the green earth. He was determined to remain romantic about the district, not being fully sensitive to criticisms of the control exercised by still-feudal landlords or by the new class of unsentimental capitalists. And it has to be acknowledged that at least a part of the reason for a complacency not totally unlike Bishop Watson's was that his changed circumstances made him less sensitive to memories of his own past.

The former inn in Grasmere (now called Dove Cottage), where he had written out his poems after composing them on walks, became too small for family and guests. So he tried several larger houses before becoming so content with Rydal Mount (from 1814) that when its owner seemed about to end his lease he bought the field in front of it and threatened to build a new house there, preserving his view. As his expenses increased he sought employment, asking the new Lord Lonsdale in 1812 to use his influence. His anxiety led him to pretend that he was willing to move anywhere, but next year Lonsdale solved the problem realistically: the poet was appointed Distributor of Stamps for Westmorland. This post, which he held for almost thirty years, involved the oversight of the agents who sold the stamped paper needed for many purposes, and Wordsworth did attend to his responsibilities as a taxgatherer although the routine work was done largely by an assistant who was also his gardener.

In the election of 1818 he published *Two Addresses* to voters as part of the Lonsdale family's successful campaign to retain control of the region. He argued that the family had changed since the time of the wicked earl, but his own family was surely right to beg him not to let his gratitude to the new earl make him vulnerable to the abuse which he received. In 1841 another unnecessary and unwise action exposed him to condemnation by the future. He published fourteen 'sonnets upon the punishment of death' in the Tory *Quarterly Review*, pleading with the public not to 'strike from Law's firm hand that awful rod'. He did not, however, go so far as to defend the situation in the 1820s, when the list of offences thought to deserve hanging had run to almost two hundred.

Some of his poetry after 1805 is significant if we are interested in his religion or spirituality, but not much of it is in that category. He was discouraged by contemptuous reviewers of his *Poems in Two Volumes* in

1807 and kept almost all his work private for seven years. As late as 1825 no publisher could be found for his collected poetry. And it seems that he thought that there would be hostility rather than indifference were he to say plainly what his religious beliefs now were, and for reasons good or bad he had no wish to offend.

The White Doe of Rylstone, largely written in the sad winter of 1807–08, was a dignified story set mainly in the churchyard of Bolton Abbey in the reign of Elizabeth I and dedicated to his devout wife. It was a tale about eight brothers who joined their father in a Catholic rebellion against the queen: all lost their lives. The remaining brother had not rebelled but was perhaps a traitor to his family. Anyway, he was killed near the abbey and buried there, and their sister Emily was to be seen mourning over the grave, according to the local legend in the company of a white doe. The doe survived the mourner's own death and is to be seen as Christ, the Christ of Easter; the symbol had been used before. But it was not a very powerful symbol.

The friends to whom he showed this poem thought it unworthy of him and it was not published until 1815 – and then in a small and expensive edition. In 1808 similar discouragement made him abandon a poem which promised to be about the future of the Church although it had the innocuous title 'The Tuft of Primroses'. The little flowers growing among the rocks to proclaim spring inspired a tribute to monks who had withdrawn from the world under St Basil's leadership long ago, to seek

> The life where hope and memory are as one,
> Earth quiet and unchanged, the human soul
> Consistent in self rule, and heaven revealed
> To meditation in that quietness.

But in the mood in which he wrote, one of sadness about the death of friends, he went on to lament the decline or death of the monastic movement in the modern world without being clear about St Basil's, or a modern, faith. The incomplete poem was first published in 1949.

The Excursion, dedicated to Lord Lonsdale and first published in 1814, was written over eight years and began with a revised version of 'The Ruined Cottage' of the 1790s. One change was to rename 'the Pedlar' who had explained the ruin; friends had said that such high thoughts could not be expected from a door-to-door salesman and he was renamed the Wanderer, with an emphasis on his life amid nature as he brought wisdom to welcoming cottages. And in the second edition nature's redeeming response to the tragedy in the ruined cottage –

> Those weeds, and the high spear-grass on that wall,
> By mist and silent rain drops silvered o'er

– was to be put second to the Redeemer himself. He now wrote that in Margaret's worst distress she had learned, with soul

> Fixed on the Cross, that consolation springs
> From sources deeper far than deepest pain.

That was written by a man well acquainted with grief. In 1812 he had lost two young children and many years later could still describe the courses of their last illnesses in detail. In 1847 his daughter Dora was to die and he was not to recover before his own death three years later.

Like the ecstasies on Snowdon or above Tintern, that vision of the ruined cottage was raw religious experience. But what did it signify? Could nature speak more clearly? How did the cross console? One of the characters in the debate which occupies most of *The Excursion* is the Pastor, but the only act of worship which this Anglican priest leads is in the open air and his eloquence is about parishioners buried in the churchyard, not about doctrines which might be taught from the pulpit. The poem includes some poetry which was as good as his most famous passages but its failure finally to affirm or to contradict the orthodoxy of the churches led to a disappointed and disappointing reception. In a review Francis Jeffrey called *The Excursion* a 'tissue of devotional and moral ravings' and we have to ask whether that is in any way a just verdict.

The narrator is taken by the Wanderer to the Solitary, a figure representing what Wordsworth might have become as a recluse who, when disillusioned and bereaved, could have failed to find any consolation except a tearful solitude. The Solitary might see in the clouds above the mountains further visions of the perfect city –

> that marvellous array
> Of temple, palace, citadel and huge
> Fantastic pomp of structure without name,
> In fleecy folds voluminous, enwrapped.

But in reality is heaven empty and is the whole scene 'the sport of Nature, aided by blind Chance'? And how is that mystery to be solved by 'imagination high or question deep'? When the French Revolution had gone wrong the Solitary had gone to America and then turned to nature in Britain, but now he wants only death, 'where all is still'.

The Wanderer responds with a layman's sermon which in its final version begins

> One adequate support
> For the calamities of mortal life
> Exists – one only; an assured belief

> That the procession of our fate, howe'er
> Sad or disturbed, is ordered by a Being
> Of infinite benevolence and power . . .

He knows as does the Solitary the 'secret attractions of the grave' but before death there is hope to be nursed and duty to be done. Man can 'above himself erect himself' so that he may 'live by Admiration, Hope, and Love' and hear 'authentic tidings of invisible things'. In English poetry that is to be the faith of Tennyson, Browning and Hopkins. But the Solitary is not persuaded – as part of Wordsworth is not, even now. He refuses to regard as authoritative

> The outward ritual and established forms
> To which the lips give utterance,

for in the churchyard to which they go he finds himself

> Here standing, with the unvoyageable sky
> In faint reflection of infinitude
> Stretched overhead, and at my pensive feet
> A subterranean magazine of bones.

He challenges the Pastor to speak truth fully about the tragedies of life and the priest does that, but his message is scarcely a proclamation of faith. Good and bad were mixed between, and within, the people he has known, now in their graves, and good and bad are mixed in all experience. 'Human life abounds with mysteries' and only the decision of faith or unbelief can begin to make sense of it. In his own case, the decision to believe has been supported by the beauty of the creation to be seen around the churchyard, so he repeats the Wanderer's appeal to the evidence of nature.

The Solitary, however, is still not persuaded, and the questions about the religious significance of nature have only grown since his day. The countryside which Wordsworth knew best lifted up hearts and minds through its mountains and at ground level encouraged comparisons between God and a shepherd, even between God and a lamb. It was kept in order, and made useful to patient and pastorally minded humans, by placid sheep which ate grass and provided wool and meat. But what if flesh-eating animals chase, tear and kill, making nature 'red in tooth and claw' (Tennyson's disturbed *In Memoriam* was published in the year of Wordsworth's death)? What if another part of nature is far less beautiful than the Lake District, and far less friendly? Or if one lives in a sordid part of a city? Wordsworth's nature-mysticism was authentic, and many people across the continents and the centuries have shared it to some extent, but by the time of *The Excursion* he had moved beyond it to a belief in the transcendent Creator, converted to that faith not on a mountain but in the valley of the shadow of his brother's death. To be convincing as a reporter of that spiritual journey, he could perhaps have merged the solitary, the Wanderer and the Pastor into himself and written the often-promised philosophical poem. Then he might have matched Milton: he was not too old, as we see when we remember that Milton did not begin *Paradise Lost* as a young man.

His *Ecclesiastical Sonnets*, composed mainly in 1821, were proofs of how far he had travelled since the 1790s, reaching the belief that for most people any revelation of God in nature needs to be strengthened by the religion of a community with a tradition. And for him, despite his unorthodoxy, only one such community was an option. His versified history of the Church of England was stoutly patriotic and mainly for this reason Protestant: at the time he was opposed to the grant of full civil rights to Roman Catholics because he regarded them as people, probably Irish, who owed allegiance to a foreign pope. The Ancient Britons were rebuked for yielding to the army of Rome and the Anglo-Saxons were preferred to their Norman conquerors, who destroyed 'ancient customs' after their invasion with a papal blessing. The medieval civilisation was applauded, but not the 'pomp' of the Mass and the monasteries, with 'rites that trample upon soul and sense'. There was joy that superstitious rites were no longer conducted in King's College Chapel in Cambridge or in Westminster Abbey, whose architecture was compared with the Alps. (He also wrote about St Paul's Cathedral when covered by 'its own sacred veil in falling snow'.) And Protestants who did not belong to this 'English Church' were urged to return to it because its beautiful buildings, traditional ceremonies and stored memories were open for all to enter and enjoy. The trouble was that the future of this, and every other, religious body was to depend on people believing that it spoke the truth – and because Wordsworth did not believe that the Church of England did this adequately in his own day, his sonnets were reticent about the heart of the matter.

Thus the ex-radical became an elegant, if insecure, a pillar of Church and State in Early Victorian England. As such, as well as because of his admitted eminence as a poet, he received a pension from the government in 1843 and next year the dignity of appointment as Poet Laureate in succession to Robert Southey. But of course that is not the reason why he has quite often seemed important to later generations.

In a bitter mood Coleridge dismissed his final message: 'Wordsworth has convinced *himself* of truths which the generality of persons have either taken for granted from their infancy, or else adopted early in life.' But in fact the basic beliefs about human life which seemed obviously true to Coleridge, and as he thought to almost everyone else, were not permanently safe. Even in the Victorian Age Matthew Arnold could hear the tide retreating over the stones of Dover Beach and reflect about the ebb of the sea of faith in God as life's ultimate explanation. Then came the time of the great wars and of the triumphs of the Nazis and the Communists, and a hundred years after Wordsworth's death in 1850 the secularisation of Europe was about to gather new force as the incoming tide. The Europe which had been Christendom was to become the world's most secular large continent. In such a future, where the sceptical Solitary was now in the majority, many would have to go on spiritual journeys, away from any fashionable beach, if they were ever to agree to the truths which Coleridge thought trite, and it would be useful to have a suggestion about where a journey might start. And that Wordsworth could supply. As Helen Darbishire wrote in 1950, his greatest poetry 'breathes the freshness of mountain air' and 'seems to spring from the earth like a mountain spring: its language is as colourless as water. The poet is looking into the heart of man and the life of nature as if indeed he saw things for the first time.'

SIX

COLERIDGE

A MOVEMENT IN LITERATURE and the wider culture between 1790 and 1825 (approximately), chiefly in Britain and Germany, was seen as a whole by twentieth-century scholars and called 'Romantic'. In its time it saw nature as a whole, felt deeply about it with a new emotionalism, found God in it if anywhere, and drew from it the faith that human nature either was glorious or could become so and be full of joy. Thus Wordsworth can be called a Romantic poet, and even compared with Beethoven the supreme Romantic musician, although in middle age he did not derive his beliefs from nature alone.

Other great Romantic poets were, however, totally incapable of writing ecclesiastical sonnets, for they were convinced that the official shape of Christianity was without an alternative – and without credibility. Byron told his estranged wife 'I do believe' and when he imagined Childe Harold in Athens and Rome he treated the Parthenon as a waste of time but St Peter's Basilica as 'the Holy of Holies'. He believed in God at least to the extent of being sceptical about total scepticism: nature is ambiguous. But by temperament he was a rebel although an aristocrat, and his sympathy was with the outcast Cain against Abel in the Hebrew myth, as with Greeks against imperial Turks in current politics. Keats made a Hellenism of the imagination his own religion: 'beauty is truth' as seen on a Grecian urn. Christianity has a worse mythology because it has been 'accommodated to the purposes of power and revenue'. And Shelley never moved from his belief as a student in the 'necessity of atheism'. To him Jesus was 'this most just, wise and benevolent of men', 'the enemy of oppression and falsehood', but 'no man of sense' could think Christianity true, as he said three months before he died.

Yet there were many points of contact between Romanticism and the Christian tradition. Both put spirituality and morality above materialism and love above commerce and war; both made 'intense and impassioned' (Shelley) responses to nature and nature's God (if there is any true God); both respected the human Jesus and the literature called the

Bible; both cared about the poor and hoped for radically better days. And connections could be expected to be specially close in Britain. In traditionally Catholic France opposition to Church and King was Deistic in religion, reserving its worship for the Supreme Being, but in England Protestant Dissenters formed a large sub-culture in opposition to the Established Church, providing a Christian alternative. Even within the Church of England there could be some spirit of rebellion. So we can end this book by taking account of two Romantic poets who were highly intelligent and definite, although not conformist, Christians. One will be William Blake, now agreed by almost everyone to be one of the giants, but it is convenient to take first his younger contemporary Samuel Taylor Coleridge, partly because of his connection with Wordsworth and partly because even if he was not a giant it can be thought that he would have been one had he not wrecked his life: Charles Lamb famously called him a damaged archangel. He was born in 1772 and might have achieved the definitive restatement of Christianity in dialogue with Romanticism.

In his lovely poem 'Frost at Midnight' he meditated during the sleep of his infant son in a silent cottage, after a snowstorm in February 1798. He hoped for that boy a childhood as happy, in a countryside as beautiful, as the one he had known himself in Devon. There his father had been both priest and schoolmaster. Almost in the shadow of a fine medieval church the boy had begun to absorb the Christian faith which never entirely left him although it changed its shape, and with his father's encouragement he had begun to be a prodigy of knowledge and speech. But before his ninth birthday he lost his father to death and he was expelled from this Eden. His brothers had not been fond of their father's favourite, who was already eccentric, and now his saddened mother also grew cold.

He was sent away on a scholarship to Christ's Hospital in London where the teaching was excellent but given as a charity and without softness. Boys who competed well intellectually were sent on to universities and boys who did not succeed in this way knew that their lives would be more lowly. Coleridge competed but emotionally he was starved. His nightmares began at that school and he remembered looking up at the stars: they provided the only beauty in sight.

He rebelled against Cambridge after a competitive start (like Wordsworth) and incurred debts after wine and women. To escape the debts he enlisted in the cavalry under a ludicrous name and proved unable to stay on a horse. Rescued by two of his brothers (one was a colonel) with the plea that he was mad, he left the university without taking a degree but soon became a notable figure in Bristol, the nation's second city. There he denounced not only the recently declared war but also the slave trade which was the city's chief source of profit. He attracted attention as a talker and lecturer, journalist and poet, and preached in Unitarian pulpits to extremely Protestant Dissenters who shared Milton's faith. His message was not about the divine Christ, but Jesus was 'a perfect example of all human excellence', his moral teaching was 'unspotted by one single error', and those who obeyed it could fix their eyes on 'the glittering summits that rise one above another in Alpine endlessness'. Young William Hazlitt walked ten miles to hear him and, although he was dismayed by his later life, on his death he called him the only genius he had known. The sermon he heard was about Jesus praying alone in the hills in defiance of the authorities of Church and State, and such a Jesus might well have blessed an idealistic plan to emigrate to America and live there in a 'pantisocracy', a Christian commune with Communist principles.

The chief organiser of this project, Robert Southey, collaborated on a play about the French Revolution, which was published along with addresses to the people by Coleridge himself (under a Latin title). But Southey then decided to go to Portugal instead and the emigration to Utopia collapsed, as did a newspaper, *The Watchman*, intended to awaken England. More seriously sad was the fact that Southey had persuaded Coleridge to become engaged to his wife's sister, Sarah; it was planned that the two women would look after them in America. Coleridge had wanted to marry Mary Evans but he told Southey that he would do his 'duty' although he did '*not* love' Sarah. He now decided that if he was to remain an Englishman after all, he would retire to read and write in the countryside with Sarah, and he was supported by an annuity from a rich young admirer who belonged to the Wedgwood dynasty of manufacturers of pottery. So we find him with the baby on that night in February 1798.

His spiritual development can be traced in his poems. 'Religious Musings' were optimistic declamations on Christmas Eve in 1797:

'Tis the sublime of man,
Our noontide majesty, to know ourselves
Parts and proportions of one wond'rous whole.

Next August he asked about this whole wonderful world

And what if all of animated nature
Be but organic harps divers'ly framed,
That tremble into thought, as o'er them sweeps
Plastic and vast, one intellectual breeze,
At once the soul of each, and God of all?

Now comes an ominous note. That poem, 'The Eolian Harp', was short, and in blank verse sounding conversational, and it has been praised as the first great Romantic lyric ever written. But it ends with a 'mild reproof' from his wife. Told that he must 'walk humbly with my God' instead of musing about nature, he feels 'sinful and most miserable'. The acknowledgement that they have incompatible temperaments is beginning. He thinks about himself but also about the divine 'Incomprehensible' and the glowing future of 'noontide majesty': she is conventionally devout and domestic.

At the end of 1796 he wrote an ode which, in his own words, 'prophesied the downfall of this country' in its war against France the home of liberty, but announced that he was recentring his 'immortal mind in the long Sabbath of high self-content'. However, this had been the year during which, when eye trouble threatened his reading, he remembered that at Christ's Hospital the doctor had given him opium. The drug worked again, it was mixed with a strong drink such as brandy, the doses were increased, and by the end of 1801 he had begun to be disastrously addicted. Portraits show that within three years his face had been coarsened and ravaged almost beyond recognition, and his notebooks show that his general health was not improved by the new medicine. While complaining about rheumatism or neuralgia he had managed to take long walks until his addiction made him indolent and fat. He had complained about dysentery but now bouts of constipation were excruciating. He made several attempts to break the habit, but could not and blamed himself.

Modern readers are likely to find it difficult to understand how a man so intelligent, and so moral, could destroy his life in this way, but in this period opium was widely used as soothing and healing medicine. Had John Wordsworth reached India on that voyage, his ship would have been given a new cargo, to take opium to China, and his hope was that his brother would finance edifying poetry out of the profits of that trade. William Wilberforce, an Evangelical whose life and writing commended a fervent religion to other members of the upper and middle classes, and whose leadership of the crusade against the slave trade has always been honoured, became an opium addict. A doctor's prescription was not needed, it was not very expensive and there were no clinics to fight the habit's grip. Even after the publication of Thomas De Quincey's explicit and widely noticed *Confessions of an English Opium-Eater* in 1821, more than forty years passed before the sale of the drug was controlled in Britain; and during this period a war was fought in order to protect the right of British traders to poison the Chinese.

Inevitably Coleridge's poetry was affected. The line it had been expected to take was shown when in November 1796 he would

fight the bloodless fight
Of science, freedom and the truth in Christ.

Next June he pictured his new-found friends, the Wordsworths, and his schoolfriend Charles Lamb, walking through the Somerset countryside which 'beneath the wide, wide heaven' has glories which are the clothes of 'the Almighty Spirit' and which can always keep the heart 'awake to love and beauty'. This healing power of nature is specially important now, for Lamb is trying to recover from a 'strange calamity': his sister had killed their mother. But later in that summer of 1797 he had a 'slight indisposition' (a stomach upset) during a walk and he treated it with an 'anodyne' – a dose of opium. He rested in a cottage, he had a dream and when he woke up he sooner or later wrote 'Kubla Khan'.

He later claimed that he had been reading a book of 1613 which mentioned the ten-acre garden of a palace in the Orient, and that he would have written more if he had not been interrupted by 'a person from Porlock', but both statements are questionable: one of the effects of opium was to blur the difference between fact and fancy. That book was too bulky to be carried on a walk or found by chance in a cottage, and research has shown that what he wrote and rewrote was a jumble of near-quotations from many books. It seems possible that he simply did not know how to end the poem, which despite many ingenious suggestions has never been shown to have any clear meaning. It sounds magical as it moves from the 'pleasure dome' down the 'sacred river' through 'caves of ice' to the 'sunless sea' but if this is about to be interpreted as the Story of Life (from youth to death) or as the Story of Art (from the pleasant to the sublime) in the song of the Abyssinian maid, that song is never heard. What is clear is that this famous poem has everything to do with opium and nothing to do with the English countryside or with 'science, freedom and the truth in Christ'.

At first the opium was not a severe depressant. In the spring of 1798, after 'Frost at Midnight', he wrote two fine political poems. 'France: An Ode' was indignant about the French invasion of republican Switzerland. 'Fears in Solitude' was a celebration of his own Britain, now threatened by the possibility of another invasion:

How should thou prove aught else but clear and holy
To me, who from thy lakes and mountain-hills,
Thy clouds, thy quiet dales, thy rocks and seas,
Have drunk, in all my intellectual life,
All sweet sensations, all ennobling thoughts,
All adoration of the God in nature,
All lovely and all honourable things,

Whatever makes this mortal spirit feel
The joy and greatness of its future being?

One evening that April he listened, spellbound romantically, to the songs of nightingales and dared to rebuke the venerated Milton for calling these birds 'most musical, most melancholy'. To him the birds' chorus was 'full of love and joyance' and it only confirmed his belief that 'in nature there is nothing melancholy'; the poem was appropriately dedicated to the Wordsworths.

However, his 'Rime of the Ancient Mariner' has become far more famous because like 'Kubla Khan' it belongs to dream-time and is as fascinating as it is enigmatic. A friend told Coleridge that he had dreamed of a ship whose crew had all died and Wordsworth suggested that this might be regarded as punishment for killing an albatross; he had been reading about such an incident. At first they agreed to write a short poem jointly but soon found that their styles and minds were too different and what resulted was entirely written and rewritten by Coleridge during the winter of 1797–98. It suggests both that the gap between the two poets was widening and that the influence of opium was helping to pull one of them away from the song of the nightingales.

An old sailor with a 'glittering' (hypnotic) eye stops a guest trying to get to a wedding and pours out a tale – not for the first or last time. His ship was blown into the Antarctic region where it acquired the albatross as a mascot accompanying it when it escaped from that world of fog, ice and snow, but the bird was shot and hung around the neck of the culprit, the sailor who seems to have been the captain. The ship was then blown into the middle of the Pacific where it was becalmed under the tropical sun in the 'wide, wide sea' without 'any drop to drink'. Then another ship appeared, a wreck manned only by a skeleton and a prostitute playing dice. On the mariner's ship the rest of the crew now died and their corpses stared at him for a week. Then 'all unaware' he blessed the water-snakes swimming in the moonlight. Rain came, the crew revived and eventually the ship reached harbour, only to sink in an earthquake. The mariner survived to ask for absolution from a hermit living in a wood, but his penance was to tell the tale again and again.

Among the many interpretations which have been offered, some seem not impossible. The hermit who prays among the trees may represent Wordsworth the 'semi-atheist' who worships nature, but if so Coleridge received no absolution: in later editions of the *Lyrical Ballads* the poem was displaced from its leading position, the medieval-sounding language was modernised, and a note was added with an editorial apology for 'great defects' including a lack of any explanation of the mariner's emotions or of the disastrous changes in the weather.

Coleridge offered several explanations, one of which agrees with what Wordsworth feared was true: he told De Quincey that it was 'a poem in delirium'. But in 1817 he added notes in the margin which show that long before that date, but also long after 1798, he had accepted orthodox Christianity. The killing of the albatross, like the water-snakes one of God's creatures, is now a crime in which the crew share because they do not condemn it until the weather has changed for the worse. The prostitute called 'Life-in-Death' in the poem is now a symbol of Resurrection and she wins the mariner's life during her game against Death. When the mariner has shown 'love and reverence to all things that God made and loveth', good angels take charge of the voyage. But in a book of 1817 he acknowledged that good angels are not the only supernatural forces in the poem: there is an angry spirit who is determined to punish any approach to the South Pole, for example. His explanation is that he was writing about people who believe that they are 'under supernatural agency', 'from whatever source of delusion'. Neither he nor the reader is so deluded, but it is the poet's task to bring about the reader's 'willing suspension of disbelief for the moment'. (In the Protestant Coleridge's eyes, that would also cover the sailors' invocations of Mary and the saints.) And years later when a lady complained to him that the poem had 'no moral' to explain everything, he replied that he regretted the inclusion of any touch of morality – which appears to suggest again that it was all a dream like 'Kubla Khan'.

Recent critics have quite often seen in this ambiguous work of art, or at least in its background, punishment for Britain's involvement in one or both of two great crimes. The slave trade inflicted savage cruelty on Africans so that they could grow sugar in the Caribbean, and the war against France could also be condemned, even now: Britain's alliance with the royalists who invaded France was one cause of the terrible developments which destroyed the idealism surrounding the start of the revolution. The slave trade is more likely to have been the main target because Coleridge could see its ships under sail in the British Channel and could read many boastful books recounting the adventures of British sailors as they began a worldwide empire, with the slave trade rivalling India as a source of profit.

It has also been seen that the poem's emphasis on the freeze near the South Pole, on the thirst in mid-Pacific, and on storms or deadly calm, by implication contradicts the idea that nature has 'One Life' which is favourable to humanity. Opium had, it seems, given Coleridge ideas which differed deeply from Wordsworth's: Kubla Khan's garden can be far more beautiful than the English countryside but the oceans of the mariner's voyage can be far more hostile.

'The Three Graves' was another poem written after an attempt in

1797 to do it jointly with Wordsworth. It imagines the growth of a superstitious story around the graves. Edward marries Mary but he and her widowed mother lust after each other. A curse is initiated by the mother but rests on them all. In the next year he completed Part I of 'Christabel', another tale of the supernatural, but Part II, postponed to 1800, needed 'labour pangs' as it was born line by line, apparently because he had no clear idea about the plot's development. Part III was, it seems, not even begun. The collapse was almost certainly due to the difficulty of handling the subject, sexuality outside marriage, acceptably. In Part I the innocent Christabel is about to be married but her sexual awakening comes when she meets Geraldine who has been raped by 'five warriors'. She takes the victim to her father's castle and to her own bed where she is embraced; both women are nude and in the preliminaries Geraldine's sinister behaviour suggests that she is a witch. In Part II the aged and widowed father is enraged by his daughter's misbehaviour but is himself attracted to Geraldine. Byron was to subsidise the printing of 'Christabel' with 'Kubla Khan' in 1816 because it seemed 'wild' It sold well but was attacked for indecency and Coleridge had to claim that it was a fairy tale.

In the 1790s he also wrote a play which after revision was eventually staged, about the love of two brothers for one woman. In real life, however, his marriage was already under strain and it began to disintegrate when he went with the half-persuaded Wordsworths to Germany in September 1798. While he was there he was in high spirits, learned German thoroughly, and drank and talked almost non-stop with the professors and students of Göttingen. He wrote almost no poetry but thought up large projects, a biography of the dramatist Lessing and a history of German philosophy which would make metaphysics intelligible even for the English. Neither of these books was ever written. He had assured Sarah that he would be back after three months, but even when she told him that their son Berkeley had died during his first year of life he prolonged his absence until it amounted to almost a year. When he reached England he did not hurry home. His attitude to her was shown by the first names of his two sons: Hartley and Berkeley were both given the surnames of eighteenth-century philosophers.

He seems to have fallen in love with another woman, Sara Hutchinson, soon after his return to England but the ill-assorted married couple tried to patch up their relationship and produced another son (Derwent, named after the river) and daughter (Sara), and when that failed there was no divorce. At first he promised to take care of his sons but of course he could not and in effect their uncle, Robert Southey, became their foster-father, largely at his own expense. An industrious and well-paid writer, the author of poems easy to understand and of books easy to enjoy (his bestseller was a life of Nelson), this ex-radical had become all that Coleridge could never be. Gradually the failed father saw that his separation from the son on whom he had doted was having an effect similar to the death of his own father on him. Hartley was to be a minor poet but was deprived of his fellowship in Oxford as an alcoholic. When Coleridge died his son had not seen him for eleven years.

In 1804 he went to Malta's sunshine for the sake of his health and was happy to serve temporarily as the senior civil servant in that island, newly acquired for Britain by the Royal Navy. But he now spent many hours alone and reached two decisions. The outward voyage had so humiliated him because of illness resulting from opium, and his dependency on the drug had become so obvious, even to himself, that he decided to become an orthodox Christian believing in God as Creator but also as Saviour and as Inspirer. He also decided to make his separation from his wife permanent. Despite his new faith, when he returned to England the effects of opium continued: while visiting the Wordsworths he hallucinated and had a vision of William in bed with Sara Hutchinson. But not many days later, in January 1807, he heard *The Prelude* being read and immediately wrote a poem of homage to 'Friend of the Wise! and Teacher of the Good!' And when he rose from listening, 'I found myself in prayer'.

He knew that in comparison he was not a great poet and never would be but he still wrote poems, mostly about grief after loss. The most pathetic was a poem about the glory of Mont Blanc seen at dawn, for he never saw it. The most tragic were perhaps 'Constancy to an Ideal Object' and the passage about Limbo in a notebook. In the former, the poet longs in vain 'to have a home, an English home, and thee'. In the latter life is 'the horror of the blank Nought'.

The marvel is that the break with the Wordsworths was so slow in coming, but it came in 1810. A plan was formed that Coleridge should now stay in London with a friend's family, but William warned the future host about the 'hopeless' addiction to opium and alcohol. So Coleridge was asked to stay in a nearby hotel, where he broke down, telling his one reliable companion, his notebook, that 'no one on earth has ever loved me' since his father's death. Eventually the kind Morgans came to his rescue and he was happier in their home. A formal reconciliation with the Wordsworths was arranged in 1812 but it meant little.

A great philosophical poem had been his suggestion to Wordsworth. Of course he ought to have written it himself, but the intellectual strength needed, including the strength of the imagination, had gone after that short but splendid flourishing in the 1790s. Now in moods of despair he could think that what he had found in history, or in nature, or even in God, and had put into the strong images of his poetry, was no more than imaginary. He had been eloquent about the power and the glory of the imagination; now he stressed only the need to destroy its power to deceive. He traced some of the possible consequences in other poems, including one on the psychological results of the denial of immortality, but the most poignant expression of his fear came in his 'Letter to Sara Hutchinson'. Did he only imagine that she returned his love? Was her, or his, real happiness possible if everything dear to them both had been as much a 'delusion' as the belief in the supernatural had been to him when he had written the ancient mariner's tale?

> O Sara! we receive but what we give,
> And in our Life alone does Nature live:
> Ours is her wedding garment, ours her shroud!

Now reality seemed 'void, dark, and drear' and in that 'inanimate cold world' he could 'see, not feel' any beauty there might be. He became haunted by this fear that the external world might in reality be meaningless Nothingness, blaming his absorption in the metaphysical philosophy of Germany (of which Wordsworth said that he had never read a word), or on his preference for similarly unearthed talk in English (about which Wordsworth said that he did not understand a syllable). But the basic cause of this pathological anxiety was his addiction to opium, which could so easily and so often produce visions of glory but also nightmares when the world seemed entirely fantastic or horrific. When asleep he could not resist 'viper thoughts that coil around my mind'. In 1803 he had already been experiencing 'The Pains of Sleep', and he had woken himself up on the third night by screaming. He had felt 'shame and terror' about 'deeds to be hid which were not hid', about 'desire with loathing strangely mixed', and he had thought that 'th'unfathomable hell within' was a just punishment on his sinfulness.

A friend, Crabb Robinson, once heard Coleridge explaining that religion is supremely important but best without 'clear notions'; it is, he claimed, like a clock which is set to work by a hidden mechanism since the power in religion comes from feelings deeper than thoughts. And that comparison illuminates everything that Coleridge could offer for the Romantic renewal of Christianity which became his central interest as he sought his own salvation from the demonic drug. In 1972 Owen Barfield called his book *What Coleridge Thought* but it is much more interesting to consider how Coleridge felt. His intellectual interpretations of his feelings may or may not convince us, but we can still feel his feelings. Even when his subject was the Void, he felt it and reported it imaginatively.

He could say that 'neither awake nor asleep do I have any other feelings than what I had at Christ's Hospital', and certainly his removal from Devon to that tough school was what began to form the character which he analysed. 'From my earliest recollection', he wrote, 'I have had a consciousness of power without strength', always with 'some dread in my mind, from fear of pain or shame'. He did not lose all self-respect but he lost self-confidence: 'I am loving and kind-hearted and cannot do wrong with impunity but O! I am very, very weak.' His unconsummated but constant love for Sara Hutchinson (who withdrew to Wales in 1810 and never married) seems to have been the only deep passion which he had after the end of his childhood, but he could write magnificently about the loves which he could not sustain for any length of time. He could be in love with nature, remembering his childhood, and he could be in love with the idea of love. To one of his friends he wrote that 'the heart, thoroughly penetrated with the flame of virtuous friendship, is in a state of glory', and he compared the habitual deeds of love with the flowers on an orange tree, immediately replaced when they fall. But if love is 'a sense of union', as he thought, he missed out. He hoped that in the future those responsible for the young would concentrate on developing the capacity to love, but he had not experienced such a blessing and so no one really loved him. Or so he felt.

He also believed that education should develop a healthy imagination more than a retentive memory. The clearest thoughts that he derived from his study of German metaphysics were about the imagination. He summed up 'the pith of my system' as 'make the senses out of the mind', since it is the mental activity of the brain that registers the impressions we receive and puts these images into some kind of order. He compared this with nothing less than the creation of the world by God, when by 'Will' what he called 'Being' makes 'Multiplicity'. So the mind's 'primary imagination' comes first in our experience and then the 'secondary imagination' is a power which 'dissolves, diffuses, dissipates in order to recreate', as we develop pictures or words in order to make sense of what the senses have given. This secondary imagination can produce 'fancy' – the association of an idea which is already definite and fixed with another idea without there being any natural connection between them. So an image of reality can be associated with an image of beauty or of evil.

The implication for poetry is that it must always be a work of the imagination, for good or bad. It need not be ashamed that it produces 'symbols' rather than completely accurate accounts of the world outside the mind, for that is all that the mind can produce. And what poetry can do at its best is highly desirable because it can give 'intellectual pleasure' in 'musical delight'.

This emphasis on imagination and symbolism has been described as nothing less than the discovery of the subconscious mind, but it was not intended to be anti-rational. Coleridge believed that even poetry, the specially imaginative arrangement of symbols, sought 'understanding' which he could define as 'the faculty of thinking and forming judgements on the notices furnished by the sense' – something very different from the manufacture of fantasies not at all related to reality. He did grandly imagine nature as 'One Life', but all the time he was recording detailed impressions in his notebooks and in addition to his studies of the Germans' *Naturphilosophie* he discussed contemporary science with friends such as the pioneer of modern chemistry, Sir Humphrey Davy. Inevitably he brought his own feelings to the facts, but he did not ignore the facts.

In 1816 he began to write his own *Theory of Life* but it was published only after his death, in 1848. Although much of the science in it now looks dated, its theme can be connected with the ideas of some scientists in our own time. He was fascinated by the evolution of organisms in nature although his idea of 'evolution' owed more to Erasmus Darwin's poetic *Botanical Garden* (1789–90) than to Charles Darwin, whose *Origin of Species* was published only in 1859. He saw evolution as a force which depends not on challenges from environments but on the divine purpose to organise ever richer combinations until life emerges. He defined life as a product of 'the power which unites a given all' into 'a whole that is presupposed by all its parts'. He saw that corals were alive because they unite the 'mineral' and 'animal' worlds, and of course he made the human body with its brain the supreme union of parts. No other poet of his age took so much interest in science.

But naturally he was more interested in literature, and here his originality was such that he was a pioneer in the development of literary criticism. Or at least he was the pioneer in the English language, for he could import ideas from Germany without acknowledging his debt. He has been severely criticised for what can be called plagiarism, but his notebooks show how carefully he read and considered many books in addition to those which he used directly.

He gave lectures on the literary heritage during a number of winters, partly in order to raise funds. Audiences seeking self-improvement could be large at first but then melt away because lectures could be cancelled on the ground of illness or be unfocused because ill prepared. But he did establish some important points, in particular about Shakespeare. While not in position to date the plays reliably, or to say much about the man's life, he attacked the mistreatment of the plays in the theatres around him with their censored texts and obtrusive scenery. Urging that the plays should be read with care if they could not be staged properly, he demolished the fashionable notion that Shakespeare had not needed to labour when he wrote them. They were created by a poet's imagination but sheer work was needed to put that creation on paper and on the stage. And on some of the characters he was more perceptive than anyone before him. Since he longed to know true love, he understood Romeo as a young man on heat while Juliet and the nurse are in their very different ways really loving. Since he knew about jealousy and anger from his dealings with Wordsworth, *Othello* was his favourite play. Since he was capable of saying in a note-book that 'there is something inherently mean in action', he understood Hamlet, 'for ever occupied with the world within him'. And since he knew despair, he was alongside Lear on the heath in the storm.

He was less good on Milton since he did not understand heroism. But late in his life he told a friend that 'I take unceasing delight in Chaucer': he admired from afar his 'manly cheerfulness' and his willingness to achieve sympathy with his characters 'by a strong act of imagination'. And in 1817 he published his first book, *Biographia Literaria*, where Wordsworth was given more space than anyone else. He bestowed censure as well as praise, usually being the first to offer long-pondered criticisms and carefully phrased tributes which have become commonplaces in subsequent commentary. Wordsworth was disinclined to accept either rebukes or compliments from Coleridge at this stage, but he did quietly revise most of the passages which were censured – and he was not so displeased with the book's main influence on his reputation. What people noticed most was that Coleridge classed his former collaborator, whose work he knew intimately, with Chaucer, Shakespeare and Milton.

The full story of the birth of *Biographia Literaria* might supply comic relief if space permitted it to be told here, but it may be said that Coleridge was himself. He announced a plan for *An Essay on the Elements of Poetry* in 1800 but delayed. Then in 1815 he wanted to write a preface to an edition of his collected poems (which did not appear until 1828). As he dictated the material grew and then the printer insisted that there must be two volumes, not one and a half. A rush to find padding followed. Yet this maddeningly disordered book is usually regarded as the beginning of the modern discipline of literary criticism, partly because Coleridge demonstrated by his many touches of auto-biography that he had an extraordinarily serious and strong feeling for literature.

The depth and width of his interests, and his combination of insight with eloquence when he was at his best, suggest that he might have written a great book about religion, where his feelings were now at their most intense. He wrote about himself that he had 'a mind habituated to the Vast', and Charles Lamb shrewdly observed that in order to convey this 'hunger for eternity' he never stopped preaching. But this was a layman preaching in short bursts, not a leisurely, well-informed and calmly reasoned restatement of Christianity with a full consideration of modern knowledge and experience – and in the Victorian Age no one else supplied what was needed although there was much churchgoing. Newman did not because he was capable of concluding his autobiographical *Apologia* with the statement that he had had no new religious opinions since becoming a Roman Catholic (although this was not strictly true). F. D. Maurice did not because his *Kingdom of Christ* was preaching by an Anglican who was broad-minded but always with the basic optimism of a clergyman in a church which could still plausibly claim to be the nation's, at the centre of an empire; so his message was, like Newman's, tied to the situation of a particular church in a period which passed. He dedicated his book in 1838 to Derwent Coleridge in honour of his father.

Some of Coleridge's feelings and thoughts about religion were expressed in journalism, for example in the three volumes published in 1818 in order to preserve articles in *The Friend*, his second unsuccessful attempt to manage his own journal. He was somewhat more systematic in four booklets – two *Lay Sermons* in 1816, *Aids to Reflection* in 1825 and *On the Constitution of Church and State* in 1829. Six years after his death his *Confessions of an Inquiring Spirit* were printed under that title in order not to cause too much offence: they were seven letters to a friend about the authority of the Bible.

He had his own reason for insisting that religion is not opium to keep the people quiet. He issued a warning that since true religion is commitment to truth, 'he who begins by loving Christianity better than truth will proceed by loving his own sect or church better than Christianity, and end in loving himself better than all'. But he was not only an intellectual: to him the supreme truth in Christianity was 'redemption', for he had experienced it. He could dismiss doctrines about Christ issuing from councils of bishops who, when able to do so, thought in the language of Greek metaphysics, for to him these were 'speculative systems'. He could also dismiss the Middle Ages, when 'the Christian world was for centuries divided into the many who did not think at all and the few who did nothing but think'. More recent pronouncements by Catholic or Calvinist thinkers seemed meaningless to him. He was as little impressed by claims that Christianity was proved to be true by prophecies being fulfilled, or by miracles being undeniable, or by 'evidences' of the machine-like perfection of nature. To the many theologians who at that time insisted on these 'proofs' he addressed the question: 'is not the creating of a new heart the one essential miracle?'

This would be a miracle both by and about God, defined by him as 'a Being in whom supreme reason and a most holy will are one with infinite power', so that 'all holy will is coincident with the will of God, and therefore secure in its ultimate consequences by his omnipotence'. And since God had become that to him, he was now sceptical about his earlier insistence on finding such a Being within the 'One Life' of nature. There had to be a clear decision about whether or not nature was a creation by the transcendent God. In his table talk he put it simply: 'assume the existence of God and then the harmony and fitness of the physical creation may be shown to correspond with, and to support, such an assumption.' Above all, there had to be a personal decision to adjust and submit one's own will to the holy will of the All Holy: in that sense the created new heart must matter more urgently than the created old universe.

In his notebooks he wrote down a number of passionate prayers of repentance, 'prostrate in the dust', apparently not after specially bad sins but after incidents which had reminded him that he was the sinner whose dreams would disclose 'the wild activities and restless chaos of my own corrupt nature', beneath any daytime morality. His *Aids to Reflection* did not mention opium but were a generalised warning to the 'studious young' who were 'at their close of their education or on the first entrance into the duties of manhood and the rights of self-government'. 'If you are not a thinking man', he asked, 'to what purpose are you a man at all?' If the young reader was full of thoughtful doubt, he should not be afraid 'if only you have the disposition to believe, and doubt in order that you may end in believing the truth'. But the truth may be unexpected, as it had been in his own case. One of his quotations from a seventeenth-century bishop (Leighton) was this: 'There is nothing in religion further out of nature's reach, and more remote from the natural man's liking and believing, than the doctrine of redemption by a Saviour, and by a crucified Saviour.'

It may seem that the young man's 'disposition to believe' would be believing before experimenting, but Coleridge is commending only the willingness to experiment while wondering. 'In wonder all philosophy began; in wonder it ends; and admiration fills up the interspace.' Christianity can be lived while wondering, for it is 'not a theory, or a speculation, but a life and a living process . . . TRY IT!' And it can be entered while one is largely evil, for the sinfulness of man is 'a known fact' recognized by every religion or philosophy aware of 'the essential difference between good and evil'.

Coleridge presents 'the crucified Saviour' as the only one available in his experience. He promises that despite our moods essentially 'the peace we have with God in Christ is inviolable', bringing 'a divine Comforter present to our inmost being and aiding our infirmities'. He quotes Leighton against despair: 'he that chooses God for his delight and portion may conclude confidently that God hath chosen him to be one of those that shall enjoy him, and be happy with him, for ever.' And in his *Confessions* he says how a thinking Christian should use the Bible in the ups and downs of life. To say that the Bible is only 'one Word' is 'superstitious and unscriptural' because actually its varied words are symbols about the mystery of the 'Great Invisible' speaking and acting in history and in human flesh. What is authoritative is the 'spirit' of the Scriptures, finding the spirit of the sinner. In the Bible 'there is more that *finds* me than I have experienced in all other books put together'. The Bible has supplied 'words for my inmost thoughts, songs for my joy, utterances for my hidden grief, and pleadings for my shame and feebleness'.

Such words are strong because they speak about experiences which he has shared, but he was less successful when he tried to apply the Bible to the current problems of Church and State. In 1816 he intended to publish three long 'lay sermons' but the third, to the people, was never written. The first claimed that the Bible was *The Statesman's Manual* but almost totally failed to discuss the questions which statesmen could not avoid at the time. The second, to the 'higher and middle classes', also had little effect. A bigger booklet looked as if it was going to cast biblical light on the constitutional questions under debate in 1829, arising from the need to give full civil rights to suitably qualified Roman Catholics if the union of Ireland with Britain was to be preserved. But on that issue Coleridge made no contribution of great value. He saw that the country around him was Christian at least in name and he was at least doubtful whether Roman Catholics could be called loyally British Christians. He saw that its civilisation depended on a property-owning elite and he was at least doubtful whether 'the Multitude' could be raised to the required level within the foreseeable future. If he had had a vision of a multifaith Britain where every adult could vote he might have treated it as one of his nightmares. He wanted the state to act morally but he had no idea that within one hundred and fifty years it would be given very extensive powers, and not far short of half the national income, to act for the benefit of the whole electorate. But on one point he was surely right: he wanted Christians to think hard with the Bible in one hand and a newspaper in the other.

He did live to see that the exclusive alliance between the Church of

England and the state was breaking down irretrievably. He saw that the international Church of Christ would survive that breakdown, with or without the Roman Catholics, but he pleaded that the Church of England should exert itself to be the National Church in deed as well as in claim – and there he was a prophet of the coming Anglican revival. He also urged that recognition should be given to the wider work of what he called the 'clerisy', spreading 'civilisation'. Anglican clergy should be the central figures in their parishes, but not on George Herbert's terms: their work had to be done in co-operation with doctors, teachers and others who did not depend for their livelihoods on physical strength or commercial acumen. There he was a prophet of the Victorian growth of 'the professions' as a wealthier and more complex society called for, and supported, many more men (not yet women) whose motives, training and standards would be at a level for which the word 'professional' had to be invented. In particular he was an enthusiast for the education of all classes up to levels which varied but were above the ignorance taken for granted in all earlier ages. He hoped that generous Anglicans would build primary schools which would in some sense revive the good work of the monasteries whose wealth had been transferred to the Crown and the gentry in the time of Henry VIII – and his hope was not entirely in vain.

What work was accomplished after April 1816 was made easier because in the Highgate suburb of London he was accepted as a patient and paying guest by a sensitive doctor, James Gillman. He was not cured but Gillman regulated his intake of opium and alcohol while allowing him to buy a little extra opium from a nearby chemist, for the sake of his self-esteem. He was encouraged to receive visitors and to go out for walks and meals with friends. He still did not compose much poetry, or write a book, but Thomas Carlyle was not being entirely ironic when he wrote that 'rising spirits of the young generation' came to listen to this 'dusky, sublime character' who seemed to be a prophet or magician 'whispering strange things' about 'German and other Transcendentalisms'.

Even greater encouragement came when his daughter Sara, clever, learned and beautiful ('a blue eyed fairy' to him), presented herself when he had not seen her for ten years and cared for him. After his death in 1834 she prepared his chaotic papers for publication where possible. She fell in love with a cousin who also appeared on the scene, they married and he made a record of the great man's table talk, also for publication. The Coleridge cult, a more intellectual companion of the Wordsworth cult, had begun. Its influence was strong on the 'Broad Church' movement which grew in some of Britain's churches, not so much Catholic or Evangelical as liberal, but liberal in a Romantic way:

the new generation was more visionary, impassioned and energetic than the 'latitudinarians' such as Bishop Watson who had made themselves comfortable in the eighteenth century. Opium had made Coleridge's life a tragedy but that did not ruin everything. His work survived as the achievement of a great might-have-been. But perhaps that is true of many human lives.

SEVEN

BLAKE

If Coleridge was an archangel damaged by addiction to opium, William Blake (1757–1827) was a genius damaged because he never had an hour's normal schooling. He could therefore be dismissed as eccentric to the point of insanity. Wordsworth thought him a better poet than Byron, but that was not a high compliment from him, and he also thought that much of Blake's poetry was 'madness'. Coleridge said that his own poetry was 'commonplace common sense compared with Mr Blake'. Through the mouth of Los in *Jerusalem* Blake explained that 'I will not reason or compare, my business is to create', but he would have created works more easy to understand if he had not so often used 'reason' as a bad word. It is of course common for non-academics to express themselves by telling stories or making oversimplified statements, and this was one of the ways in which Blake was like Jesus. But almost all his readers have been to school and not a few have been professors.

He was left to live and die in obscurity. In 1783 two admirers paid for the printing of his early *Poetical Sketches* but that promising collection was not put on sale and the only other books of poetry by him which he ever saw were books of which a few copies were sold, mainly for the sake of the illustrations. Some of his best poems remained in notebooks. The first full-length biography, by Alexander Gilchrist, which appeared in 1863, presented him as an innocent eccentric, 'a man without a mask' as Samuel Palmer put it, but made no great claims for a place in history. His art was discovered by the pre-Raphaelites who were themselves pioneers in Victorian England, and rediscovered by twentieth-century modernists of the stature of Nash, Spencer and Sutherland, but it has always been difficult to locate it on the usual map of art which puts pictures either on the solid territory of the representational or in the wide ocean of the abstract; his art has even been called ugly. His poetry was picked up by Yeats at the end of the nineteenth century and some of his lyrics have been in many anthologies, but the first academic study which could be called monumental was Northrop

Frye's *Fearful Symmetry*, published 120 years after his death. Only after the 1940s was his genius widely acknowledged. Even since then the tendency in literary criticism has been to say that Blake's thought was far less symmetrical than it was made out to be in Frye's 'unified scheme', and subsequent debate about what he really meant has left many readers uncertain about what simple conclusions – if any – should be drawn. 'Those seeking answers,' wrote the editor of *The Cambridge Companion to William Blake* (2003), 'should keep their distance.' He urged students to 'keep faith with Blake's fundamental unreadability'.

Blake pretended not to be hurt about the public's treatment of him: 'that which can be made explicit to the idiot is not worth my care.' But since he reckoned himself to be at least the equal of painters whose greatness was admitted, he resented having to exercise his art on commissions secured for him by friends who did not wish to see him starve. He was as bitter about the almost total lack of response to his poems. His masterpiece was his *Milton*, about which he could write 'Mark well my words! They are of your eternal salvation' – but only four original copies have survived. He said much about his tough life when he declared that he was 'born 28 November 1757 and has died several times since'. He said even more when he put these words into the mouth of Enion in the Second Night of *Vala*:

> What is the price of experience? Do men buy it for a song
> Or wisdom for a dance in the street? No, it is bought with the price
> Of all that a man hath, his house, his wife, his children.
> Wisdom is sold in the desolate market place where none come to buy
> And in the withered field where the farmer plows for bread in vain.
>
> It is an easy thing to rejoice in the tents of prosperity:
> Thus could I sing and thus rejoice: but it is not so with me.

A lifetime of such experience seems to have left him without any ambition to share his wisdom by talking what would commonly be regarded as sense when he thought he was being patronised. Crabb Robinson, a London barrister with a gift for friendship, including friendship with poets, brought about the formal reconciliation between Wordsworth and Coleridge and he recorded his impressions after a few visits to Blake during and after 1825. He found that the old man habitually had 'an expression of great sweetness' but could be agitated when he referred to the spirits who spoke to him with encouragement from eternity, or to fellow mortals who were in his judgement spiritless, not true poets or artists. Robinson respected his dedication to his art as a very sensitive creator of beauty who lived in squalor and could say 'I want nothing whatsoever.' But this lawyer could be shocked when Blake was obviously teasing: 'there is no use in education', 'reason is the only evil or sin', 'I do not believe that the world is round.' Himself a Unitarian like the young Coleridge, he was more deeply scandalised when Blake was blasphemous: 'Christ took much after his mother and in so far was one of the worst of men', 'Jesus Christ is the only God and so am I and so are you', 'nature is the work of the devil.' Blake mentioned casually that he had often seen Milton, who had asked him to correct his poetry but 'I said I had my own duties to perform.' After only a little of this, Robinson was 'not anxious to be frequent in my visits' to a little, dirty room where the talk was outrageous. He had not found a new friend.

Since Blake's death, 'going out of one room into another' as he put it to Robinson, experts have been divided as to whether or not he seriously thought he was going to heaven as envisaged in Christianity.

On the one hand, he is reported to have been happily singing shortly before his death and he sounds really serious when he puts this on record: 'If I myself omit any duty to my station as a soldier of Christ it gives me the greatest of torments.' Or this: 'I see the face of my Heavenly Father, he lays his hand on me and blesses my works.' A striking phrase which can be quoted to prove that he was an atheist – 'God only acts, and is, in existing beings and men' – deserves some thought about its context and then it may be understood as meaning that the Divine, the Infinite, 'the Prolific,' must submit to the limitations of the material, the finite, 'the Devourer', in order to be known in 'weak and tame minds' as either existing or taking action.

However, Northrop Frye interpreted him as meaning that 'Man in his creative acts and perceptions is God, and God is Man,' so that 'we do not perceive God' but 'perceive *as* God'. Thus 'the worship of God is self-development' and 'heaven is this world as it appears to the awakened imagination.' The *Cambridge Companion* of 2003 included a glossary explaining Blakean terminology. In it 'imagination not only perceives the divine, but is the divine.' Also, Blake's 'Eternal Great Humanity Divine' means that 'the imagination perceives Jesus as all humanity in one man.' So if we are to accept Blake's wish to be counted as a follower of Jesus and a worshipper of God, we must sum up his life.

He grew up in the centre of London, in an environment almost totally different from the background to Coleridge or Wordsworth. That was why he annotated a copy of the latter's collected poems in 1826: 'natural objects always did, and now do, weaken, deaden and obliterate imagination in me.' He could call Wordsworth a 'heathen philosopher' who did not understand even the nature which he claimed to know so well: 'what he writes valuable is not to be found in nature.' Instead of the Lake District he had London, and instead of mountains and lakes he had the Bible to feed his imagination.

In *Blake and Tradition* (1963) Kathleen Raine explored possible links between his work and an esoteric or occult tradition of spirituality which had run underground in Europe for many centuries as an alternative to official Christian doctrine. She showed that he was for a time intimate with Thomas Taylor the 'English Pagan' who also influenced the young Coleridge. Taylor must have drawn his attention to the suggestiveness of symbolism which he was to use in his own art or poetry. It cannot be a mere coincidence that images to be found in the writings of Plato, Plotinus, Porphyry or Proclus now reappear. Also, as an impressionable apprentice Blake is known to have worked on engravings to illustrate Jacob Bryant's *Ancient Mythology* (1774–76), and later he admired the mystical writing of the more recent Jakob Boehme in an English translation. Such influences must have helped him to move away from biblical fundamentalism. He became insistent that Scripture must be interpreted in a sense both spiritual and humane; if it is obeyed as a set of laws 'exclusive of conscience', it becomes 'an abomination'. Yet he read the Bible far more frequently and attentively than he read any other book and his message, inspired by the Bible, was illustrated by biblical symbolism more than by images derived from other books. This overwhelming influence on him was inherited from his parents who were Protestant Dissenters rejecting the Church of England. They relied on their own private reading of the Bible to guide them as they ran their moderately successful hosiery business and brought up five children.

In this family William was the dreamy one. As an adult looking back on his childhood he was to be enthusiastic about Wordsworth's Immortality Ode, for unlike Wordsworth he thought he could remember his own life before birth. It was his conviction that 'Man is born like a garden already planted and sown.' His visions seemed only to confirm this. At the age of four he saw the face of God in a window (upstairs). Other visions of eternity followed, for example 'Milton lov'd me in childhood and showed me his face.' The boy was also sensitive to any message from mere mortals which he did not like, and for that reason was kept away from the discipline he would have experienced in a normal school. But he was taught at home to read and love the Bible and he educated himself by hours deep in lesser books whose authors became his friends and teachers. In 1803 he was to say 'I dare not pretend to be other than the secretary while the authors are in eternity.' The Bible remained by far his most decisive reading but this was because, as he wrote later, 'the whole Bible is fill'd with imaginations and visions from end to end and not with moral virtues.'

Visions came to him during many solitary walks. As he got to know the sordid poverty of many parts of London which were next door to scenes of power and extravagance, and as he witnessed crimes and riots, the author of a haunted poem on 'London' was being educated. He also walked in the meadows which were then quite close to the city's centre although polluted by the city's refuse. He saw angels in a tree and was nearly thrashed when he got home for telling such an unlikely tale, but throughout his life his visions did not cease to occur and to be reported, no doubt with some colouring. They convinced him that 'eternity exists, and all things in eternity, independent of creation which was an act of mercy.' He attacked the 'modern philosophy' which supposes that 'a spirit and a vision' are 'a cloudy vapour or a nothing'. On the contrary, 'Man has no body distinct from the soul for that called Body is a portion of Soul discerned by the five senses.' And what matters about nature is its soul. His declaration that he never saw the sun looking like a coin has often been quoted but deserves to be seen in its original setting. This was the defiant climax of a catalogue of an exhibition of his work which was a commercial disaster:

> I do not behold the outward creation . . . it as the dirt upon my feet, no part of me. 'What', it will be question'd, 'when the sun rises, do you not see a round disk of fire somewhat like a guinea?' O no, no, I see an innumerable company of the heavenly host crying 'Holy, Holy, Holy is the Lord God Almighty'.

When he had agreed to attend an art school from the age of ten he became really good at drawing, so that he might have developed into a professional painter, perhaps becoming as rich as Sir Joshua Reynolds (whom he detested). But his family could not afford the further training needed, so at the age of sixteen he was apprenticed to an engraver. His talent for drawing meant that he could be trusted to make pictures of medieval tombs in Westminster Abbey for later engraving and the experience gave him a lifelong love of things 'Gothic', considered less 'mathematic' and 'mechanical' than the art of Greece and Rome. The most elaborate of all his engravings depicted the start of *The Canterbury Tales* and in a commentary on this in 1810 he wrote that 'Chaucer was very devout and paid respect to a true enthusiastic superstition. He has laughed at his knaves and fools as I do now, but he has respected his true pilgrims.' Indeed, much of his later work can be assessed as an extension of the 'Gothic' or 'pre-Romantic' rebellion against the official culture of the eighteenth-century Enlightenment which preferred neatness, elegance, understatement and rationalism in art and literature as in architecture. When he was in his sixties he was to be treated as the patriarch of the Ancients, a small group of young artists led by Samuel Palmer, who wore medieval dress and lived a semi-medieval life in a village in Kent, singing in the cornfields by moonlight. He had much in common with William Langland across the gap of four hundred years.

Blake no doubt sympathised with the rioters who in 1791 burned down the mechanised Albion Flour Mill near his home in Lambeth, and he could count the human cost of the Industrial Revolution from the viewpoint of a one-man factory. The difference between him and most workers was that his work was boldly creative. By hard work he not only mastered the technique required from an engraver if a picture and lettering were to be cut into a copper plate which could then be taken to a printer: he invented his own method of making 'illuminated' books. This involved putting a picture and any text on the copper by the use of a special ink which remained on the plate when the level of the rest of the copper had been eaten away by nitric acid; a lifetime of inhaling that acid seems to have destroyed his health. The page could then be printed by the engraver in his shop and if necessary sold by him. The procedure was time consuming (the text had to be written backwards) but it became his almost daily occupation for the rest of his life, until in old age he became a wood engraver, again with a new method: he had the skill needed to cut the picture into the wood.

Such manual work had psychological effects. Some of these were negative. He had no energy left to take physical exercise. He knew why for many people manual and repetititive labour was 'sorrowful drudgery', often for fourteen hours in a factory full of noise and foul air. He could neglect commissioned projects because he preferred to enjoy and describe his own territory, his visions of eternity. He insisted on making engravings which would reflect these visions wherever possible, so he had to rely increasingly on commissions from his friends. He was never able to set up a profitable business, although less gifted and original men could prosper. For many years he had to survive on the equivalent of an agricultural labourer's wage, and in the end he had to sell the large collection of prints from which he had often gained inspiration when his visions were inadequate. But he had compensations. Working with his hands creatively every day gave him an experience very different from that of a gentleman walking through an attractive landscape or sitting to contemplate it passively and at leisure. What he had to do and be shaped his own version of Christianity, where his emphasis was on the exuberant creativity of God, calling for a human response in the same style.

His experience of marriage also fed his thinking. The first poem which he illustrated and printed, *The Book of Thel* (1789), was about a young woman's very confused feelings as she descends from innocence and virginity: 'does the eagle know what is in the pit?' His own feelings in his early years were also confused and he said that he had married Catherine because she had answered yes to his question 'Do you pity me?' She was a market-gardener's daughter who in 1782 signed the marriage register with a cross, but she learned to read and write, and to help, understand and support him. They had no children but he made no secret of his enjoyment of sexual union – 'cominglings from the head even to the feet' – and endorsed the idea that the original Eternal Man, older than Adam, had been partly female. He also believed that this complete union would be restored in heaven. His pictures could be erotic and some, it seems, were destroyed after his death along with some bawdy poems. In theory he advocated 'gratified desire' outside marriage and could say 'Sooner murder an infant in its cradle than nurse unsatisfied desires.' There are hints that in the early years he could practise what he preached, and his wife protested, but there is no evidence that when the marriage had matured he was actively unfaithful to his Kate, on whom he came to depend.

What we can know is that his experiences of being absorbed in difficult work or in ecstatic sex fed his serious doctrine about the need to 'annihilate' the egotism which he called 'selfhood'. But that he did not mean that people in general, or he himself, should not express, and strongly assert, their individuality: 'one Law for the Lion and Ox is Oppression.' Nor did he mean that everything is finally merged into uniformity: 'in eternity one thing never changes into another thing.' But he did mean that the self must be turned outwards and that selfishness must be sacrificed. It was reported about him that his urges to create and communicate were so strong that his hands were never idle during the day and that during the night he would get up in order to write, with his patient wife at his side in order to calm him down. And when many disappointments had taught him not to expect much from those with whom he wanted to communicate, in old age he entered the 'sort of pious and humble optimism' which Crabb Robinson found in him, with 'undescribable grace'.

Although in this book there is not much space for Blake the artist, it is important to remember that his pictures were his own interpretation of his words and that most of his average day was given to the creation of art. For a time he clung to the ambition of becoming a professional painter and in 1779–80 he studied in the new school opened by the Royal Academy, but while there he lectured the lecturers and refused to base his paint on oil because he thought that too sensuous. Only later did he learn how to add carpenter's glue, thought to be more spiritual like the masterpieces of the Renaissance. He did not flatter potential patrons and objected to subjects which he thought sentimental. So he had to fall back on the work of an engraver, often working on other men's designs. But he developed new painterly skills in that humble trade, adding watercolour to engravings or managing to print in colour. His own drawing developed; for example, he learned how to add muscles to flesh and most of the figures in his later work were either nude or draped thinly. He fully shared the belief of the Renaissance that the human skin is a robe woven in heaven.

Some of his most beautiful pictures illustrated the poems to which we now turn. Apparently naïve, they were written in middle age and their rich collection of metres was not the only sign of an adult sophistication – which is not to deny that he loved children and must have grieved that he had none of his own. The *Songs of Innocence* of which a few copies were sold in 1789 would have been more accurately called songs about innocence and were perhaps best understood when sold together with the later, disillusioned *Songs of Experience*. They were introduced as 'songs of happy cheer' as if they were intended to make children glad, good and able to enjoy written words and simple pictures, but it turns out that even in childhood experience provides many reasons to be in 'grey despair'.

In the spring this poet once again hears the birds singing 'merrily, merrily' and the woods and streams laughing 'Ha, Ha, He!' And this Wordsworthian mood can return. When he notices a dead bird on the ground he can reflect that the glow-worm is still alive. When he sees the shepherd caring for the flock he can hope that the lion will one day also care. But there is a terrible other side revealed by experience. The tiger's eyes burn bright as he stalks his prey and a human life begins not in 'infant joy' but with the baby wailing, struggling and sulking. This man without worldly ambition can admit that if they are not to be little clods of earth under the cattle's feet people have to learn 'only self to please', and they must deceive their enemies by politeness before poisoning them. In order to learn how to survive and prosper in such a world the white schoolboy must be kept from the joys of play while the little black boy has to be prepared by his loving mother to face a lifetime of slavery. The 'charity children' who look and sound so sweet as they sing in the cathedral must become aware that they have been rescued by a charity whose real motto is

> Pity would be no more
> If we did not make somebody poor
> And Mercy no more would be
> If all were as happy as we.

In that time boys who could be only five years old were sent up chimneys in order to bring down the soot. The law said that they must be over eight, washed once a week, not worked for more than seven hours a morning, and not stimulated by fires being lit beneath them, but the enforcement of the law was not strict. When fires were not needed, the boys were left unemployed and uneducated: it was the London of *Oliver Twist.* Tom, Dick, Joe, Ned and Jack (Blake knows their names) may try to cheer each up as they 'do their duty' but the reality is that these 'apprentices' have been sold by their parents into misery and diseased, stunted and shortened lives.

Blake's vision of his London sees its class structure as a human (not divine) invention, 'mind-forg'd manacles' which could be discarded, yet in every street he meets 'marks of weakness, marks of woe' because the manacles remain. The chimney-sweeper's call for help bounces off the wall of the 'black'ning' church and the paint of the revolutionary slogan scrawled on the wall of a palace runs down it like a soldier's blood. A bridegroom goes to marriage diseased because he has been with a young prostitute whose weeping 'blasts' the crying of her unwanted child but goes unheard down 'midnight streets'.

Moments of happiness are ended soon enough by mortality. The children at play have to go to bed; the old people who watch them will soon sleep in death; as the sunflower turns towards the declining sun, the virgin is turning towards a grave under the snow; even the pretty rose tree has thorns and is destroyed in its 'crimson joy' by a worm in the night. A fly is brushed off an arm – is that human life? Should a human be happy because in death he will become as thoughtless as a fly?

Blake's harshest words are, however, reserved for the churches. A chapel has been built on what used to be a playground, with '"Thou shalt not" writ over the door'. A heretic is burned 'where many had been burn'd before'. In a poem which he wrote but dared not print he sees a 'chapel all of gold' where a priest vomits 'poison' over the eucharistic bread and wine – and Blake prefers a pigsty. God himself would prefer people to go to the ale-house which is 'healthy and pleasant and warm', for he is a God of love and 'children of the future age' will be astonished to learn that '"Love! Sweet love!"' was once regarded as a crime in London's churches. Years later, when he was commissioned to illustrate Dante's visit to hell, he refused to accept the medieval Catholic's belief that Francesca would be everlastingly tortured because when her husband had been consistently cruel she had committed adultery; instead, Blake provided for the lovers a kind of escalator which would elevate them out of trouble.

What, then, should the churches be teaching about God? Blake did not advocate that they should preach Trinitarian theology in the orthodox style, with three 'persons' in the Godhead. Nor was he a Unitarian as the old Milton and the young Coleridge were, regarding Jesus as the most heroic of men but not as the Second Person of the Trinity: he could say that 'God is Jesus' as well as 'Jesus is God'. When the admittedly ambiguous evidence is taken as a whole, the probability seems to be that he meant to be in the final analysis essentially orthodox: the human life of Jesus is God's supreme self-expression. Without this declaration of love, the Creator is nobody's father, 'Nobodaddy'. Such a 'silent and invisible' God does not deserve worship even if he demands it as 'the Father of Jealousy'. But if God's love is embodied in Jesus, that means that an extremely close link is at least possible between divinity and humanity, and what is not humane cannot be true about God. It seems that this is what is meant seriously by a saying such as 'after Christ's death he became Jehovah.'

A song of innocence can be happy about the God revealed in Jesus:

For Mercy has a human heart,
Pity a human face,
And love, the human form divine,
And Peace, the human dress.

And it is to the good God so pictured that 'every man of every time' prays when in distress. But a song of experience which he decided not to make public shows how well he knew that the image of God as a man can have a far more menacing character:

Cruelty has a human heart,
And jealousy a human face;
Terror the human form divine,
And secrecy the human dress.

He once reflected that 'you cannot love' a cloud unless you think of 'a holy man within the cloud' but that it does not follow that the man is there. So when under the darker clouds in life he faced the question at the heart of any intelligent religious belief: is God there, an invisible parent?

Any answer must be personal but to many readers it has seemed that Blake's final answer is indicated by the emotional intensity of his image of God as a mother in 'On Another's Sorrow':

Can a mother sit and hear
An infant groan, an infant fear

without weeping herself? 'Never, never can it be!'

And can he who smiles on all
Hear the wren with sorrows small,
Hear the small bird's grief and care,
Hear the woes that infants bear,

And not sit beside the nest,
Pouring pity in their breast;
And not sit the cradle near,
Weeping tear on infant's tear? . . .

He doth give his joy to all;
He becomes an infant small;
He becomes a man of woe;
He doth feel the sorrow too.

Think not thou canst sigh a sigh
And thy maker is not by;
Think not thou canst weep a tear
And thy maker is not near.

O! he gives to us his joy
That our grief he may destroy;
Till our grief is fled and gone
He doth sit by us and moan.

Through a fortnight in February 1787 he watched his brother Robert, to whom he was devoted, die at the age of nineteen. It was an experience like William Wordsworth's grief for his brother and Blake, too, thought more deeply about life after death as a possible defiance of the laws of nature. Only three years earlier he had included himself as 'the Cynic' in an attempt to reproduce smart conversation (*An Island on the Moon*). But now when the spirit left Robert's body, he thought he saw it 'clapping for joy'. Thirteen years later he told William Haley, whose son had just died, that 'I lost a brother and with his spirit I converse daily and hourly in the same spirit and see him in remembrance in the regions of my imagination.' This was more than remembering by imagination. Eternity seemed so real that he could assure Haley that 'our deceased friends are more really with us than when they were apparent to our mortal part.'

This bereavement appears to have been the main reason for a temporary fascination with the teachings of a Swedish engineer who became a mystic and independently minded theologian, Emmanuel Swedenborg, based on his own conversations with the dead and on his conviction that a new age had begun in 1757. But Blake had his own conversations to pursue and did not last long as a member of Swedenborg's 'New Church' in London: he rapidly recovered his conviction that 'every man may converse with God and be a king and priest in his own house.' A church of independents has always been a paradox.

He recovered the energy needed for life on earth and in 1793 his independent thinking resulted in the little collection of illustrated sayings called *The Marriage of Heaven and Hell.* Beginning with a denial of the everlastingness of the tortures in hell, it developed into an attack on any oversimplified contrast between good and evil. Of course he could distinguish between right and wrong: he called the claim that 'God will torment Man in eternity for following his energies' wrong; it was 'the voice of the Devil'. What is true is that 'energy is eternal delight'. And of course he knew that the full truth can be complicated: 'reason and energy, love and hate, are necessary to human existence.' But his emphasis was on creative energy. There is truth, although not the whole truth, in 'proverbs of hell' such as these: 'The road of excess leads to the palace of wisdom', 'If a fool would persist in his folly he would become wise', 'Exuberance is Beauty', 'Damn braces: Bless relaxes', 'Eternity is in love with the productions of time'. And this was Blake's own vision:

> The pride of the peacock is the glory of God.
> The lust of the goat is the bounty of God.
> The wrath of the lion is the wisdom of God.
> The nakedness of woman is the work of God.

As he put it more soberly elsewhere, people 'are admitted to heaven not because they have curbed and govern'd their passions, or have no passions, but because they have cultivated their understandings'.

He could have thought up proverbs of heaven to balance these, but the earthiness seemed to be more necessary because in the spirit world Swedenborg had 'conversed with angels who are all religious' instead of learning the facts of life from devils. From this period of recovery from mourning comes a reliable story that William and Catherine were discovered one day in their little garden in Lambeth (then a suburb) as naked as Adam and Eve in Paradise. Another story tells of him parading in the street wearing the red bonnet of a revolutionary.

He began a poem about the French Revolution. It was intended to be long and sympathetic but only the introduction was set in type by the printer and the project was abandoned, partly (it seems) because the publisher saw that it would never sell but also because Blake had a 'nervous fear' about the reactions of a British government now at war with France. However, like Milton he now wrote poems which would escape the censor by being elaborately and mysteriously mythological. Although a revolutionary message couched in bewildering language, and priced quite highly, was unlikely to attract many purchasers, this coded response to current affairs could be sustained for a time because Blake did all the work and bore all the costs himself – which at least proves his sincerity.

In *A Song of Liberty* 'the fire, the fire' is falling on Paris and expected to fall on London; it falls even on African slaves. 'Empire is no more!' for 'every thing that lives is holy.' In *Visions of the Daughters of Albion* there is a potent mixture of such anti-colonialism with feminism: English women weep in sympathy with the raped coloured girl who is the 'soft soul of America' and she gets a name (Oothoon). This linkage between imperialism and sexual violence is not explained clearly but the two things are connected by Blake's belief, anticipating modern psychology, that aggression can result from a lack of fulfilment in love. The British may feel the need to conquer an empire because they are not happy in bed.

One reason why he does not make matters clear is that he knows that he may be censored. In *America, a Prophecy* 'the shadowy daughter of Urthona stood before the red Orc' but no official glancing at that first line would immediately know that the daughter (not named here) is American, that the name of her American father comes from 'Earth-owner', and that Orc the 'hairy youth' embodies the spirit of rebellion. He is about to break free of his chains and have sex, and the independence of the USA is about to be proclaimed by George Washington, who in this poem sounds like a Communist agitator.

But the spiritual and cosmic dimensions of the Age of Revolution interest Blake far more that the details of revolutionary events. At the end of *America* we meet Urizen who is the God of British colonialism and of the earlier Spanish conquest, because he is the God of law, order, force and inhumanity. We meet him again in *The First Book of Urizen* and *Europe, a Prophecy* (both 1794). In the beginning he wins a struggle against more likeable Eternals, rules imperially, imposes 'iron laws', makes innocent people feel guilty, and presides over wars which make them really guilty. War is now devastating Europe because what ought to have been the European Revolution, after the example set by the victorious USA, has degenerated into the terror in Paris and the violent reaction by the remaining monarchies. Orc has to struggle to rescue the revolution – and to struggle energetically, because his mother is Enitharmon, the spirit of the repressive *ancien régime* and the female part of the supreme monarch, Urizen.

The frontispiece in *Europe* is a portrait of Urizen, often reproduced as 'The Ancient of Days'. He is a majestic old man who owes much to the sculpture of Michelangelo (in Blake's eyes the greatest artist ever) and he kneels inside the sun. But he has created a tempest: the mighty wind of Genesis 1:2 blows through his white hair and he has to reach down into the storm with his designer's compass. A later picture of 'Elohim Creating Adam' shows Urizen in action on the created earth. He presses his body down on the earth and is not smiling as he makes Adam out of the mud. For his part, Adam does not seem to enjoy being created, particularly because the evil snake of the Fall is already imprisoning him. The thought behind these two pictures was to be stated by Blake with a characteristic indiscretion in 1810: 'Thinking as I do that the Creator of this world is a very cruel Being, and being a worshipper of Christ, I cannot help saying "the Son, O how unlike the Father!" First God Almighty comes with a thump on the head. Then Jesus Christ comes with a balm to heal it.'

In *The Book of Urizen* (1794) when eternity is peopled only by the Eternals Urizen has a quarrel with most of them. He separates himself, which is the first Fall, and starts the creation of the material universe as something inferior to eternity. Another of the Eternals, Los, intervenes but creates further divisions. Time is split up into years, days and hours, and the body of Adam into the five senses and the two genders. Urizen sees the sorrows which now afflict humans but his hypocritical tears create something 'like a spider's web, moist, cold and dim' – the 'Net of Religion' to make the captivity of the creation worse, as laws and divisions increase.

At the end Urizen's son Fuzon makes a brief appearance as a rebel against his father, and his fate is described in *The Book of Ahania* (1795). He manages to castrate Urizen and separates him from his female part, Ahania. The enraged Eternal then kills this son and nails his body to the Tree of Mystery. But in *The Song of Los* and *The Book of Los* (also 1795) there is some hope. Los is an eternal blacksmith who can make something better than the Net of Religion – poetry. He sings songs of liberty to Africa, Asia and Europe, and the fire he lights in Europe moves to Jerusalem the traditional centre of the world, where the dry bones of humanity are quickened into life. And in *The First Book of Urizen* this is seen at work in the primal liberation, which is the emergence of life, and of human life, out of fire, water and rock:

> Many sorrows and dismal throes,
> Many forms of fish, bird and beast
> Brought forth an infant form
> Which was a worm before.

It seems possible to find a path through this jungle of names, images and ideas, if we cling to simple facts known about Blake. He welcomed the American and French Revolutions as explosions of energy which could renew the world. He saw the world as a place of confusion, struggle and suffering, but he hoped that a time was coming when people would be freed from all forms of slavery, from all laws and divisions, to pursue the peaceful happiness of creative work and of non-violent sex. He saw this as the assertion of human dignity in a movement which must fall short of eternity's perfection but is greater than anything to be found in the rest of nature or of history. And it is the task of poets to inspire a new spirituality as an essential part of this Age of Revolution which must include a revolution in religion. But after completing this series Blake was exhausted mentally and financially; the poems of 1795 were printed more cheaply than their predecessors. His nervous fear of the government was probably another factor. He had not named himself as the author but in the hope of sales – of which there were very few – he had to state that these revolutionary visions were 'printed by W. Blake'.

His energy now went into the making of a series of magnificent colour-prints, almost all of which were left unsold. One is a portrait of Nebuchadnezzar, the ravingly mad, beast-like emperor who in the Bible tries to rule the world. Another is of Isaac Newton, the scientist who is mad in a quieter style: he sits on a rock at the bottom of the sea, he stoops down like Urizen, he measures the sand – but he misses what he might see if he looked up. He is the emperor of materialism. And yet another picture is of the risen Christ being adored by six disciples after his own revolution, the overthrow of the old order by energetic, creative, all-embracing love.

To earn money Blake had to work on other people's ideas and that could be frustrating: of his 537 designs to illustrate Edward Young's *Night Thoughts* only 43 were accepted for engraving. But in 1799 he began to paint fifty biblical pictures in watercolour, calling them 'visions of eternity' and bringing to the story of Jesus a tenderness he had learned from the art of Fra Angelico.

Plainly his hope was that Jesus would catch the imagination of that violent age with his gospel of forgiveness, love and hope. He did not argue intellectually, believing that 'Christ addresses himself to the man, not to the reason', but he put that person-to-person appeal into pictures about stories, convinced that 'the Old and New Testaments are themselves the great Code of Art' – not a theological book. He could say that 'Christianity is art' and that 'prayer is the study of art' because that was how he and many other people were touched. He did not mean that anything whatever which can be called art must be treated as truth. He could be very critical about fellow artists, however famous: he condemned Titian, Correggio and Rubens, and even Rembrandt, as being too worldly. But he was sure that true religion must produce and use good art, in pictures or words. He wrote that 'I know of no other Christianity and of no other gospel than the liberty both of body and mind to exercise the divine arts of imagination.'

In 1800 he was so depressed by the commercial failure of his poems, and by the lack of patrons for his art, that he accepted an invitation from William Haley to work 'under my auspices' in the little village of Felpham near Chichester in Sussex. Haley was a rich patron of poets and artists, in particular of those who, because they were like him eccentric if not insane, could be expected to be grateful for financial and emotional support. In some ways this invitation was to Blake's benefit. Haley commissioned this newfound protégé to decorate his library and his new book of ballads about animals, and secured other jobs from his friends. He taught Blake some Greek, Latin, Hebrew and French. He gave him his first sight of the sea and his first time in the countryside, and at first Blake who had been in a 'deep pit of melancholy' did respond as expected, loving in particular his walks by the sea and the little garden of his rented cottage. But his enthusiasm did not last. He increasingly resented being patronised by Haley who was a man entirely pleased with himself and with his own attempts to be a poet. The fees were too low, the cottage was damp, Catherine was rheumatic, and after three years it was decided to return to London, independence and poverty.

The literary fruit of those years was not a lyrical response to nature. It was the expansion of *Vala*, a poem begun in a mood of despair, to become *The Four Zoas*, 'an immense poem' of epic proportions and content, a history of the world related largely in terms of his own mythology. His praise of it showed why he could be thought mad: 'I am more famed in heaven for my works than I could well conceive. In my brain are studies and chambers filled with books and pictures of old, which I wrote and painted in ages of eternity before my mortal life and these works are the delight and study of archangels.' But the new poem was inspired at the rate of about a dozen lines at a time and written on scraps of paper, so that almost everyone who has ever tried to read it is dismayed by its chaos as well as by its length. Perhaps all that need be said now is that it is a semi-Miltonic history of a Fall into materialism from origins in a Golden World. The four eternal 'zoas' are Urizen, Los who used to be Urthona, Luvah (Lover) who used to be Orc, and a new Eternal, Tharmas the spirit of nature. Each is accompanied by a shadowy self, his 'emanation' who is the feminine part of his personality: for example, Luvah the spirit of imaginative love is accompanied by Vala the spirit of sexual passion.

The reasons for the Fall into materialism are no more simple than the characters of these Eternals who are more or less in control. Blake blames a combination of smugly institutional religion with coldly impersonal reasoning, a combination found in the 'enlightened' Church of England which he knew from a distance (the only Anglican services which he is known to have attended were his baptism, wedding and funeral). The results are perversions of what humanity ought to be. The powers of the imagination are destroyed as work becomes mechanical and war becomes disaster on a new scale. Albion, the Eternal Man in this poem, dies. But that is not the end, for in the part of the poem written when he was back in London with a more assured faith Blake splendidly imagined the crucifixion and burial of Jesus followed by his resurrection and a festival in the restored Golden World, the new Jerusalem which is his bride (as in the Revelation of John). Through Jesus the Eternal Man awakes from death. 'The children of six thousand years who died in infancy' are now vindicated; tyrants, warriors and priests are not; horses, bulls, tigers and lions beat 'the iron engines of destruction' into instruments of agriculture; 'all the slaves from every earth in the wide universe' sign a new song as they 'laugh in the bright air' (a picture repeated from *America*); 'the evil is all consum'd.' But the poem which told of his own transition from despair to faith with a hundred illustrations, did not seem satisfactory, or at least not saleable, and it was not published before 1899.

His departure from Felpham was amid great anxiety, for he had ejected a drunken sailor from his garden and was accused of having done so with treasonable words about the king. A jury acquitted him. Then he was worried about money, not doing any more commercial engraving for another eleven years, but he threw himself into his longest poem, *Jerusalem*, with work which spread over another sixteen years although not continuously.

It incorporated parts of *The Four Zoas* but had a clearer focus for essentially it was about Jesus 'the God of Fire and Lord of Love' in relation to England. In 1802 he had told Thomas Butts that 'I shall to all eternity embrace Christianity and adore him who is the express image of God' and now he did precisely that in a lay sermon addressed to four audiences each of whom was given a preface. Readers drawn from the public were asked to understand his enthusiasm about Jesus and to remember that they would one day be like the sheep blessed or the goats cursed by Jesus. Jews were invited to join the construction of a new Jerusalem in an England where in ancient times the authentic religion of Jesus flourished as liberation from religion as sin-and-punishment. Deists who believe in 'natural' religion and morality were told that they really accepted human idolatry and all evil, for 'Man must and will have some religion: if he has not the religion of Jesus he will have the religion of Satan and erect the synagogue of Satan, calling the prince of this world God.' And Christians were told that they must never despise art and science, for 'to labour in knowledge is to build up Jerusalem'. So 'let every Christian, as much as in him lies, engage himself openly and publicly before all the world in some mental pursuit' to that end.

The 'golden string' which he promises will lead us through the maze of the poem's complicated eloquence can be grasped. Albion is the giant who personifies England and Jerusalem is the feminine part of him. But he is seduced by Vala who is Mother Nature at her least spiritual (so much for Wordsworth!) and as he sleeps he has nightmares (like Coleridge). Finally he is murdered. But Los the spirit of poetry labours on and the poem looks forward to the triumphant return of Jesus, to the rebuilding of London as the City of God, and to the renewal of a purified nature, 'tree, metal, earth and stone', all somehow awakened into 'the life of immortality'. Later he was to explain that this universal resurrection would be into the spiritual body of Christ, within the Godhead.

Blake also laboured at his own 'mental pursuit', the creation of Christian art. He became a recluse, distancing himself from the radicalism of the 1790s: 'I am really sorry to see my countrymen trouble themselves about politics . . . If men were wise, princes who are fools would not hurt them.' This aloofness was not the result of any new conservatism in his politics. It was caused by his conviction that what was needed most was not attempts to resist the Tory government now firmly in power. It was efforts to meet the spiritual crisis by showing what could be meant by an imaginative Christianity as inspiration for the renewal of England. That might influence the rest of the world in which England was now the richest and most powerful nation, but first it had to influence England and that was the difficulty. Shortly before his death Blake wrote with bitter irony about the country's 'happy state of agreement' with the men with power – 'to which I for one do not agree'.

For Thomas Butts (an imaginative civil servant) he completed another series of very beautiful biblical pictures and for other patrons (hopefully) a series on the Last Judgement although the largest, depicting almost a thousand people, has been lost. 'The Ancient Britons', an immense picture of grandeur, has also disappeared. It idealised pure Christians of the type praised in *Jerusalem* as being the glory of England before the Druids took over with their religion, alleged to be a religion of human sacrifices to angry gods, but now the Britons, having retreated to Wales in their near-naked majesty, are defeated by iron-clad Romans. (The picture was painted for a house in Wales.) As he laboured to create such art, his wife allowed herself to make a complaint: 'I have very little of Mr Blake's company; he is always in Paradise.'

Then Blake's difficulties increased. A bookseller who wanted illustrations for a new edition of another man's poetry rejected Blake's specimen engraving as being too original and his designs for the book, although used, were reviewed as 'absurd'. His magnificent engraving of Chaucer's pilgrims was made only after another painter had used his original design, and when he mounted an exhibition of his work in 1809 not one picture was sold. It was not that his art had ceased to be in the first class. In 1820 he produced inventive, and very lovely, wood engravings for a translation of Virgil's *Pastorals* designed to attract schoolboys to the text; in 1823 he began 23 more normal engravings to illustrate the biblical book of Job; in 1824 he illustrated Bunyan's *Pilgrim's Progress*; in 1825 he began work on Dante's *Divine Comedy*, learning some Italian in order to do so, but died before he could finish. His imagination dwelt among the great artists in words and he could match them by his art, but he could not make enough money to live in comfort. What strengthened him for this struggle was the faith which he expressed in *Jerusalem*:

> Jesus said: 'Wouldest thou one who never died
> For thee, or ever die for one who had not died for thee?
> And if God dieth not for Man and giveth not himself
> Eternally for Man, Man could not exist; for Man is Love
> As God is Love . . .

That should be remembered when we read the drafts of *The Everlasting Gospel* which he wrote in 1818, while still writing *Jerusalem*. It was a lighter-hearted poem and he kept it private in a notebook. He knew that his vision of Christ would be at enmity with other visions, for his Christ had 'a snub nose' just like his and also, unsurprisingly, a message just like his. He wrote short lines and in rhyming couplets, not the right medium for leisurely, solemn and cautious theology, and his tone was very different from the traditional piety of his deathbed. But he had urged that others should 'turn inwardly thine eyes and there behold the Lamb of God' and this what he saw when he himself did that:

> When twelve years old he ran away
> And left his parents in dismay . . .
> He cursed the scribe and Pharisee,
> Trampling down hypocrisy . . .
>
> For he acts with triumphant, honest pride
> And this is the Reason Jesus died . . .

If he had been Antichrist, Creeping Jesus,
He'd have done anything to please us . . .

So far he was quite close to the Bible. But the poem goes on to say that in Gethsemane the Father told Jesus to be a man:

Thou art a man, God is no more,
Thy own humanity learn to adore.

These lines have been interpreted as a revelation of Blake's atheism, of a belief that 'God' is no more than a man imagined to be in the sky. But the context is a part of the evidence which goes against this suggestion. Jesus is not talking to himself; he has 'humbled himself to God' in prayer, and God is speaking. He does not deny that he is eternal and he reminds Jesus that 'thou also dwell'st in eternity.' Then he reminds him that he is human as well as eternal and urges him to be brave as humans can be – with the supreme example of God's own courage. He must not let his humility defeat his courage:

Humility is only doubt
And does the sun and moon blot out . . .

But when Jesus was crucified,
Then was perfected his glittering pride.

That is an unconventional interpretation of Gethsemane and Calvary, but it is not atheism. It seems possible that Blake wrote 'God is no more' because he was in a hurry to find a word rhyming with 'adore'.

In one draft of this poem the gospel of forgiveness, love and courage is illustrated still more sensationally when Jesus forgives his mother for having conceived him after adultery (this was a story circulating among non-Christians in the Roman empire to explain why according to Matthew Joseph was shocked by Mary's pregnancy). In another draft the mission of Jesus is seen as a radical protest against all earthly authorities although not against the authority of the true, eternal God. 'Ask Caiaphas, for he can tell' says Blake without disagreeing:

He scorn'd earth's parents, scorn'd earth's God,
And mock'd the one and the other's rod;
His seventy disciples sent
Against religion and government . . .

But more soberly, a note in prose is added. 'Forgiveness of sins: this alone is the Gospel . . . If you avenge you murder the Divine Image' (Jesus) but 'he rises again' although 'you deny that he is arisen'.

Here was a vision of Christ opposed to the more usual image of the upholder of Family, Church and State. Elsewhere he wrote that 'State Religion is the source of all cruelty' and that 'the modern Church crucifies Christ with his head downwards'. Like everybody else Blake selects from the evidence but the people of London might have heard him gladly, had his voice reached them. And there is no heresy in the moral which he drew from the story of Jesus in other poems which he never published:

Seek love in the pity of others' woe,
In the gentle relief of another's care,
In the darkness of night and the winter's snow,
In the naked and outcast, seek love there!

As Los says in *Jerusalem*, 'He who would see the Divinity must see him in his children.' But those who reckon that Blake was ultimately an atheist whose compassion was not essentially Christian need to ponder 'Auguries of Innocence'. It is one of the poems which he kept in his notebook, so that it cannot be said to be a public performance fearing censorship. Not only does it value space and time as revelations of eternity:

To see a world in a grain of sand
And a heaven in a wild flower,
Hold infinity in the palm of your hand
And eternity in an hour.

It also immediately values all God's creatures in accordance with the belief first stated in the *Song of Liberty* that 'everything that lives is holy':

A robin red breast in a cage
Puts all heaven in a rage.
A dove house filled with doves and pigeons
Shudders hell thro' all its regions.
A dog starv'd at his master's gate
Predicts the ruin of the state.
A horse misus'd upon the road
Calls to heaven for human blood . . .
Kill not the moth nor butterfly
For the Last Judgement draweth nigh.

To Blake it is obvious that if a moth is loved by God all humans are also holy, as is said in 'The Divine Image':

All must love the human form,
In heathen, Turk or Jew.

Where Mercy, Love and Pity dwell,
There God is dwelling too.

And if humans suffer the most, that is the cost of the imaginative sensitivity which makes them divine:

Man was made for joy and woe;
And when this we rightly know
Thro' the world we safely go.
Joy and woe are woven fine,
A clothing for the soul divine.

He did publish – in his usual, very small, way – a long poem called simply *Milton*. Completed in 1808 or 1809, its first edition in 1811 was expanded seven years later. It was stimulated by two recent experiences as well as by the love-and-hate affair with Milton since boyhood. He had been irritated by William Haley's totally uncritical book on Milton, making him more aware that the poet had been as self-centred as this very minor author. In 1807 he was commissioned by Thomas Butts to paint 38 pictures based on Milton's works and this made him study the texts yet again, with reverence and realism. He had once pictured the spirit of Milton entering his right hand to inspire his own writing but in the new poem the spirit enters the left foot so that Blake can 'walk forward thro' eternity' and boldly summon his proud fellow poet to leave heaven for the sake of his soul.

He wrote a materialist poem, taking Milton out of a purely spiritual heaven, and a feminist poem, rebuking Milton for insensitivity towards three wives, three daughters, Eve and Dalila. It was also a pacifist poem, demanding repentance after the pleasure taken by Milton in his accounts of the war in heaven. But it was above all a religiously unorthodox poem, attacking Milton for depicting God as 'the Forbidder' and 'the Punisher' whose anger could not be appeased except by the death of his Son. Milton's God seemed to be Urizen or Nobodaddy.

These criticisms of *Paradise Lost* are unfair. Milton forgave his immature first wife, was devoted to his second wife, and would have been helpless without his third wife and his daughters to run the house and write the dictated poem, and he may be forgiven if in his blindness he was not always a perfectly uncomplaining man. He was more sympathetic with Eve than Blake thought and when he enjoyed the defeat of Satan the monarch of hell, it was partly because he wanted the defeat of royalism in England – which Blake also wanted. And when Adam fell by wanting to please his wife, Milton made both the Father and the Son less wrathful than was to be expected. Nevertheless, it is understandable that Blake was one of the readers who have disliked what Milton had told the public about God, since the revelation of Milton's 'heresies' in *De Doctrina* was not known until 1823, five years after the last revision of *Milton*. Thus he did not know that, like him, Milton thought that the doctrine that the Son died in order to appease the wrath of the Father was 'horrible'.

What matters most, however, is not whether Blake misrepresented the historical Milton but whether he misrepresented the historical Jesus. Within this book it can only be said that this poet thought that he was being loyal to Jesus when he attacked religion as legalism and respectability, the subordination of women, enthusiasm for war and the representation of God as the hostile Judge. His idea of the 'Great Humanity Divine' may be understood as saying that what is truly divine is, although very mysterious, not incompatible with what humans reckon to be humane, for example in loving parenthood. (The greatest theologian of the twentieth century, Karl Barth, could towards the end of his spiritual journey write powerfully about 'the humanity of God'.) The idea is also compatible with the passages in the New Testament about the worthiness of a human life to express the glory of God, and about the dignity of all humans (male and female) as being in the image of God, and about the capacity of humans to be united with the Father through the Son in the power of the Spirit, finally partaking of the divine nature (2 Peter 1:4). There seems to be no good reason to claim that in the final analysis Blake contradicted the Bible which he is known to have loved from boyhood.

What is arresting in *Milton* is the drama of Milton's salvation. It would be mistaken to suppose that Blake was basically hostile to a poet whose work he illustrated in many beautiful watercolours commissioned by Thomas Butts, who shared his love. The most moving is *Milton in His Old Age*, blind but with a 'raptuous prophetic' vision. But in this poem Milton is persuaded that his mistakes while on earth were sins so great that he must go to 'eternal death' and, on the way, go back to earth. He must go as Jesus was willing to go but he cannot be certain 'when, O Lord Jesus, wilt thou come?' One thing Milton now knows: he must die if there is to be new life.

> I will go down to the sepulchre to see if morning breaks:
> I will go down to self annihilation and eternal death,
> Lest the Last Judgment come and find me unannihilate,
> And I be seiz'd and giv'n into the hands of my own selfhood.

Now he sees that 'I in my selfhood am that Satan', for in his selfishness he had been diabolical. As he goes back into space and time, life and death, Oothoon the 'Shadowy Female' who is the classic temptress

(Milton's Eve?) 'howls in articulate howlings' and proposes to go after him but she is urged to put on the true 'Female Form'. She must wear not 'sexual garments' but 'garments of pity and compassion like the garment of God'. And Miton, too, must strip: he must 'put off the Not Human'. Then Urizen 'the Demon' emerges from the land of rocks and snow and tries to freeze Milton's brain with the icy water of the river Jordan, but instead the poet is covered in red clay which becomes flesh (as when Adam is created in Genesis or when God the Word becomes flesh in John's gospel). Ololon, the collective name of Milton's wives and daughters, decides to die for him and with him – but as she joins him on earth Jesus comes with her.

He does not come as the Judge who is eager to condemn. Ololon has just told Milton that he is like everyone else, a sinner: 'Thou goest to Eternal Death and all must go with thee.' So she comes in 'clouds of blood' – but so does Jesus, weeping. And they come to the seaside village where Blake had been happy for a time, 'to Felpham's Vale' from which 'the lark mounted with a loud trill': it is spring, it is resurrection. Not only birds know it:

> All animals upon the earth are prepar'd in all their strength
> To go forth to the great harvest and vintage of the nations.

For Jesus comes as the embodiment of the true God,

> For God himself enters death's door with those that enter
> And lays down in the grave with them, in visions of eternity,
> Till they awake and see Jesus and the linen cloths lying
> That the Females had woven for them, and the gates of their
> Father's house.

Urizen has been exposed as a false God, as the true Satan, so that Milton can teach him this:

> Such are the laws of eternity, that each shall mutually
> Annihilate himself for others' good, as I for thee.
> Thy purpose and the purpose of thy priests and of thy churches
> Is to impress on men the fear of death, to teach
> Trembling and fear, terror, constriction, abject selfishness.
> Mine is to teach men to despise death and to go on
> In fearless majesty . . .

So in his preface to *Milton* Blake can issue a summons to the youth of England to think and live in that fearless majesty: 'Rouze up, O young men of the new age!' They must use their God-given imaginations along with 'the daughters of inspiration', for only so can they enter 'these worlds of eternity in which we shall live for ever in Jesus our Lord' – and only so will God's kingdom come on earth. Even Shakespeare and Milton had been 'curb'd' in their imaginations by 'infection from the silly Greek and Latin slaves of the sword', instead of turning to 'the Sublime of the Bible'. Was the boy Jesus brought to England by Joseph of Arimathea, as the old legend tells? Did 'the countenance divine' then 'shine forth' upon the 'clouded hills' of England? 'Was Jerusalem builded here' – the City of God? It does not really matter, for if it was, that Jerusalem was destroyed by the cruel priestcraft of the Druids. What matters now is that the young men and the daughters of inspiration should stand and fight alongside Blake, destroying the 'dark Satanic mills' (factories) where men, women and children, created in order that they may share divinity, are made to work in a way which is utterly evil. The English Revolution is still needed, so

> Bring me my bow of burning gold:
> Bring me my arrows of desire:
> Bring me my spear: O clouds unfold!
> Bring me my chariot of fire.
>
> I will not cease from mental fight,
> Nor shall my sword sleep in my hand,
> Till we have built Jerusalem
> In England's green and pleasant land.

SOME BOOKS

1 Chaucer

The best text is now *The Riverside Chaucer* in its 1987 edition, the best *New Introduction to Chaucer* is by Derek Brewer (2nd edn, 1998), the best critical *Life of Geoffrey Chaucer* is by Derek Pearsall (1992), as is a good survey of *The Canterbury Tales* (1985). Also useful are Gillian Rudd's *Complete Critical Guide to Geoffrey Chaucer* (2001), the one-volume Blackwell *Companion to Chaucer* edited by Peter Brown (2000) and the three Oxford Guides: Alastair Minnis, *The Shorter Poems* (1995), Barry Windeatt, *Troilus and Criseyde* (1992), and Helen Cooper, *The Canterbury Tales* (1989). Corinne Saunders edited extracts from recent criticism of *Chaucer* (2001). Such criticism includes David Aers, *Chaucer, Langland and the Creative Imagination* (1980), Lee Patterson, *Chaucer and the Subject of History*, John Hill, *Chaucerian Belief* (both 1991), S. H. Rigby, *Chaucer in Context* (1996) and Derek Brewer, *Chaucerian Tragedy* (2002). E. T. Donaldson discussed Shakespeare's use of Chaucer in *The Swan at the Well* (1985), and Malcolm Godden studied *The Making of Piers Plowman* (1990). *The Oxford Companion to Chaucer* edited by Douglas Gray (2003) is a compact encyclopedia.

2 Shakespeare

The best text is now *The Riverside Shakespeare* in its 1997 edition. Stanley Wells introduced *Shakespeare for All Time* (2002) and edited *A Bibliographical Guide* (1990) and with Gary Taylor *The Complete Works* (1986), to which the best one-volume companion is the Oxford Guide to *Shakespeare* edited by him and Lena Cowen Orlin (2002). The best biography of *Shakespeare* is by Patrick Honan (1998) but Katherine Duncan-Jones, *Ungentle Shakespeare* (2001), is sterner. Recent essays are conveniently assembled in the Cambridge Companions to *Shakespearean Comedy*, edited by Alexander Legatt (2000), *Shakespeare's History Plays*, edited by Michael Hattaway (2003), and *Shakespearean Tragedy*, edited by Claire McEachern (2002), and in the four larger Blackwell Companions to the *Tragedies, Histories, Comedies* and *Poems, Problem Comedies and Late Plays*, all edited by Richard Hutton and Jean Howard (2003). John Drakakis edited another collection on *Shakespearean Tragedy* (1992). Other treatments of the plays have been studied by Brian Vickers in *Appropriating Shakespeare* (1993) and by Jonathan Bate in *The Genius of Shakespeare* (1997). John Ross, *After Shakespeare* (2002), is an anthology of reactions. Harold Bloom, *Shakespeare: The Invention of Humanity* (1998), and Frank Kermode, *The Language of*

Shakespeare (2000), and *The Age of Shakespeare* (2004), are specially impressive recent treatments. G.K. Hunter, *English Drama 1586–1642: The Age of Shakespeare* (1997), surveyed the background. David Bevington, *Shakespeare* (2002) and Stephen Greenblatt, *Will in the World* (2004), used the plays to explore the psychology.

Other studies include Roland Frye, *Shakespeare and Christian Doctrine* (1963), and Roy Battenhouse, *Shakespeare's Christian Dimension* (1994). Peter Milward, *Shakespeare's Background* (1973), stressed the Catholicism, as did Richard Wilson, *Secret Shakespeare* (2004). A special relevance may be found in J. E. Bishop, *Shakespeare and the Theatre of Wonder* (1996), Jonathan Dollimore, *Radical Tragedy* (2nd edn, 1989), William Elton, *King Lear and the Gods* (1996), R. A. Foakes, *Hamlet versus Lear* (1993), Robert Hunter, *Shakespeare and the Comedy of Forgiveness* (1985) and *Shakespeare and the Mystery of God's Judgements* (1976), Ivor Morris, *Shakespeare's God: The Role of Religion in the Tragedies* (1972), and Helen Vendler, *The Art of Shakespeare's Sonnets* (1997).

3 Herbert

F. E. Hutchinson edited *The Works of George Herbert* (2nd edn, 1945), but the Penguin *Complete English Poems of George Herbert* edited by John Tobin (1991) includes *The Priest to the Temple* and Izaak Walton's *Life*. To its bibliography may be added Elizabeth Clarke, *Theory and Theology in George Herbert's Poetry* (1997), Christopher Hodgkins, *Authority, Church and Society in George Herbert* (1993), Christina Malcolmson, *Heart-Work: George Herbert and the Protestant Ethic* (1999), Michael Schoenfeldt, *Prayer and Power: George Herbert and Renaissance Courtship* (1991), Harold Toliver, *George Herbert's Christian Narrative* (1995), Patrick White, *Predestination, Policy and Polemic: Conflict and Consensus in the English Church from the Reformation to the Civil War* (1992), and the essays on *George Herbert: Sacred and Profane* edited by Helen Wilcox and Richard Todd (1995). John Roberts edited *George Herbert: An Annotated Bibliography of Modern Criticism* (2nd edn, 1988). The only recent *Life of George Herbert* is by Amy Charles (1977). Studies of his brother include Robert Bedford, *The Defence of Truth: Herbert of Cherbury and the Seventeenth Century* (1979), Peter Harrison, '*Religion' and the Religions in the English Enlightenment* (1990), and Eugene Hill, *Edward, Lord Herbert of Cherbury* (1987).

4 Milton

The best text is now *The Riverside Milton* (1998) but there are many smaller editions, e.g. the Penguin *Paradise Lost* edited by John Leonard (2nd edn, 2003). Vol. vi of *The Complete Prose Works of John Milton* edited by Dan Wolfe (1953–82) translates *De Doctrina Christiana*. The best *Life of John Milton* is by Barbara Lewalski (2nd edn, 2003) and Cedric Brown's *John Milton* (1995) surveys his work. Also useful are Richard Bradford's *Complete Critical Guide to Milton* (2001), the *Cambridge Companion to Milton* edited by Dennis Danielson (2nd edn, 1999) and the Blackwell *Companion* edited by Thomas Corns (2000). Recent criticism includes Simon Achinster, *Milton and the Revolutionary Reader*

(1994), *Milton and Republicanism* edited by David Armitage and others (1995), Dennis Danielson, *Milton's Good God* (1982), *Milton and Heresy* edited by Stephen Dobranski and John Rumrich (1998), Stephen Fallon, *Milton among the Philosophers* (1991), Stanley Fish, *Surprised by Sin* (2nd edn, 1997) and *How Milton Works* (2001), Christopher Hill, *Milton and the English Revolution* (1977) and *The Experience of Defeat* (1984), William Kerrigan's psychoanalysis in *The Sacred Complex* (1983), John King, *Milton and Religious Controversy* (2000), William Kolbrener, *Milton's Warring Angels* (1997), Barbara Lewalski, *Paradise Lost and the Rhetoric of Literary Forms* (1985), David Lowenstein, *Milton and the Drama of History* (1990), Anthony Low's study of *Samson Agonistes* in *The Blaze of Noon* (1974), Lucy Newlyn, *Paradise Lost and the Romantic Reader* (1993), C. A. Patrides, *Milton and the Christian Tradition* (1966), John Rumrich, *Milton Unbound: Controversy and Reinterpretation* (1996), John Steadman, *John Milton: The Self and the World* (1993), and J. G. Turner's study of Miltonic sexuality in *One Flesh* (1987). J. Martin Evans edited *John Milton: Twentieth-Century Perspectives* in 5 vols (2003).

5 Wordsworth

The standard scholarly text, including drafts, is the *Cornell Wordsworth Edition* with Stephen Parrish as the general editor but a convenient collection, *William Wordsworth* in the Oxford Authors series, was edited in 1984 by Stephen Gill, who in 1975 edited the first volume for Cornell. The best biography is now his *William Wordsworth: A Life* (1989), the best guide is *The Cambridge Companion to Wordsworth* which he edited (2003), and he surveyed *Wordsworth and the Victorians* (1998).

A good introduction is A. S. Byatt, *Unruly Times: Wordsworth and Coleridge in Their Time* (1989). The *Cambridge Companion* includes an annotated bibliography by Keith Hanley, the author of *William Wordsworth: A Poet's History* (2001). Duncan Wu was more detailed about *William Wordsworth: An Inner Life* to 1814 (2001) and Juliet Barker about his domestic circle in her *William Wordsworth: A Life* (2000). Jonathan Wordsworth's Penguin edition of *The Prelude* (1995) is convenient but facts have been uncovered by research including Kenneth Johnston, *The Hidden Wordsworth* (2dn edn, 2000), and critics who have read between the lines include Marjorie Levinson, *Wordsworth's Great Period Poems* (1986), David Bromwich, *Disowned by Memory* (1998) and Ashton Nichols, *The Revolutionary I* (1998).

John Williams surveyed recent criticism of *William Wordsworth* (2002). Older books include John Beer, *Wordsworth and the Human Heart* (1978) and *Wordsworth in Time* (1979), and Jonathan Wordsworth, *William Wordsworth: The Borders of Vision* (1982). William Ulmer drew attention to *The Christian Wordsworth* (2001) and Stephen Prickett to his influence on the Church in *Romanticism and Religion* (1978). His thinking about society was studied by David Simpson in *Wordsworth's Historical Imagination* (1987), about science by Trevor Levere in *Poetry Realized in Nature* (1981) and about nature by Jonathan Bate in *Romantic Ecology* (1991). Heather Glen connected him with Blake in *Vision and Disenchantment* (1983) and Nicholas Roe linked *Wordsworth and*

Coleridge: The Radical Years (1988) with results studied by Gene Ruoff in *Wordsworth and Coleridge: The Making of the Major Lyrics* (1989). William Richey and Daniel Robinson edited *Lyrical Ballads and Related Writings* (2002).

6 Coleridge

The English Romantic movement was interpreted as a move towards secularisation in M. M. Abrams, *Natural Supernaturalism* (1971) and Thomas McFarland, *Romanticism and the Forms of Ruin* (1981), but as a struggle to renew religion in Robert Ryan, *The Romantic Reformation* (1998), and in a broader way by Marilyn Butler, *Romantics, Rebels and Reactionaries* (1981), and Jerome McGann, *The Romantic Ideology* (1985). Duncan Wu edited *Romanticism: An Anthology* (1994), *Romanticism: A Critical Reader* (1995) and the Blackwell *Companion to Romanticism* (1998).

Kathleen Coburn was the general editor of the Princeton series, *The Collected Works of Samuel Taylor Coleridge* (1969–2002), but a convenient selection of *Coleridge's Poetry and Prose* with some criticism was edited by Nicholas Halmi, Paul Magnuson and Raimonda Modiano (2004). The best biography is Richard Homes, *Coleridge: The Early Visions* (1989) and *Coleridge: Darker Reflections* (1998). Lucy Newlyn edited *The Cambridge Companion to Coleridge* (2000).

Relevant studies include J. Robert Barth, *The Symbolic Imagination* (1977), *Coleridge and Christian Doctrine* (2nd edn, 1987), and *Coleridge and the Power of Love* (1988), John Beer, *Coleridge the Visionary* (1970), James Boulger, *Coleridge as Religious Thinker* (1961), Kelvin Everest, *Coleridge's Secret Ministry* (1979), David Jasper, *Coleridge as Poet and Religious Thinker* (1985), Ben Knights, *The Idea of the Clerisy in the Nineteenth Century* (1978), Thomas McFarland, *Coleridge and the Pantheist Tradition* (1969), Stephen Prickett, *Words and the Word* (1986), and Bernard Reardon, *From Coleridge to Gore* (1971). Paul Fry edited *The Rime of the Ancient Mariner* with criticism (1999).

7 Blake

David Eerdman edited *The Complete Poetry and Prose of William Blake* (2nd edn, 1988) and Mary Johnson and John Grant a 600-page selection of *Blake's Poetry and Designs* with some criticism (1979). The most readable biography is now Peter Ackroyd's *Blake* (1995) but G. E. Bentley was more detailed and severely factual in *Stranger from Paradise* (2001). Morris Eaves edited *The Cambridge Companion to William Blake* (2003).

Other studies include Northrop Frye, *Fearful Symmetry* (1947), although Kevin Hutchings found Blake to be less fearful in *Imagining Nature* (2002). J. G. Davies defended his orthodoxy in *The Theology of William Blake* (1948) but John Beer disagreed in *Blake's Humanism* (1968). E. P. Thompson found him rebellious in *Witness Against the Beast: William Blake and the Moral Law* (1993), as did Michael Ferber in *The Social Vision of William Blake* (1985). The prophetic books were illuminated in *Blake's Sublime Allegory*, edited by Stuart Curran and J. A. Wittreich (1973), and in Morton Paley, *The Traveller at Evening* (2004).

The background in radicalism was studied by James Bradley, *Religion,*

Revolution and English Radicalism (1990), Jon Mee, *Dangerous Enthusiasm* (1982), and Saree Makdisi, *William Blake and the Impossible History of the 1790s* (2003).

INDEX